PURSUING A BETTER TOMORROW

BLANCA DE LA ROSA

Copyright © 2024 by Blanca De La Rosa

All rights are reserved, and no part of this publication may be reproduced, distributed, or transmitted in any manner, whether through photocopying, recording, or any other electronic or mechanical methods, without the explicit prior written permission of the publisher. This restriction applies to any form or means of reproduction or distribution.

Exceptions to this rule include brief quotations that may be incorporated into critical reviews, as well as certain other noncommercial uses that are allowed by copyright law. Any such usage must adhere to the specified conditions and permissions outlined by the copyright holder.

ISBN: 978-1-83556-236-9   Paperback
ISBN: 978-1-83556-237-6   Hardback
ISBN: 978-1-83556-238-3   eBook

Book Design by HMDPUBLISHING

DEDICATION

I want to dedicate this book to my children and grandchildren so they will know a portion of our family's history. I encourage them to reach out for a better tomorrow with confidence, knowing that I will always be there to guide them in finding the courage, strength, and inspiration to forge ahead.

This book is lovingly dedicated to the memory of my husband. For 52 years, he was a steadfast companion, supporting my educational and career goals. He taught me invaluable lessons about love and relationships and was not just my best friend but also my most ardent supporter.

To immigrant children who find it difficult to see success in their futures, as they are so engrossed in the learning of a new language, acclimating to a new environment, and feeling the weight of what appear to be insurmountable obstacles to overcome.

To children growing up in poverty and dealing with circumstances that no child should have to experience. I hope that my story and my words can be a beacon of light and inspiration.

CONTENTS

PREFACE 6

AN ADVENTUROUS LIFE ON THE MOVE

01. The Dilemma 10
02. The Reality of Military Service 12
03. Galicia, Spain 16
04. An Agonizing Decision 20
05. The Voyage 25
06. A Life of Reckless Abandon 30
07. Home Sweet Home 40

A WOMAN AHEAD OF HER TIME

08. A Hypocritical Society 55
09. A Woman Ahead of Her Time 59
10. Embracing New Beginnings 69
11. The Gouging of Her Soul 73
12. A Martyr of Life 82

A LIFE OF FALSE DICHOTOMY

13. Daddy's Little Girl 91
14. The Betrayal 94
15. Unmasking the Witch 109
16. Sam Rosa: Humble Beginnings 120
17. Fleeing an Unstable Political Environment ... 124
18. Adapting to Life in New York City 128
19. Coming Full Circle 134
20. The End of a Long Journey 141
21. Gone with the Wind 147

A LIFE OF UNTOLD BLESSINGS AND OPPORTUNITIES

22. New York City: The Early Years 156
23. The Concrete Jungle 162
24. Too Young to Marry 177
25. Major Decisions and Points of Inflexion 184
26. The Joys of Parenthood 197
27. Reclaiming My Identity 205
28. Spiritual Awakening.. 210
29. The End of My Life as I knew It 215

MY PROFESSIONAL JOURNEY

30. Taking the Girl Out of the Projects 221
31. From the Projects Blossomed a White Rose 225
32. A Near-Miss Experience.. 238
33. Positive Disintegration. 242

EPILOGUE

34. In Pursuit of a Better Tomorrow 249
Bibliography References 253
Blanca De La Rosa - Biography 256
Blanca De La Rosa – Bibliography.. 258

PREFACE

I often wonder what life would have been like for me had my family not emigrated to the US from the Dominican Republic, where many of its citizens live below the poverty level.

Like many other Dominicans, my family emigrated to the US in the early 1960s in search of a safe environment, economic improvement, and stable government. Despite the lack of a supportive Latino community to help in the transition, we could overcome the challenges we faced as immigrants.

Although my story contains excerpts of other people's lives, it's portrayed from the perspective of my reality—how I perceived and experienced life. Even when we share experiences, we will each have a perceived reality of the situation. Each of us sees the world through the lens of our unique perspective. My experiences led to my reality, and the experiences of my family, friends, and coworkers led to theirs. My story, experiences, and perspective, as relayed in this book, have absolutely nothing to do with those referenced therein. It is about me, my reality, and how I perceived specific events.

The novel spans more than one hundred years in the lives of three generations of my maternal lineage. The story begins with my maternal grandfather in Spain and culminates with my life in the US. Along the way, I document our humble beginnings and, in some cases, our struggles to survive in a foreign land. It details some hardships experienced by immigration, the sense of displacement, and the confusion of identity suffered by immigrants as they struggle to assimilate.

The text consists of four interconnected short stories, each of which focuses on one of the main characters of the era. The novel's major themes include immigration, acculturation, coming of age, and the self-discovery of the characters' psychological and moral growth.

In compiling the history of our family, I traced my maternal grandfather's journey from late nineteenth-century Spain, Cuba, and the Dominican Republic to the twenty-first century in the US, unfolding in a story of aspirations and humble beginnings, where the characters dare to dream of a better tomorrow.

Both of my grandmothers died before I was born. Although both of my grandfathers lived to be in their eighties, they lived in the Dominican Republic, and I had no interaction with them as I was growing up in New York City. I learned about the lives of my maternal grandparents through the researching and writing of the stories of their lives.

As I embarked on the journey of researching, I was transported to a world and time long forgotten. In my virtual journey I traveled to a time in rural Galicia where the primary focus of each day was meal preparation and consumption—to a time in the Dominican Republic at the height of machismo, the cultural indoctrination that allowed the males to play a dominant role within the family, a practice encouraged by their society.

The intense emotional connection and relationship that I developed with my grandparents, even if it was on paper and in my mind, caught me by surprise. I could see their lives with the benefit of hindsight. I felt their pain, joy, and disappointments. It was the most rewarding and enlightening experience.

In tracing my maternal grandfather's footsteps from Spain to the Caribbean, I traveled to Galicia, Spain. I visited his childhood family home in the village of Nocedo, where the family home's external structure still stands. The inside of the house has deteriorated to the point where the floor of the second level has completely disintegrated. I interviewed a neighbor who could give a glimpse into the Fernandez family life. I also met and interviewed my Galician cousins who still live in Galicia.

Regrettably, my in-depth research started in 2017, long after many of the subjects had died. However, through interviews and a great-uncle's diary, I could find more than sufficient information to document the stories of their lives. There was a lot of back-and-forth in the quest to reconcile everyone's memories. My Galician cousins were generous with their time and patient with my questions.

My primary source of information about the life of my grandparents came from my mother's recollection of her childhood and oral history relayed by her father as she grew up in Santo Domingo.

As I researched and wrote about the lives of my maternal grandparents and great-grandparents, I struggled with the accuracy of the portrayal of their lives and conversations. Where I included dialogue, it has been constructed based on the general knowledge of those interviewed and logical inference of what may have transpired. It's not intended to be verbatim but merely to help the story flow.

I have used pseudonyms for those family members, friends, and co-workers who are still living, and I have used actual names for those who have long passed away. In some cases, names and identifying details may have changed. Some characters are composites which have passed through the characters' lives. Time and events were compressed to keep the story moving.

In researching my personal family history, I wanted to understand the how and why of our blended cultural genetics. Recalling the history of the Spanish Empire and its impact on the shaping of the Western Hemisphere gave me a clear understanding of my Hispanic roots.

Interspersed within the narrative is a readable historical overview of the Taíno, the conquistadors, early settlers, the Spanish Empire, and the Dominican Republic, which unfold through the perspective of the character of the era.

In detailing my story, I hope that immigrant children, the children from the projects, and other children who doubt that there is success in their futures can believe in their dreams.

Children constantly look to those around them to serve as role models. I want to be a role model to that child who looks around for someone to emulate. I genuinely hope that my words can motivate and encourage others to believe in themselves, have big aspirations, and strive for success because achieving the American dream is attainable.

Destination: The American dream

Passport: Education

Travel Partners: Hard work, dedication, and stick-to-it-ivity.

Blanca M. De La Rosa, Fairfax, Virginia

PART I
JOSÉ FERNÁNDEZ CARNERO
1900–1983

AN ADVENTUROUS LIFE ON THE MOVE

CHAPTER 1
THE DILEMMA

Damn the Spanish government for putting him and his family in this position. His resentment of the Spanish government was a tangible force that dominated his every thought. He fiercely opposed this invasion and violation of his rights and freedom of speech.

José plunged the pitchfork into a bale of hay as he contemplated his predicament. He fed the animals and worked the fields as if in a trance, unaware of his physical movements. As he wandered through the hilly landscape and open fields, he was lost in a world of his own, contemplating his future.

His eighteenth birthday was rapidly approaching, and the agonizing thought of having to report to the military for Spain's compulsory service weighed heavily on his mind. He considered himself a pacifist and anti-militarist. Regardless of his personal feelings, failure to enlist would cause his immediate incarceration.

Like many others of his time, José was a conscientious objector who claimed the right to refuse to perform military service on the grounds of freedom of expression, conscience, religion, dislike for the government, an unpopular war, or the violation of his rights.

For over two thousand years, Spain had been militarily involved in battles both at home and in its former and current colonies and territories. Although Spain remained neutral during World War I (1914–1918), it was militarily active elsewhere during the early part of the twentieth century. Since 1909, Spain's primary war engagements had been related to strengthening its position in North Africa.

José gathered the firewood for the evening, as he racked his brain, trying to figure out an alternative to enlisting. Could he report to the Spanish government and offer to pay a fee instead of service? Rumors abounded that the rich escaped conscription by paying money to the government. He quickly dismissed this idea, as he recognized it was unlikely that the son of a peasant farmer could get away with bribing his way out of military service.

The compulsory enlistment for three years of active duty and then potentially being transferred to reserve forces was so much more than he wanted to commit. He did not want to enlist for even one day.

José recalled the lively discussions and dilemmas surrounding his older brother's enlistment. Juan had not wanted to join either. Instead, he had wanted to travel to Cuba, but their father, Salvador, would not hear of it. José was ten years old, but he clearly remembered the discussions before Juan had joined the military. He also recalled the heated discussions when Juan had returned on leave a year later.

Maybe it was Juan's words and experience that shaped José's outlook about the military, or perhaps it was his way of rationalizing his desire to escape the stiff, ridged, and stifling environment his father had created with his strict rules and iron grip on the family. Nevertheless, José was adamant about not enlisting in the military. Juan's experience was sufficient for him to make his decision.

CHAPTER 2
THE REALITY OF MILITARY SERVICE

The dreadful conditions of military life were quite clear to Juan six months into his tour of duty. In 1910, Spain had engaged Morocco in war (the second Rif War), even though the effort was unpopular with most of the Spanish population. The Spanish army was ill-equipped and suffered heavy losses to a fierce and skillful enemy equipped with superior weapons. The second Rif War claimed the lives of approximately 2,500 Spanish soldiers.

After ten months of service, Juan had been defeated and overwhelmed by the heavy burden placed on him and the other Spanish soldiers. He wished his parents had facilitated his trip to Cuba.

Juan waited impatiently for his leave. He was eager to go home and demand that his father help him wake up from the nightmare of war. He didn't know how his father could be stupid enough to think that joining the military was better than going to Cuba. His father had claimed that serving in the military would afford Juan the glamor of travel. Well, Juan had news for his father—there was nothing glamorous about military life.

Finally, at the one-year mark, Juan could take his leave and travel to his hometown of Orense. He walked through the fields, toward home and the family farm, practicing in his head what he would say to his father.

Donning his full military garb and the experience of the previous year did not stop him from feeling like a child in his father's presence. To his astonishment, he was still afraid of his father's wrath. His father's reactions were unpredictable, especially when one questioned his authority. Now that Juan was back at the farm, he questioned which was worse—the military or his father's temper. He even debated whether he should leave without approaching his father.

It took Juan an additional day to summon up the courage he needed to speak with his father. He would have preferred to speak with his father in private; but given the size of the house and the time of day, both his mother and José were in the kitchen. Nevertheless, he forged ahead, as it was now or never.

As he cautiously approached Salvador, Juan appeared calm, but his rapid pulse and sweat-dampened shirt betrayed him. "Papa, I need to speak with you."

"Juan, you have been fidgeting and moping around for the last couple of days. What's on your mind?"

Juan opened his mouth to speak, but nothing came out. He cleared his throat and said in a quaky voice, "Papa, I do not want to return to my post. The past year has been a nightmare. Men are maimed and dying daily. Each day, I ask myself whether it will be my last day. I want you to help me travel to Cuba."

"I will do no such thing. You committed to the military, and now you must complete your tour of duty. How do you think your desertion will look? It will make you look like a coward."

Juan noted that Salvador's voice was softer than usual. Could it be that his father was feeling sympathetic to his plight? Emboldened by the tone of his father's voice, Juan responded, "Frankly, I do not care how it will look. Enlisting in the military was the wrong decision. I should have gone to Cuba instead."

"Juan, there is no such thing as a right or wrong decision in life. Life is about choices, options, opportunities, and what people eventually make of them. You must now make the best of your time in the military."

If Salvador's conciliatory tone and words of encouragement were meant to make Juan feel better about his military service, it only increased Juan's agitation. At that precise moment, Juan despised his father more than ever; no longer threatened or afraid.

The rage that welled up in Juan gave him the courage to stand up to his father. With arms flailing and a pointed finger, he angrily retorted, "How dare you preach to me about options and choices? You made this decision for me. I wanted to go to Cuba, and you refused to help me, insisting that I enlist in the military. You think you know it all, and everything has to be your way. If you had given me the option to make my own decision about my future, I wouldn't be here complaining about my military service. But this was your decision, not mine."

When he finished candidly saying what was on his mind, he stepped back and braced himself as he waited for his father to lunge at him. To his surprise, his father's response was a tepid one. Could it be that his father regretted having forced Juan to enlist? Or was he respecting the fact that his mother and José were witnessing the interaction?

Salvador stood from his chair, chest puffed, and in his sternest tone said, "First and foremost, let this be the last time you speak to me with such disdain and disrespect. Don't think for a moment that your military uniform will stop me from giving you a good beating. I did what I believed to be in your best interest and that of our family. Notwithstanding that decision, the choices you make from this day forward will dictate the outcome of your military service and the rest of your life. My advice is that you try to make the best of this situation. You can be brave and get honorably discharged. Or you can be a coward and run away from your reality. Juan, running away from your reality is not the solution to a difficult situation. People with true resolve, determination, and strength of character will find a way to resolve any problem when presented with a difficult or unpleasant situation. So, what's it going to be, Juan?"

Juan was still seething and did not immediately respond. He had to take some time to compose himself and think about his prospects. His father's refusal to help him was not what Juan had expected. Juan had naively imagined himself on a beach in Cuba, believing he would not be returning to his post.

At that specific moment, Juan both hated and respected his father. His father was an uneducated brute and a strict disciplinarian who did not hesitate to use corporal punishment for the slightest infraction. But he was also a wise and ethical man who instilled in his sons the value of keeping their word and commitments.

Juan was both disappointed and encouraged. He had to go back and make the best of his years in the military. He did not know exactly how, but if he changed his attitude, the remaining time of his military service would be easier to endure.

"Papa, I understand your reasoning but am extremely disappointed. You did not support my decision to go to Cuba then, and you are not supporting me now. But I urge you to reconsider your position when the time comes for José and Miguel to enlist. I do not want my brothers to live through what I have had to endure."

Juan dramatically turned to José and said, "I know you are only eleven years old and may be too young to understand this right now, but I want you to remember this evening and everything we have discussed here tonight. I want you to understand the reality of life in the military. I do not want anyone else in this family to live the horrors of Spain's senseless, insane, and irrational wars."

As the oldest sibling, Juan was protective of his brothers. He wanted to shield them from their father. Their father's autocratic rule made them feel as if they did not have a life of their own; he always had to have the last word. In Juan's mind, it was them against their father. Juan vowed to help his brothers should they want to travel instead of enlisting for military service.

Juan reluctantly returned to his post

CHAPTER 3
GALICIA, SPAIN

José Fernández was the second of three sons born to Salvador Fernández Souto and Francisca Carnero Fernández. He was born on August 20, 1900, in Nocedo del Valle (Nocedo), an agricultural village in Orense, one of the four provinces of Galicia, Spain.

Spain is a complex nation with a rich culture. The Iberian Peninsula, the second-largest European peninsula, is located in the southwestern part of Europe. Portugal and Spain comprise most of the territory, with Andorra and a portion of France along the peninsula's northeastern edge, as well as Gibraltar on its south coast.

The peninsula, bordered by the Atlantic Ocean, the Mediterranean Sea, and the Pyrenees Mountains, gives Spain a strategic advantage. The peninsula connects the Mediterranean with the Atlantic and Europe with Africa.

Columbus' discovery of a route to the Americas and Caribbean in 1492 launched from the Iberian Peninsula.

Historically, Spain's geographic location on the Iberian Peninsula has attracted the migration of the many diverse peoples that have contributed to Spain's diversity. Throughout history, people from other nations have been drawn to Spain, creating a multicultural, multireligious country with many distinct regions. The rich multicultural tapestry of Spain resulted from many years of migration, integration, and settling.

Spain is a diverse country composed of seventeen different autonomous regions. The regions vary in economic and social structures, languages, and historical, political, and cultural traditions.

Galicia is one of Spain's seventeen autonomous regions. It is in the northwest and is bordered and culturally influenced by Portugal. The provincial capital, Orense, is the largest population center, while the rest of the province is predominantly rural.

The official language of Galicia is Gallegan, one of the Romance languages. Gallegan has many similarities to Portuguese, of which it was historically a dialect. Gallegan is not a dialect of Spanish, nor is it badly spoken Castilian; the language merely shares Latin roots with those languages.

Galicia has rolling hills, meadows, and mountains with oak, myrtle, and pine forests. Despite the lush green landscape, the land does not produce in abundance, as the earth is rocky. The excessive rain permits the ground only one harvest per year.

Despite the difficult, rocky soil, the Celts settled and thrived in Galicia, building their mountain townhomes from stone. The men hunted and fished, and the women did agricultural work. Traces of Celtic roots still abound in Galicia. The local musical instrument is the bagpipe, some of the stone houses in the green countryside simulate those of Ireland, round stone huts still dot the hilltops, and many of the Gallegan words have Celtic roots.

During the early twentieth century, Galicia remained relatively impoverished and isolated by Western European standards. Its climate and topography made farming the primary source of the region's revenue; cattle raising, pig breeding, and agriculture dominated the economy. The economy of Galicia was an agricultural system with a tradition of self-consumption. The predominantly rural population reaped their primary source of income from the commercialization of wine and the breeding of cattle.

Orense, with an approximate area of 2,800 square miles, is surrounded by mountains and is the only landlocked province in Galicia. Historically, these mountains isolated the territory from the more populated Galician coast, with no connecting roads to the other regions. The northwest province of Galicia is mountainous, and mountain ranges surround the central plains. The topography isolates each valley, increasing each village's tendency to think of itself as autonomous.

During the early 1900s, the lack of progress in the region was staggering compared to the rest of Spain. Galicia was so far behind that it was difficult to believe that it would someday attain a reasonable standard of living, let alone catch up with the rest of the country. The mountainous terrain and isolation kept the province economically challenged and encouraged many to immigrate to other parts of Spain and the New World.

The village of Nocedo, located on a plain irrigated by the Tamega River that crosses the valley of Monterrey from north to south, was a rural community comprised a group of houses made primarily of stone, pizarra granite, and wood. Nocedo's economy consisted of the autonomous production and consumption of perishable goods, bartering, and breeding cattle and pigs. Theirs was a subsistent economy that relied heavily on local natural resources to provide for the town's basic needs.

Nocedo was a community of approximately three hundred inhabitants. There were no clinics, hospitals, or government offices. The town's inhabitants had to travel approximately three miles by foot or mule to the town of Verín to conduct official business and receive medical attention.

The Fernández home in Nocedo was a two-story structure typical of the rural Galician household. Their way of life was reflected in the internal organization of the house, with fully used spaces all under one roof. An interior partition separated the upper and lower levels, connected by an internal stone staircase accessed through the back of the house.

The family's living quarters were on the upper level and consisted of one bedroom with three cast-iron beds, a large kitchen area, a combined living and dining room, and a balcony that surrounded the entire perimeter of the house. The lower level stored the agricultural tools necessary for daily survival, together with granaries, haystacks, and livestock such as chickens, pigs, and cattle.

Theirs was a cozy home that met their needs even if it felt as if they were living in cramped conditions, one on top of the other. Most, if not all, of their neighbors, lived under similar conditions.

The kitchen was the focal gathering point for the family, as food consumption and food preparation were at the center of their daily lives. Everyone in the family contributed to the production and preparation of the meals.

Salvador and the boys spent most of their time outdoors, working the fields, tending the livestock, planting, gathering firewood, bartering, or selling produce and livestock.

Their mother, Francisca, tended the house, spending most of her time in the kitchen. Cooking dominated Francisca's time, and her typical day began before sunrise, as preparing meals was time consuming. The seasonings had to be ground up using a mortar and pestle, as well as the butter churned, meats cured, bread baked, and the water for cooking fetched from the well. Properly baking the bread and maintaining the simmer in the stew required stoking the flame and making constant angle adjustments for the stew pot hanging by the trammel hook.

With an oversize hearth and a chimney that effectively drew out the smoke, the kitchen was a spacious room. In the kitchen, there was a wooden bench that had a backrest and a storage compartment underneath its flip top. The space-saving kitchen table was a wooden board secured to a wall, so it could be lifted and lowered as needed.

The hearth served multiple purposes: cooking, roasting, and heating the house during the cold winter months. The primary cooking utensil was a three-legged cast-iron Dutch oven pot used to prepare several types of food and allowed cooking from both the top and the bottom. Other cookware and utensils hung above the fire, suspended from a crane fitted with a chain with large links. Swinging back and forth above the flame, the iron bar with adjustable hooks served as the crane.

The hearth was the hub of the family's home life, making the kitchen the heart of the home and the natural place to spend time during the long winter nights. They shared many memorable and tense moments in the kitchen. They gathered in front of the hearth before bed to warm up, tell stories, and plan their activities for the following day and their future. Some of the family's most crucial decisions were made in the kitchen, sitting by the hearth.

CHAPTER 4
AN AGONIZING DECISION

The Fernández boys had a short-lived childhood, as they were required to work at a young age. For the most part, the boys did not receive a formal education. Both Juan and José were withdrawn from the village elementary school to help their parents work in the fields.

The basic and simple daily life of Nocedo hardly made school necessary for an eminently rural peasant population. Formal education did not improve the economic situation of the average farmer of Nocedo. Besides the financial burden and loss of manpower that sending children to school posed for the rural population, most families carried a heavy tax burden.

Salvador and Francisca were determined to do the best they could for their boys. They taught their children the value of money, hard work, and a strong work ethic. Their rural and farming lifestyle was an arduous one, but they felt safe and protected within their limited universe.

That her children would venture outside of their controlled environment of their village had caused Francisca many sleepless nights. Throughout the years, Francisca had agonized over the idea of having to send her sons to the military because of Spain's never-ending involvement in one conflict or another.

Despite the mild weather, Francisca shivered as she tightened her shawl around her shoulders. Francisca paced and fidgeted as she asked, "Salvador, when will these stupid wars end?"

Let's not delude ourselves, Francisca, into thinking that someday this will end. We have to be practical and prepare to help José and Miguel avoid fighting in these senseless wars."

She was visibly agitated by the discussion. As she continued to pace the kitchen floor, she acknowledged, "Salvador, I know we talked about sending the boys away, but I wonder if there isn't some other way."

His voice softened as he replied, "If there is another way, I don't know what that could be. Francisca, try to control your emotions. You are going to worry yourself sick, and the boys haven't even left yet. The time has come for us to act. I, too, have dreaded this day, but we have to do what is best for our sons."

Francisca recognized Salvador's sympathetic tone as his way of trying to appease her. But as the time for the boys to leave came closer, forcing them to make a final decision, she became more agitated.

Francisca was mild-mannered but having to send her boys away infuriated her. She immediately became protective. Though she was barely five feet tall, when protecting her offspring, she felt a surge of invincibility that made her feel like a giant.

She furiously banged her fist on the table as she snapped, "I hate the Spanish government for forcing the timing of my sons' independence. If José and Miguel go away, I will be sentenced to a lifetime of never-ending agony, not knowing if they are safe, hungry, or ill. I don't think I can survive the blow of sending my children away forever. Losing our little girl to illness at four years of age was devastating, and I do not think I could survive the loss of another child."

Salvador, always portraying an air of confidence so Francisca could calm down, stoically insisted, "Francisca, stop being so dramatic. You will not die. I know that losing our daughter was hard, but you survived. You'll survive this too. So, what is the right or fair time to let our children become independent?"

Francisca stared at Salvador with disdain and exclaimed, "Stop being sarcastic; you know I do not know what the answer is. What I know is that allowing our children to become independent and sending them away forever are two distinct realities." With tears streaming down her cheeks, she sobbed, "The Spanish government has decided that the right time is eighteen years of age, and I do not know what this means to me as a mother."

Salvador put his arms around his wife. "It means that as a mother, you must let the boys find their way in life. Whether they are eighteen or twenty-five, we have to let them make their own choices in life. There will be times when we will worry and others where we may feel a baseless dread. But we can also choose to remember the happy times."

"Salvador, I know our children will someday be on their own. But if they go overseas, it is likely we will never see them again. We will miss out on so much of their adult lives."

Salvador did not immediately respond to Francisca. Instead, he slowly sat back and rubbed his temples. "Francisca, given the economic conditions in Galicia and the compulsory military service, we should give the boys the option of leaving Spain. I believe that the best option for the boys would be Santiago de Cuba."

Santiago de Cuba had a supportive Spanish community. Many Galicians had immigrated to Cuba during the middle of the nineteenth century, as Spanish emigrants could only travel to Spain's remaining colonies. As such, migrant laborers moved to Cuba and Puerto Rico to work in the sugar plantations.

Despite the supportive Galician community, as parents, both Salvador and Francisca had a difficult time accepting that they would never see their sons again.

Salvador had saved sufficient money for a full third-class passage plus initial seed money. Unfortunately, it was what they could afford. Imagining the experience of the third-class voyage was enough to give anyone nightmares. But what other choice did they have? The boys could take their chances on the voyage or go to war.

Francisca and Salvador had reason to be concerned. The transatlantic liners did not have a good reputation with third-class passengers. The liners had a reputation for poor sanitation, and diseases were said to be common. Also, the transatlantic liners treated the steerage passengers as human cargo.

Saving enough money through scrimping and scraping, they provided José with the option to decide his fate. They were confident that José would repay the loan. They also agreed that if José were going to travel to Cuba, it would be best if he did so a couple of years before the mandatory enlistment age of eighteen to avoid any potential conflict with the military authorities.

On a quiet evening in March 1916, as they were sitting by the fire, Salvador and Francisca presented José with the option of traveling to Cuba instead of enlisting in the military.

Even though he had contemplated these options over the years, José still struggled to reconcile the two options before him. Both required that he live away from his family. Joining the military was temporary, while fleeing Spain was permanent. Fleeing the country to avoid conscription was a criminal offense, and the Spanish government would demand his immediate incarceration if he ever returned to Spain.

"Papa, mama, I know that living away from home will not be easy. But I also know that serving in the military is something I'm not willing to do. I saw what military service did to Juan, and it makes me hate the Spanish government that much more. So, I will accept your offer and travel to Santiago de Cuba."

Francisca sat at the table, biting her lip and holding back tears. With a quivering voice, she encouraged her son, "José, we could not give you a formal education, but at least you know the basics of reading, writing, and calculating numbers. Your strong work ethic and willingness to work hard will serve you well."

After everyone had gone to bed, José sat by the fire, contemplating his future and that of his family. Who would help his father work the fields and tend the livestock? Working in the fields and taking care of the animals had been José's responsibility. Although his father was physically fit and healthy for his sixty-eight years, he still needed help with the farm. Juan lived in Verín and had joined the military police. Miguel was only nine years old and attended elementary school. José's parents now acknowledged the value of formal education and wanted to allow Miguel to study.

Venturing into unknown territory at the young age of sixteen would be painful and scary. José accepted that his fate was not in Spain, but the devastation of not seeing his parents ever again was painful. José would not see his parents grow older, be there to take care of them when they could no longer fend for themselves or attend their funerals when they died.

Recognizing and appreciating the sacrifice his parents had made, José arranged his trip to Cuba. His parents depended on him to work the fields, and the selfless act of helping him move to Cuba was priceless.

On the day of his departure, José left the house before his family awoke. He could not bear to say goodbye to his family, especially to his mother. Seeing the pain in his mother's eyes or hearing Miguel begging him not to leave would break his heart. Instead, he took a long last look at his sleeping family and mouthed "goodbye" as he quietly sneaked out of the bedroom. The discussions of the previous few days had been hard enough and would have to suffice.

José left his boyhood home with his parents' blessings.

CHAPTER 5

THE VOYAGE

José walked the three miles from Nocedo to Verín to board the train that would take him to the Port of Vigo. He was leaving Galicia with a heavy heart, a lump in his throat, and many fond memories; not caring what the Spanish military may or may not think. Surely, they would not travel to Cuba for a peasant such as him.

In May 1916, three months before his sixteenth birthday, José embarked on a harrowing sea voyage destined for Santiago de Cuba.

His palms sweated, and his heart raced as he walked up the gangway and looked into the sea of people below. Boarding the ship was slow, as the people in front of him stopped every five seconds to glance back and wave goodbye to their loved ones.

José nervously turned to look back, beyond the sea of people, as he was unsure what the future had in store for him. He wanted a last look at Spain. As he gazed out toward the horizon, he was doubtful that he would ever return to his beloved Spain. Boarding the ship represented the end of his relationship with Spain. It represented the first day of his life without the support of his family. He did not know what future awaited him in Cuba, but he was looking forward to the adventure.

As he approached the immigration officer, he noticed that the officer was checking papers and identification and asking questions. José could not overhear what was said, but a sudden paralyzing thought overcame him. He broke out into a cold sweat at the sudden thought of the officer questioning him about the nature of his trip. What would he say if the officer asked about his return date to ensure he enlisted in the military? What if the officer demanded proof of his return?

José felt ill-prepared, as he had not discussed this with his father or Juan, and he had no idea what he should say. They had not entertained the possibility that anyone would ask why he was traveling without a plan for meeting his obligation to the Spanish government. It was a long five-minute wait as he stood panic-stricken and sweating profusely despite the unseasonably cool weather.

When José finally reached the top, the officer asked to see his passport and boarding pass. As the officer examined his boarding ticket and passport, he commented, "You appear to be nervous. Are you all right?"

José exclaimed, "Yes, I'm fine. It's that I've heard many horror stories about the unsanitary conditions of the ship."

With a hearty laugh, the officer teased, "Is that it? What do you do for a living?"

"I work the fields and tend the livestock on my parents' farm."

The officer laughed harder at José's response. José was puzzled. He did not get the joke. What was so funny?

The officer joked, "Then you will feel right at home. You appear to be a healthy and strong young man. If you can stand the stench and mess the animals make, you should be fine on this voyage. There will also be about one thousand four hundred ninety-nine other steerage passengers to share your misery. Have a great trip and good luck in Cuba."

José still did not understand what was so funny. Nevertheless, he thanked the officer and quickly walked away before the officer asked him any more questions.

He then descended a narrow stairway down to the steerage compartment, where the third-class passengers resided in the cheapest possible accommodations. A steward directed him to the bow of the ship, where the single men lived for the duration of the voyage.

On his way to the steerage, José noticed with concern the grilled door fitted at the bottom of the stairs.

He asked one of the stewards, "What's the purpose of the grilles?"

The steward informed José, "Ship regulations require that third-class passengers remain in their area of the ship. Once third-class passengers have boarded and settled in their berths, a steward closes and locks the grilles to prevent the classes from mingling. But don't you worry; we immediately open the grilles in the event of an emergency."

José thanked the steward, but as he continued to move toward his cabin, he replayed the steward's words in his mind. The steward's response was not comforting to José, as he recalled the fate of the third-class passengers on the maiden voyage of the *Titanic*, which had collided with an iceberg on April 14, 1912. Rumors were that the first-class passengers had been given priority boarding on the lifeboats, while the third-class passengers were confined behind locked grilles and sank with the ship the following day. The rich spared at the expense and suffering of the poor. Although these were rumors, the locked grilles concerned him.

Lost in dreadful speculation, he reached his assigned cabin and berth. As he explored the sleeping arrangements, he was glad to see that each berth had a clean mattress, blanket, pillow, utensils, and bucket. He unpacked and settled into the six-foot-long and two-foot-wide berth, acknowledging that this was where he would be living for the next twenty days. So far, so good.

At dinnertime, José ventured out with utensils and bucket in hand to find the dining facilities, where the daily menu consisted of soup or stew and sometimes bread, biscuits, or potatoes.

Throughout the voyage, the berths received little to no attention from the stewards. He realized poor sanitation was most likely the leading reason the transatlantic liners had diseases such as cholera and typhus.

The stench of the vomiting was overpowering because the stewards did not immediately clean up after those that had been seasick. José's lungs begged for fresh air, but as a steerage passenger, he could not go up to the main deck of the ship. The best he could do was go onto the poop deck when it wasn't overcrowded. Only the fresh breeze from the sea overcame the sickening stench, which was so much worse than his parents' barn.

It was then that he understood what the officer had found so funny. But the officer had been wrong; this was much worse. At least back home, he could open the door and air out the barn.

The steerage area accommodated approximately fifteen hundred people. In the confined space, any sound that reached José's ears was irritating beyond endurance. There were loud, grating wails from children crying and running around; men were arguing and yelling profanities; women were screaming, trying to ward off unwanted advances; the daily hustle and bustle of the crew; and the sound of the ship's engines. José wished he could avoid it all, but there was no place to hide.

He longed to be back at the farm, with its sounds of nature, his neighbors conducting their daily duties, and the quiet, peaceful, starlit nights. The only pleasant and calming scenery and sounds on the ship were those of the sea—the crescendo of the rising wave and its thunderous roar as it finally crashed against the side of the vessel.

Before he'd embarked on this voyage, José had heard the horror stories of the ocean liners treating third-class passengers like human cargo. However, nothing could have prepared him for the overcrowded and unsanitary conditions below deck.

By the seventh day of the voyage, everything was dirty, sticky, and disgustingly disagreeable to the touch. The dining area was a cesspool of germs. The only clean area José could run to for shelter was his berth, but his cabin was not immune to the stench that permeated the entire lower level of the ship.

Given the unpleasant conditions on the ocean liner, the twenty-day voyage from Galicia to Cuba had been the longest twenty days of José's life.

As the ship neared the port in Santiago de Cuba, José recalled discussions he had heard over the years about the Spaniards' colonization of the Caribbean islands. There were two distinct opinions about the Spanish conquistadors' colonization of the Americas.

~◆~

The argument promoted by Juan Ginés de Sepúlveda—philosopher, theologian, and proponent of colonial slavery—was that the native people were inherently inferior and should be placated forcefully by a civilized master. Their inferior intellect made them natural slaves, as nothing better could be expected of them. Their sins as pagans warranted subjugation and conversion to Christianity. Spain's ingrained religious culture dominated the crown and its military. The conquistadors forced their religious beliefs and ethics on the indigenous population, pressuring them to convert to Christianity or perish.

On the other hand, Bartolomé de las Casas, a sixteenth-century colonist who acted as a historian and social reformist, was fiercely opposed to the Spanish conquistadors' intensely violent and abusive methods of colonization, which inflicted considerable losses on the indigenous population of the islands.

Bartolomé de las Casas published A Short Account of the Destruction of the Indies, wherein he chronicled his personal experiences during the first decades of the Spanish colonization of the Americas. In this account, de las Casas documented the atrocities committed by the Spanish settlers against the indigenous people.

Based on José's knowledge of the Spanish government's method of operations, he was inclined to believe Bartolomé de las Casas's point of view, as slavery was a widely accepted practice in sixteenth-century Spain.

José would have to develop his own opinion once he was in Cuba and could see and hear firsthand how the Cubans chronicled their history.

CHAPTER 6
A LIFE OF RECKLESS ABANDON

José arrived at the Port of Santiago de Cuba with little money, few personal belongings, and many fond memories of his family and his hometown. As the vessel approached the port, he was in awe of the beauty of the turquoise waters and the green, mountainous island with its white, sandy beaches.

Santiago de Cuba's landscape was spectacular with its combination of sea, mountains, and urban structures. On one side, he faced the enormous bay of the Caribbean Sea with the Sierra Maestra Mountains as a backdrop. When he turned to the other side, he faced urban colonial structures. How could one not be awestruck by the contrast of colonial architecture and the majesty of nature? The landscape was enough to make the horrendous twenty-day voyage worthwhile.

The city was muggy, hot, hilly, and exhausting. He was going to miss the changing seasons and cold weather of Galicia.

Santiago de Cuba was the second-largest city in Cuba after Havana, lying on the Santiago de Cuba Bay. Besides the existing agricultural and mining industries, it was also industrially and commercially developed as early as the nineteenth century.

The quality of life in Santiago de Cuba was good, and there were plenty of other Spaniards with whom José could identify and associate. He could not have asked for a more welcoming community.

Despite the warm reception, José found it difficult to get emotionally involved with the people and activities around him. Never having traveled outside of his farming community in Orense, Galicia, everything he encountered was new to him. Maybe it was his rural nature fighting the change to an urban lifestyle that made him feel so out of place. Despite living in a city surrounded by many people, José's life in Cuba was a lonely existence.

As José walked around Parque Céspedes, the main square in Santiago de Cuba, he admired the historical buildings. Further along, he was amazed by the colonial-style buildings with arches and balconies painted in bright, luminous, pastel colors. Though he appreciated the beautiful construction and colors, he felt like an intruder because he did not think he belonged among them.

There were always many people strolling in the plaza. He strolled with them, hoping that he would shake the feelings of displacement and homelessness. He walked around the city, trying to find a place that would attract him to forge a connection. However, he always ended up as he'd started, feeling like he did not belong anywhere.

As he lay in his hammock under a blanket of stars, a voice in his head told him that Cuba was not where he was supposed to be. When he heard that voice, he had that unsettling craving for a place that eluded him. He had an intuitive calling to be elsewhere, except he did not know where that was.

He missed the safe surroundings of the farm and village in Galicia. A distant Fernández relative lived in Santa Clara, Cuba, but when he first visited to introduce himself, his father's family did not welcome him wholeheartedly.

With its magnificent beaches, culture, and Spanish colonial architecture, Cuba was an exotic and permissive playground. It was a contrast to his native Galicia.

Contrary to his Nocedo life of stability and routine, in Cuba, José became a vagabond, traveling with his personal belongings and a hammock in a sack. He was a rolling stone that refused to settle down in one place or with any one person wherever he hung his hammock was his home.

The first year was the hardest, as he drifted in search of something familiar to him. He preferred to live one day at a time. Many times, he relied on the women he met or gambling buddies for temporary shelter. José felt physical pain in his chest when he reminisced about his family, but because of his vagabond lifestyle, he found it difficult to communicate with them.

José secured employment with the Linea Ferro Carrill, Cuba's tramway company, in Santiago de Cuba. Although this was backbreaking labor, the job was perfect for him because it supported his nomadic lifestyle. Constructing the rail tracks required constant movement. For the next eight years, José worked for the company in various labor positions. The first year, he lived frugally so he could save the money needed to repay his parents.

In May 1917, José traveled to Santa Clara to visit his distant cousin and get advice on the best way to send a package to his parents.

"Good afternoon, Cousin Manuel. How are you doing?"

"We're well; thank you. How about you? How is Cuba treating you?"

José was surprised to see that his cousin appeared genuinely glad to see him. Maybe José had misjudged him when they had first met. He said, "Since I last saw you, I have been working hard with the tramway company. I move around frequently, so I have not had the time to visit."

"Not a problem, José. I understand you've probably had a lot to contend with during the last few months," Manuel replied.

José was a bit confused by his cousin's somber tone and his comment about a lot to contend with but chose to ignore it. "Well, work and figuring out where to sleep each night keeps me busy. Other than that, it's been great. I've been working extra hours to save the money I owe my parents."

José then sat straight up in his chair and proudly declared, "The reason for my visit is to get your help in delivering this letter and money to my parents. I'm not sure how to send it safely to them. My parents will be proud to hear that despite my young age, I've been able to support myself and save the money they provided for my trip."

Manuel stood up from his chair and paced as if trying to understand what José had said. He asked a clarifying question. "José, do you mean to say you have not communicated with your family since you left Galicia?"

"Yes, it's been a year since I left Galicia. Since then, I've been living the life of a vagabond with no permanent address. I've been trying to survive day-to-day. They would not understand or approve of this lifestyle. I could have made up a story, but I did not want to lie to them. I wanted them to be proud of me. I've saved the money I owe my parents and want to repay them and share the news of how I have become financially independent."

Manuel listened intently and slowly nodded as if he had come to some realization. "José, you are an immature and foolish idiot. What made you think that not communicating with your parents was the right thing to do? Did you not think that your mother would be worried sick not knowing of your welfare?"

José could not understand the change in Manuel's demeanor and tone. He innocently defended himself. "Yes, I've struggled at times, not knowing where my next meal was going to come from or where I could safely sleep, but for the most part, I've been fine. I was waiting to have good news to share, since I wanted my parents, especially my father, to feel proud."

Manuel sternly rebutted, "You see, José, you may know that you are fine, but your parents do not know how you are. I bet that you have no idea how they are doing. Do you?"

José lowered his gaze and bowed his head at the realization of his selfishness and irresponsibility. He had inadvertently put his parents, especially his mother, through unnecessary worry. He lamented, "You're right. I do not know how any of the members of my family are doing."

At the revelation of the enormity of José's ignorance, Manuel somberly approached José, placed his hands on José's shoulders, and said, "My boy, I am so sorry to have to break this news to you. Your mother,

Francisca, suffered what appeared to be a stroke approximately two months after you left Galicia. She was bedridden for six months before she died in January. The seventeenth of January, to be exact."

José was speechless. How could this be? Had his mother suffered a stroke because of him? Was she so worried about his welfare that she made herself sick? He had overheard his mother say that she did not think she could survive if she had to send one of her children away.

The news was utterly devastating. José was numb and disoriented. For a moment, he forgot where he was as his brain tried to process the news. His mind could not accept the fact that his mother's life had been abruptly cut off. Yesterday, she had been alive and vibrant, at least in his mind. Today, there was a new reality in his life. She was gone. His experience and perspective on life changed in an instant.

Throughout his first year in Cuba, he had felt frayed at the edges of his being, but the news of his mother's death ripped the seams of his soul.

Just as he had felt good about himself and his accomplishments—as he had felt somewhat secure about his future—his mother had died, thrusting him into the depths of despair and loneliness. The isolation from his family and his inability to travel to Galicia magnified his hopelessness. Dealing with his mother's death without the support of his family was harder than he had ever imagined.

For the next year, José was tortured and grief-stricken, working through his pain and guilt. He had known that moving to Cuba would mean he would not be around when his parents passed, but he had not expected that either of them would pass so soon after his departure from Spain.

He felt guilty for not having written and for not being with his family when his mother had died. He worked long hours and engaged in gambling and drinking to cope with the unrelenting grief as he made the journey from a naïve seventeen-year-old to a mature adult.

The holidays and birthdays marking another year without his family were the worst. He lived with constant yearning and grieving over the loss of his mother, his family, and the only life he'd known. He even mourned the loss of his daily routine and mundane life back at the farm in Nocedo.

He had learned his lesson and was now in constant communication with his family. He learned of his father's marriage of convenience shortly after his mother's death. His father needed help around the house and also needed someone to help take care of Miguel.

He learned of Salvador's death at the age of seventy-three in 1921, four years after Francisca's death. Juan took custody of fourteen-year-old Miguel upon their father's death.

The inability to assist Juan in dealing with their parents' deaths left José feeling helpless. Juan had a heavy load to carry with his own family, raising Miguel, and dealing with their parents' demise.

The shock of his mother's death was like a sucker punch from the universe. In contrast, his father's death was neither shocking nor devastating. José felt sad by the news of his father's passing, but he did not feel the sorrow he had felt when his mother had died. His father had not been a loveable person. He had been hard to talk to and hard to love. His father's rage and wrath had been terrifying.

The death of his parents ended the chapter of his life in which he was a son. He was now an orphan with no back-up support system. He felt alone, with no one to give him guidance and direction. The feeling of being orphaned was strange, and not something he had expected at the age of twenty-one.

José felt liberated. He no longer had to contemplate what his parents might think of anything he did or did not do. It no longer mattered whether his parents approved of his behavior. Even though he had been independent and beyond his father's influence, he had continued to wage a virtual battle against his oppressive father. José was now free of the self-imposed battle with his father, a struggle that, in reality, had ended when he had moved away from Galicia.

The onslaught of mixed emotions had blindsided José. He had to give himself time to work through it all. When he was not working, gambling, drinking, or consorting with loose women, he tried to learn about Cuba and its history.

He was keen on learning the history of the island without the Spanish government's tainted view so that he could settle the opposing views he had heard as he was growing up in Galicia. He was interested in the conquistadors' and early settlers' actions.

The more informed he became about the local history, the more incensed he grew. How could the Spanish settlers have treated the indigenous people with such disregard and cruelty? Sometimes he was embarrassed to claim his Spanish heritage.

Working conditions for José were acceptable, but his fellow Spaniards were cruel to the people of color. As a team leader at work, he did what he could, but he was powerless to make a significant change or difference. The discrimination against the people of color persisted, even though it had been over four hundred years since the Spaniards had established colonies in Cuba.

Cuban society was a racial contradiction: institutional racism had been abolished from society but not from the hearts and actions of those wanting to whiten the race. "Bettering or 'whitening' the race denoted social mobility upward, while 'blackening' equated with backwardness, poverty, and underdevelopment." [25]

José's coworkers, knowing he was a Spaniard, freely shared what was on their minds, blaming "his people" for the atrocities committed against the Taíno people and for the torturous death of Hatuey, a Taíno chief. José was not sure how he was supposed to respond or react to the accusations. Was he supposed to apologize for the actions of the Spanish settlers and conquistadors? He opted to say nothing, letting them vent their beliefs and frustrations. He'd heard so much about the history of the early settlers and Hatuey that he'd been compelled to travel to Baracoa City to visit the Hatuey monument.

Although Cristóbal Colón (a.k.a. Christopher Columbus) had landed in Cuba and claimed the island for Spain on October 29, 1492, the island had not been settled and colonized until 1511, when Diego Velázquez had been appointed the governor of Cuba by Spain. Velázquez had set out from the island of Hispañola (today, the Dominican Republic and Haiti) to conquer the island of Cuba.

When Hatuey had learned of the Spaniard's plan to travel to Cuba, he had fled Hispañola with his family and members of his tribe to warn the Cuban Taíno of the atrocities committed by the Spaniards on the Taíno of Hispañola.

The Taíno people had inhabited the island of Hispañola since the seventh century, and by the end of the fifteenth century, they had been organized into five tribes and were considered to have been on the verge of civilization and central government.

The word Taíno meant "good" or "noble" in their language, and not only were the Taíno peaceful and generous in their hospitality, but early Spanish chroniclers documented that no Spaniard ever saw the Taíno fighting among themselves. For thousands of years, the indigenous people had lived in harmony and peace with the spirit of the land. Approximately two hundred thousand Taíno had welcomed Columbus on his first voyage to Hispañola in 1492.

The Spanish settlers had enslaved the Taíno population, taking advantage of their mild manner. Discouraged by their plight, many Taíno committed mass suicide, as oppression was not part of their soul's contract with destiny. The cruelty of the Spaniards had broken the Taíno's spirits.

Hatuey had witnessed what the Spaniards had done to the Taíno of Hispañola. He had wanted the Cubans to organize and attack the Spaniards guerilla-style. In his quest to enlighten the Cubans regarding the Spaniards' real motives, Hatuey had shown the Cuban Taíno a basket of gold and jewels, saying,

> Here is the God the Spaniards worship. For these they fight and kill; for these they persecute us, and that is why we have to throw them into the sea… They tell us, these tyrants, that they adore a God of peace and equality, and yet they usurp our land and make us their slaves. They speak to us of an immortal soul and of their eternal rewards and punishments, and yet they rob our belongings, seduce our women, violate our daughters. Incapable of matching us in valor, these cowards cover themselves with iron that our weapons can't break.

The Cuban Taíno, who had been a pure, happy, and peaceful group of people, could not conceive of such violence, and most of the Taíno chiefs had refused to heed Hatuey's warnings.

Hatuey and the few who had joined him had been ill-prepared to fight the Spaniards, who used advanced weaponry and armor to their advantage. The Taíno were not accustomed to combat and had not known how to organize a proper attack, but Hatuey had refused to back down. For approximately three months, Hatuey and his men had fended off the Spaniards.

On February 2, 1512, Hatuey had been captured, tied to a stake, and burned alive. Before lighting the fire, a priest showed him the cross and asked him to accept Jesus and go to heaven.

Hatuey asked, "Are there people like you in heaven?"

"There are many like me in heaven," responded the priest.

Hatuey rejected the offer, stating that "…he wanted nothing to do with a God that would allow such cruelty to be unleashed in his name."

The Cubans celebrate Hatuey as the first freedom fighter and Cuba's first national hero.

By the mid-sixteenth century, Cuba's indigenous population had dropped to less than a few thousand because of disease, mass suicides, and Spanish exploitation.

The trip to Baracoa City settled the matter for José. After learning the details of how the conquistadors and early settlers had colonized Cuba, there was no doubt in his mind that Bartolomé de las Casas's account of colonization was accurate. The Spanish had been intensely violent and abusive and had inflicted significant losses on the indigenous population.

Again, the Spanish government had infuriated him. Protesting irrational wars was one thing but hearing firsthand what the Spanish conquistadors and early settlers had done to the indigenous people was another.

~❖~

José was disoriented, unsure of where he was. It had been a long night of gambling, drinking, and women. As he gathered his belongings, he noticed there were holes in both of his socks. How long had those holes been there? He had not seen how and when they'd happened.

As he looked around the unfamiliar room, he saw a woman he did not recognize or remember sleeping on the bed. Who was she? How had he gotten to this room? When and how did he get trapped in this toxic, self-destructive cycle of impulsive and reckless behavior? His life was spiraling out of control. That same day, he decided to get clean, sober up, and turn his life around.

He could not continue this destructive lifestyle. It was not getting him anywhere. In contrast, his brothers were excelling in life. He was proud to read the letters from back home detailing their accomplishments.

José had expected he would have an established career, a place of his own, and a committed and stable relationship by his mid-twenties. Maybe if he were back in Galicia, that would have been the case.

Despite the distractions, and no matter how hard he tried, he could not get ahead or feel at home in Cuba. He could not quite identify what was missing. His inner self was begging him to move on.

He had nothing to show for the last eight years. He had squandered his time in Cuba, caught up in a cycle of gambling, drinking, and fast women. He had used these distractions to escape his most uncomfortable emotions, which led to losses and more gambling, reckless behavior, despondency, and despair. It was insane that he had measured the success of his days based on how much he had won or lost at the gambling table.

He was not thriving in Cuba. He was barely surviving. There were too many days he had to contend with no food or shelter. He had to get out of this never-ending cycle of destructive behavior. He needed to settle down, have a family, and live a cleaner, healthier life. He needed a change of scenery and influence. He had to take charge of his life.

Finally, in 1924, he recognized that he could no longer continue to live a meaningless life. To appease the emptiness and clamoring of his soul, he decided to move on. But to where?

CHAPTER 7
HOME SWEET HOME

Though José had not yet discovered where home was, he was certain that he would recognize it once he got there. After eight years of heaviness and sorrow that no amount of alcohol, women, or gambling could dissipate, he was ready to move on.

José had not made an emotional connection with the island. At twenty-four, he still felt lost and displaced, with no sense of direction or guidance.

In 1924, José chose Cartagena, Colombia as his destination, for no other reason than the knowledge that Cuba was not where his instincts were commanding him to be. He did like the Caribbean lifestyle, and Cartagena, with its beaches and fishing community, offered something similar. For a month, he worked long hours, abstained from alcohol and gambling, and saved as much money as he could to prepare for his trip to Cartagena.

He purchased a one-way, third-class passage and boarded a ship destined for Cartagena, Colombia. The conditions on the ship were like the voyage from Spain, but at least the trip to Colombia would only be three days, not including a several-day layover in Port-au-Prince, Haiti.

At a barbershop on José's first day in Haiti, his barber suggested, "You may want to consider going to the Dominican Republic and waiting for your ship at the Port of Santo Domingo."

"Now why would I want to do that when I'm quite comfortable here?"

As the barber finished brushing the loose hairs from José's neck, he replied, "Yes, you could stay here and wait for your ship. But you may feel more comfortable in the Dominican Republic since they speak your language. You may even bump into some of your compatriots."

The more José mulled over the suggestion, the more it appealed to him. "You make a good point. Thank you for the suggestion."

Given the ancient history between the Spanish and the French concerning the ownership of the island, he agreed that being on the Spanish side made sense. The last thing José wanted was to get into emotionally charged discussions with the locals about ancient history. He'd had enough of that in Cuba.

Fate had opened a new door to which his intuition led him to cross; traveling to Santo Domingo that same day. He purchased his fare and traveled to the Port of Santo Domingo, Dominican Republic. The trip gave him time to stop and reflect on the last eight years of his life and his new adventure.

He recalled what he had learned while in Cuba about the history of the Dominican Republic and the role his fellow Spaniards had played there. He was not proud of the suffering inflicted on its people by the exploitative colonization of the Spanish conquistadors and settlers.

The Dominican Republic had certainly had its share of hard times and bad breaks in its quest for independence.

The Dominican Republic occupies the eastern two-thirds of the island of Hispañola (the colonial name for the island), which it shares with Haiti.

Christopher Columbus had explored the Dominican Republic on his first voyage in 1492. The capital—Santo Domingo, founded in 1496—is the oldest European settlement in the Western Hemisphere. The Spanish had built an elegant medieval city, which they had turned into Spain's New World capital. Santo Domingo was known as the "Gateway to the Caribbean."

Expeditions that led to Ponce de León's colonization of Puerto Rico, Diego Velázquez de Cuéllar's colonization of Cuba, Hernando Cortez's conquest of Mexico, and Vasco Núñez de Balboa's sighting of the Pacific Ocean had launched from Santo Domingo. The country had a rich history.

The Taíno people called the island Quisqueya, meaning "mother of the earth." Dominicans still refer to the island as Quisqueya, and the national anthem, "Quisqueyanos Valientes," is a testament to the original name of the island.

The Taíno people had inhabited the island for at least five thousand years before Columbus's arrival in 1492. The Taíno people who had welcomed Columbus on his first voyage had inhabited the island since the seventh century. They had been descendants of the Arawakan Indian tribes in the Amazon that had traveled through the Orinoco Valley in Venezuela.

The Taíno's longevity on the island had not stopped Columbus from claiming the island for Spain. Fueled by greed, ego, and self-enrichment, Columbus had declared the land by proclamation. He had argued that the indigenous people had not objected to his pronouncement. In all likelihood, the native people had not understood what Columbus was saying or doing.

The Spanish throne had offered Columbus 10 percent of the revenue derived from conquered lands in perpetuity for him and his descendants. Columbus had a strong financial incentive to conquer as much land as he could, regardless of the impact on its inhabitants.

The native population had been overpowered overnight by the conquistadors' ruthless actions and the introduction of the smallpox disease to the colony in 1518. The Taíno had not had the immunities to the diseases that the Spaniards and their animals had carried to the island.

Forced into slavery and hard labor, the Taíno could not engage in agricultural activities, and famine had accelerated the death rate of the indigenous population. To escape from the Spaniards, some Taino had adopted the tactic of burning their villages and crops and relocating to less hospitable regions, where they had formed new villages.

These runaway slaves mounted the most successful resistance against the Spaniards in 1519, led by Enriquillo in the Baoruco Mountain Range near the present border of Haiti. In 1534, after fourteen years of defeating the Spanish, Enriquillo and his tribe negotiated the first truce between the Taíno and the Spanish. The Taino were pardoned and granted their land.

Within twenty-five years of the arrival of the Spaniards, fewer than fifty thousand Taíno remained on the island. Within less than a century, the Spaniards had exterminated the Taíno population.

By 1603, Hispaniola's importance as a colony had diminished as the Spaniards abandoned the island, leaving devastation in their wake. The Spanish had left a rigid racial class structure, with most of the population considered mulatto (the offspring of Africans, Europeans, and the indigenous people).

In 1821, after three centuries of Spanish rule, the Dominican Republic became independent, but it was quickly taken over by Haiti.

Since Spain had ceded the Spanish colony of Santo Domingo to France in 1795 in the Treaty of Basel, Toussaint L'Ouverture and his followers invaded the eastern portion of the island, claiming that it was French territory. He abolished slavery and incorporated the Dominican Republic into the Black Republic. The entire island was under Haitian control and domination for twenty-two years.

Toussaint was a black Frenchman who had abolished slavery in Haiti and had run the white plantation owners off. Napoleon had mounted a large expedition to conquer the blacks and reinstate slavery. The black army had defeated the French, and the blacks had declared their independence on January 1, 1804, establishing the Republic of Haiti on the western third of the island of Hispañola.

Juan Pablo Duarte, born in Santo Domingo on January 26, 1813, was the son of Juan José Duarte, a Spanish retailer born in Spain, and Manuela Diez y Jiménez, a native of the Dominican Republic. Duarte, a prominent personality within the exclusive social circles of the time, was extremely patriotic and opposed Haitian domination of the country. Duarte's opposition came not from racial differences but the cultural differences.

His philosophy was that a union between Dominicans and Haitians was not possible because of the cultural differences between the Spanish and French philosophies. The political doctrines learned from Spain: Romanticism, Liberalism, and nationalism were the foundation of the Dominican Republic and Duarte's philosophy.

Duarte helped to organize, direct, and lead a secret society called La Trinitaria, a reformist movement in the city of Santo Domingo. The reformists were independence fighters whose motto was "God, Mother Country, and Freedom" ("Dios, Patria y Libertad").

After a failed revolution against the Haitian president in 1843, Duarte and his companions were jailed and then exiled.

Approximately one year later, Duarte returned to the Dominican Republic. On February 27, 1844, the underground resistance group led by Juan Pablo Duarte overthrew the Haitian government, and independence in the Dominican Republic was declared once again. Duarte penned the constitution of the Dominican Republic modeled on that of the United States and put forth in November 1844.

José dismissed thoughts of the island's volatile history as he arrived at the Port of Santo Domingo and caught his first glimpse of the coastline, the beautiful, pristine land, and peacefulness of the island.

For the first time since he had left his hometown in Galicia, José had that warm, safe, comfortable feeling inside. He welcomed and relished the sensation. After eight long, arduous years, José still missed his family, but he no longer felt physical pain. He no longer grieved the loss of his family, parents, and life in Orense, Galicia.

José was giddy and jumped around in the sand. He did not fully understand the utter bliss, but he welcomed it after the years of grieving.

José wanted to enjoy each moment and do as much as he could before boarding the ship to Cartagena, Colombia. He had made the right decision to wait for the ship in the Port of Santo Domingo instead of Port-au-Prince.

He spent his days on the beach of Boca Chica, located on the southern coast of the island in Andrés. The beach was approximately twenty miles east of the capital city, Santo Domingo, and considered "the beach" of Santo Domingo. Boca Chica was an ideal destination to escape the daily hustle and bustle of the city.

The tropical beach, with its pristine white sand, was fringed by gently swaying coconut palm trees. The hot, lazy days evolved into spectacular sunsets radiating colors that tinted the waves of the ocean orange, red, and purple.

José welcomed the fresh ocean breeze with a hint of salt under the hot Caribbean sun. Lying in his hammock, with its lazy sway mimicking that of the palm trees, he says to himself, "This is one of the most beautiful beaches I have ever seen."

As he enjoyed the beach, it dawned on him that this was the first time in eight years he had taken a vacation. He was relaxed, enjoying himself without thinking about where to sleep, going to work, gambling, or the stress of debt.

One afternoon, while he lazily enjoyed the beautiful weather on the beach, José could not resist an intense poker game outside of a local pub. He vicariously enjoyed the game as the men played their respective hands intently. He could tell these were experienced players.

When a seat opened at the table, one player turned to him and asked, "Hey, *España* (Spaniard), do you want to play?"

José was excited about the opportunity to play and took the empty seat at the table. The game was a five-card draw, with five players at the table. He was fortunate to be sitting to the right of the dealer, so he was the last player to make a move in the first round. This position gave José the advantage of seeing everybody else's move before he had to decide on his own.

The dealer dealt the first-round cards, and the betting ensued. Someone bet, two players called (matched the bet), one folded, and then it was José's turn. José had three queens, one four, and one seven in his hand an initially strong hand, allowing him to stay in the game. A win would help him recover some of the money he had lost on the voyage from Cuba.

José knew that the game of poker was about deception. He also recognized that a strong starting hand, such as three queens, was rare, so he wanted to maximize the opportunity to increase the pot.

At this juncture, José had two options: raise or call. By raising, José could win the pot outright, albeit with less money. By calling, he would guarantee another round of betting, thereby increasing the pot. Calling could also backfire, as it would allow the other players to improve their hands.

José strategically called rather than give away the strength of his hand by raising too early. Calling ensured he proceeded into the next round of betting with the three remaining players.

To prepare for the next round, the dealer asked the remaining players if any wanted to exchange their cards. José exchanged two cards: the four and seven. When he looked at his two new cards, he saw two eights. Amazingly, he had significantly improved his hand to queens full over eights (or a full house). The odds of someone having a better hand were slim. José was elated and could barely contain himself from imagining the looks on the faces of these older, experienced players when he won the pot.

As the betting ensued, the first player placed a large bet. The second player called. Emboldened by the third player folding, José convinced himself that he had the best hand and wanted to go all-in and bet his remaining chips.

In a zealous moment of overconfidence, he raised with everything he had in his pockets, including his passage to Colombia. José was confident that the remaining two players would fold and declare him the winner or that one or both would call his raise, further increasing his winnings. In José's mind, it was a win-win scenario for him. Either way, he would come out on top.

After José placed his bet, the first player folded, but the second one called. José flipped over his cards with the utmost confidence, showing his full house. The other player, after a slight hesitation, said, "Not so fast, España," and laid down a hand revealing a higher full house: aces full over sixes. José was incredulous, staring at both hands to convince himself that his eyes did not deceive him and that he had lost.

José walked away from the table slowly and deliberately; shoulders slumped—dejected, shocked, speechless, and penniless. He trudged down to the beach to think through what had transpired. A sudden wave of exhaustion came upon him, his legs so heavy that he could barely put one foot in front of the other.

As he walked away from the table, he reprimanded himself for falling into his old habit of reckless behavior. Whatever had possessed him to enter a game of poker and bet his entire pot of money, including his passage to Cartagena? He'd left Cuba to abandon that reckless lifestyle and break the cycle of gambling. Less than one week after leaving Cuba, he was already acting irresponsibly. Here he was yet again, destitute and homeless because of his gambling addiction.

When he reached an empty hammock, he slumped down, utterly drained of energy. The outcome of the game had changed everything for him.

As the afternoon wore on, and the sun started to set, José was mesmerized by the gradient of colors from dark gold to yellow. He had an unobstructed view of the ocean and was soothed by the soft breeze under the swaying palm trees and the rhythmic sound of the gentle waves. The clouds played with the sunlight shimmering in the water, with the palm trees' silhouettes in the background. A beautiful and relaxing setting.

Lying in the hammock amid the hypnotic sunset, he suddenly heard his mother's voice saying, "José, my son, you left Cuba because you needed to set a new trajectory for your life; you wanted a fresh start. You must let go of the habits of the last eight years so you can embrace your new beginnings. Go back to the core values and ethics we taught you in Galicia."

In disbelief, José thinks, "Was that my mother's voice? I must be hallucinating."

Whether it was his mother, his imagination, or him thinking what his mother would have advised at such a moment was irrelevant. He had to change. As he looked around, continuing to enjoy the scenery, he thinks, "This is not bad." It could be worse, like back in Spain with the Spanish Army.

The atmosphere, the warm breeze, and a spectacular sunset lifted his spirits. José acknowledged how fortunate he was to be in such a beautiful place. The warm, cozy, comfortable sensation he'd experienced when he had first arrived in Santo Domingo engulfed him. But, this time, the intensity encapsulated his mind, body, and soul. It was as if an unseen entity was giving him a welcoming hug. It was a moment of transcendence, an experience of spiritual connection and awareness, unlike anything he had ever known. Again, he heard a voice saying, "Welcome home."

José did not attempt to explain what he had just heard and experienced. At that precise moment, he recognized that he was home. Home sweet home!

In an instant, he felt a surge of energy throughout his entire body. He had never experienced such an indescribable feeling of invincibility.

The synchronicity and confluence of the events that had brought him to this point in his life amused him: the overwhelming need to leave Cuba, the layover in Port-au-Prince, the barber's suggestion to wait for his ship in Santo Domingo, and, finally, the outcome of the poker game. José's love for the game of poker and the hand of fate combined had determined his destiny.

It was clear that despite his original plan, the universe had a much better option for him. He would not be traveling to Cartagena, Colombia—not only because he no longer had the passage, but because he was home. Going to Cartagena was merely an adventurous whim. No one was waiting for him, and he had no compelling reasons to travel to Colombia specifically.

In three days, José had fallen in love with the island and its people. It had been love at first sight. The women, the scenery, the accent, and the slow-paced lifestyle enchanted him. The locals had welcomed and taken him in. They even christened him with a new name, "España." He liked the sound of it. With his heavy Galician accent, José would never be exactly like the typical Dominican. Nevertheless, he was willing to work at becoming a local.

At that moment, he vowed to himself and the memory of his mother that he would live a healthy, productive lifestyle. He did not know why he felt so comfortable and welcome, and he would not try to understand or explain it. The feeling was a welcome one after eight years of emotional isolation.

He had spent the last eight years unwittingly searching for his place in the New World. Now, for the first time in eight years, he felt at home. José was confident that he could settle down and set roots on this beautiful island.

His mind raced as he tried to formulate a plan and determine his next steps. The first thing he had to do was find a job so he could support himself and rebuild his savings. He also had to find a place to live in; fortunately, he had his hammock, which would suit him well in the event nothing panned out.

José remembered a Spanish family he had befriended on the beach the previous day. He rose from his hammock in search of the Lopez family. The sun had recently set, and it was possible that they could still be at the beach. He scanned the faces of the remaining beachgoers and quickly recognized the Lopez family. Mrs. Lopez was packing, but Mr. Lopez was still lying on the hammock. He cautiously approached the Lopez family and asked, "Señor Lopez, can I please speak with you in private?"

José noted that Señor Lopez was annoyed about having to get up from his hammock. "Tell me; how can I help you?"

José recounted, "Yesterday, I mentioned to you my plan of traveling to Cartagena on the ship arriving tomorrow afternoon. But as it turns out, I will not be able to board that ship since I have done a reckless and foolish thing. You see, I lost my money and my passage to Cartagena in a poker game."

After José finished recounting his dilemma, he could see that Señor Lopez changed from somewhat annoyed to visibly unnerved by José's gambling. His hand waving José away, his body language said: "I walked over from my relaxing hammock for a gambler? I hope he is not going to ask me for money."

José continued sheepishly, "Señor Lopez, please hear me out. I assure you I am not going to ask you for money. The first day we met, you mentioned you had a family business, La Commercial, which I believe you said was a bodega. I want to ask whether you could use some help at that bodega of yours? Even if it's temporary work until I can get on my feet."

Lopez said, "A gambler? Probably also a heavy drinker, as they usually go hand in hand. Some of the sleaziest people I know are gamblers. José, you appear to be a healthy and strong young man, and I could use someone to help me with the heavy lifting. But I have to be honest; your irresponsible actions make me question your integrity, ethics, and trustworthiness. I run a serious business and can't afford to have someone that will be there one day and not show up the next because he is either too drunk or was up-all-night gambling."

José pleaded, "Señor Lopez, I understand and don't blame you for thinking that I am not trustworthy. You are correct that the predicament I have put myself in was irresponsible. I am penniless and homeless and ask that you permit me the opportunity to change your mind about me. I grew up on a farm in Nocedo, where I handled the fieldwork and tended the animals for my parents, so I am not afraid of hard work. I have also spent the last eight years doing backbreaking work, laying the tracks for the tramway in Cuba. I assure you that if you give me the opportunity, you will not be disappointed. I promise to work harder than anyone else in your bodega."

Lopez, not convinced, said, "I don't know. I've seen many men like you who say they will change and can be trusted. They get off to a great start; then after a month or two, they are back to their irresponsible behavior."

José again pleaded, "I am sure that you have seen your share of irresponsible employees, but I have vowed to myself and the memory of my mother, Francisca, to change. I am asking you to give me a chance."

Cautiously, Lopez agreed. "Fine, José. Only because you are a fellow Galician, and I know the work ethics of our people. I will take you on a trial basis. You will be on probation until I have developed confidence in you. I will also rent you a room in one of our boarding houses. Keep in mind that I will end your employment and kick you out of the room at the first sign of irresponsible behavior, no matter how slight. If you can agree to those terms, then you have a temporary job and a room to live in."

José was thrilled and thanked Señor Lopez for the opportunity. Not only did he get a job but also a place to stay. Despite losing his money, this was a good start.

He spent the next three years at the bodega, learning everything he could about running the business. La Commercial sold everything from food to hardware, catering to the needs of the town's residents. Besides stocking shelves, he learned how to manage the inventory, order new products, and take care of the other duties required to operate the bodega. It was hard work, but he enjoyed it. He enjoyed it so much he vowed that someday he was going to save enough money to purchase a bodega of his own.

After he had stabilized his finances and set aside some savings, he decided to move on. He was grateful for the help provided to him by his compatriots, but the time had come for him to explore the island on his own.

His second job was at the sugar mill, Central de Azúcar, in Andrés, where he worked as a welder on the construction of the mill's chimney. Since he still lived in Santo Domingo, he had to commute to Andrés, as he could not secure a room at the local boarding house. After six months at the mill, José learned that one of his coworkers would be moving out of the local boarding house. He made a mental note to stop by the boarding house after his shift and speak to the owner, María Acosta.

That same afternoon, when his shift was over, he walked over to the boarding house to inquire about a room. The entrance to the boarding house was through the cantina. As he walked through the cantina, he noted that men from the sugar mill occupied its ten tables, enjoying a drink and light dinner. He followed the corridor to the boarding house. It was modest but clean.

When José came upon María's office, he stood at the door, staring at her as she rifled through some paperwork. The room was small with no window, a desk, a small desk lamp, a chair, a cabinet, and a calculator.

He was not sure why, but he was immediately intrigued by María. She was not a beautiful woman, but she had a certain charm and eloquence that was attractive. She wore a simple dress with an apron. She was about five feet tall, had luxurious dark hair, and olive skin. Her face, illuminated by the desk lamp, revealed her dark brown eyes, high cheekbones, and angular jawline. Maybe she had Taíno heritage.

Sensing that someone was watching her, María turned and looked José up and down with a puzzled look on her face.

"Can I help you?

José confidently walked into the room and said, "Yes, of course. My name is José Fernández, but most people call me España because I am a Spaniard."

María responded matter-of-factly, "Tell me, Mr. España; what I can do for you?"

"I work at the sugar mill, and I need a place to live. Do you have a room available for rent?"

María was busy, and as she riffled through some paperwork, she responded without shifting her gaze. "Yes, I have one room available. It's not one of our best rooms, but it's practical and suitable for one person. It's yours if you want it. The rent includes breakfast and is payable weekly by the end of the day on Fridays. Would you like to see the room?"

José was elated and quickly said, "No, I do not need to see the room. I will take it. I need a place to live, and this location is convenient for me. I am not concerned with the size of the room." He only had his personal belongings to carry and moved in the following day.

As the weeks and months passed, José watched María from afar. He watched as she managed the staff that helped in the kitchen and dining areas and cleaned the rooms. He was amazed at her instincts and survival skills. She was skilled at presenting herself in a way to get what she wanted from the people around her.

Unlike many of her peers, María did not appear to abide by the social and cultural norms of the time. She owned her own business and liked to drink, smoke, dance, and have a good time.

He also noticed that she had a tender side, as she nurtured and interacted with her four children. He did not know how she managed to run a successful business and mind four children at the same time.

José had to admit that he was somewhat intimidated by her independence and no-nonsense, businesslike attitude. He had never met such a self-assured, independent woman. He was impressed by the efficiency with which she ran the boarding house and the adjacent restaurant that fed its residents and employees of the sugar mill.

There was nothing dainty about María. She was one of the most confident and shrewd women he had ever met. He did not know that women could possess these qualities. Granted, he had spent the last eight years of his life consorting with a different type of woman. Unlike those women, María had a wholesome, natural appearance wearing no makeup.

She was a fantastic woman. He saw her as someone who would make a great wife and business partner. It did not matter to José that she was the mother of four children. He was intrigued by her and was willing to work hard at getting to know her on a personal level.

Was there a Mr. Acosta? José had never seen a man around the boarding house, cantina, or with the children. Who knew? Maybe there was no Mr. Acosta. He wanted to get to know her marital situation before he could even contemplate a relationship with her.

PART II
ROSA MARÍA ACOSTA SEGURA
1894–1956

A WOMAN AHEAD OF HER TIME

CHAPTER 8
A HYPOCRITICAL SOCIETY

María's decision to elope with a married man was a great disappointment and embarrassment for her parents. How could she humiliate the family this way? Where had they gone wrong? Their little girl was going to be someone's mistress, despite the years they had spent grooming her to be a respectable wife.

She had been an independent, free spirit from the day she was born. As parents, they'd had a difficult time controlling her. She most certainly did not espouse any of the traits of her upbringing.

Throughout the years, they had been disturbed by her sense of right and wrong with actions unsuitable for a respectable young lady. Despite these misgivings, they had always hoped and prayed that María would mature, come to her senses, and settle down with a respectable man—hopefully, one with sufficient means to secure her future.

Rosa María Acosta Segura had come into the world on August 30, 1894, in Santo Domingo, Dominican Republic. María was the second of five children and the oldest daughter of two born to Emilio Acosta and Victoriana Segura Fernández.

Emilio and Victoriana had had the wherewithal to give their children a middle-class upbringing. Emilio had spared no expense on the education of the boys. They had attended the best schools in the city, as they would someday marry and have a family to support.

Despite his financial position, Emilio did not believe in giving the girls a formal education. In his view, this was a waste of money. The girls would grow up and get married, and their husbands would take care of their financial needs. Instead of formal education, the girls had received daily lessons in the skills necessary to make good wives and successfully manage a home and domestic staff.

From the age of thirteen, María had spent her mornings in the kitchen, learning how to bake and cook. She learned how to cook traditional Dominican dishes and bake pastries, cakes, and other desserts. She would help prepare the noon meal, which was the main meal of the day. She had also learned how to set the table to serve a formal dinner.

Her afternoons consisted of tutoring in the basics of simple math, reading, and writing. Her parents believed that a good wife should be able to handle some of the administrative aspects of running a household. Besides learning the basics of academia, the girls had been taught to suppress their intelligence and follow the male figures in their lives.

The evenings had been more relaxing, as they had learned the arts of knitting and needlepoint to pass the time.

This daily routine had left María feeling claustrophobic, trapped in a lifestyle her parents and society dictated. Why was it acceptable for boys to enjoy greater freedom and be given considerable latitude in their behavior, while the girls were not permitted to socialize without a chaperone?

There had been days when María had felt she would suffocate if she did not get out of the house and away from the duties and daily routine. At times, she would sneak out after her brothers to see what they were doing. Crouched behind a bush, she had vicariously enjoyed their freedom as she watched them play tag, baseball, soccer and go to the corner store for candy. How she had wished she could join them.

Upon noticing María's absence, Victoriana would send the housekeeper to find her. When María returned to the house, not only would she get the scolding of a lifetime, but she would also be assigned extra chores. María had not cared. Escaping the confines of her daily routine for even one moment to enjoy her brothers' adventures had been worth it.

Victoriana had regularly monitored and watched the girls to protect their virginity. María and her sister had had to entertain friends, especially male visitors, in the presence of a chaperone. The goal was to maximize the chances of a favorable marriage proposal that would lead to a formal engagement, a religious wedding, and an elaborate fiesta.

It had driven María crazy to see that her mother espoused and accepted that it was a man's world. Victoriana had treated Emilio like a king and her sons as princes. Emilio had been the head of the household and had had the last word on major decisions—right, wrong, or indifferent. End of discussion.

Why did women have to accept this restrictive lifestyle without question? She had not understood why a woman had to obey and praise the man's leadership, no questions asked, even if he was a complete idiot.

Machismo, the cultural indoctrination that allowed the males to play a dominant role within the family, was endemic in their society. The treatment of the boys and girls within her own family was living proof that this differentiation of the sexes began early in life and deeply ingrained in their society.

As the boys developed into men, having numerous premarital and extramarital sexual adventures was acceptable. It was socially acceptable for a man to father many children and maintain several women as concubines. Not assuming the role of head of the family and supporting his children was socially unacceptable. The irony was that these same men expected their brides to be virgins. This expectation was the height of machismo in a hypocritical, duplicitous society.

Throughout the years, María had had young men from good families as suitors. These men would have made excellent husbands, but they were too dull, serious, and controlling for María. They had expected her to conform to and abide by society's rules of behavior. María had unapologetically bucked societal norms and refused to suppress her free spirit. Consequently, each relationship ended in disappointment for both families.

Emilio and Victoriana had cautioned María that she would end up being a spinster if she continued to shun her suitors. They had tried to convince her that her role in life was to get married and have children of her own. Anything short of this domestic role was considered abnormal, unfulfilling, and suspect.

María had not let her parents' admonitions scare her. She took the ideals of love and marriage seriously and was not going to let anyone pressure her into a loveless and controlling union. María was not going to compromise her standards, even if the price was never getting married.

She was not afraid of the old maid title, even though she would have been far from the stereotypical spinster. María was an extrovert who dressed fashionably and was comfortable with herself. She refused to let society control her lifestyle and decisions.

CHAPTER 9
A WOMAN AHEAD OF HER TIME

With each whirl and twirl, she displayed the beautiful, silky nylon and lace layers of her petticoat. After all, petticoats were not underwear. Petticoats were meant to be displayed and admired. The fancier the garment, the more to show off.

As she was whirling and twirling to her favorite merengue, María bumped into an older gentleman dancing with his wife; María offered a hasty apology without breaking her rhythm.

Later in the evening, the gentleman approached her and introduced himself. He said, "Good evening, Señorita, my name is Juan Batista, and this is my wife, Dionisia Batista. We wanted to make sure that you were okay."

With a curious look, María responded, "Yes, I'm fine. Thank you for asking. I don't recall ever meeting you; are you related to the groom?"

"We are friends of the groom's family," said Juan.

Dionisia added, "We are having a great time; it's a fantastic fiesta."

María thanked Dionisia and said, "My mother's obsession with the planning of our weddings started on the days we were born. Throughout the years she has planned for everything wedding related. It had to be perfect. Look at my sister. She looks stunning. Not a hair out of place."

Dionisia turned to look at the bride. "Your sister looks amazing. We have a daughter and hope to have a wedding as fancy and elaborate as this one someday. Please give my congratulations to your parents; they have done an excellent job. So, María, what about you? Are you married?"

"Oh no, Señora, I don't even have a boyfriend. But that doesn't stop my mother from planning my wedding. She is driving me crazy, trying to engage me in wedding planning discussions. She is hopeful that I will someday say yes to one of my suitors."

Dionisia smiled at María's characterization of her mother's obsession with planning her wedding. "Well, I'm sure you will meet the right person someday and give your parents the pleasure of hosting another grand fiesta."

Juan said, "We will let you continue enjoying the fiesta. But before we leave, would you grant me the opportunity to dance with you before the evening is over?"

María turned to Dionisia and said, "Only if there are no objections from Señora Batista."

"Señorita María, no objections from me; you can dance an entire set or two with him so that I can take the opportunity to rest my tired feet," said Dionisia, with a thankful look on her face.

Juan happily replied, "That settles it. I will take Dionisia back to our table and come back for that dance."

María studied the couple as they walked away. He was a good-looking man, and she was a beautiful woman. They made a handsome couple.

Twenty minutes later, Juan returned in time for the band to resume playing.

"Señorita María, are you ready for that dance you promised?"

"Yes, Señor Batista. Let's hope that you can keep up," she teased.

"Don't worry about me; I can keep up."

During the first dance, María quickly recognized that she was dancing with an expert dancer. He commanded the dance floor, leading her with a firm grip. Guiding her, he initiated intricate transitions to different steps. He even improvised dance steps. He was the perfect lead. Steering her by the waist, he conveyed choices and direction through subtle physical signals. Their smooth coordination must have led onlookers to assume that Juan and María had been dancing as a couple for many years.

After the band finished playing their set, Juan escorted María back to her table.

"Señor Batista, you are an excellent dancer."

"Thank you, but please call me Juan. You were not too bad yourself. You are easy to lead and perfectly fell into step. I'm impressed at how you were able to keep up with the complex transitions, change of pace, and direction."

"Señor Batista—I mean, Juan—I love to dance and relish any opportunity to do so."

"What else do you like to do other than dance?"

"My life is pretty boring with my parents constantly watching over me, pressuring me to get married. Instead, tell me about yourself and your family."

"I am not a native Dominican. I emigrated from the French island of Corsica in the Mediterranean Sea. I have been fortunate here in the Dominican Republic. I have established several successful local businesses." Juan leaned in a little closer to her ear and said, "Why don't you stop by my bodega so that I can show you around?"

Sensing a change in his demeanor, María reverted the conversation to his family. "How long have you been married? Any children?"

"Dionisia and I have been married for ten years and have two children, Martina and Felix," Juan said, then touched her elbow lightly and again invited María to his bodega.

María looked away from Juan, not sure how to respond to his offer. After a few seconds, she thinks, "What harm could there be in going to the bodega? After all, it is a public place." She then turned to face Juan and said, "Well, I could use a few items. I may stop by to see what you have to offer."

Juan softly smiled and added, "I'm usually in my bodega on Wednesdays and can be there if you agree to stop by." As he again leaned in closer to her ear, he said, "I'd love to help you pick out some of those items."

María knew that Juan was flirting with her, but she followed along for the fun of it. "Okay, I will see you on Wednesday at about three o'clock at your bodega."

As Juan walked away with a huge grin on his face, María could not believe she had agreed to go to Juan's bodega with the bogus excuse of needing to make a purchase. What was she thinking? Señor Batista was a married man with two children. She had met and spoken with Señora Batista. Maybe it wouldn't hurt to go to his bodega, purchase those items, and say a final goodbye; and that is how, in 1916, at the age of twenty-two, María met Juan Batista.

After the wedding reception, in the solitude of her room, María replayed the events of the day. Her sister had looked beautiful. María was glad that her sister's wedding had been a success, and everyone had had a good time. Her mother's planning and obsession with the details had paid off. For María, the highlight of the day had been meeting Juan Batista. Juan was a true gentleman, easy to talk to, and a fabulous dancer.

Over the next few days, she was excited about the prospect of seeing Juan again. But, in the back of her mind, she second-guessed whether she was doing the right thing. Despite some initial trepidation, on Wednesday morning, she woke up invigorated and looking forward to her afternoon outing.

During the noon meal, she advised her parents that she would go to the Centro Commercial to purchase a few items. Her parents agreed to let her travel, but only if she had a chaperone.

She arrived at the bodega at precisely three o'clock, and there was Juan, waiting as happy to see her as she was to see him. He gave her the grand tour of his store. She was impressed with the layout and selections. Before she knew it, two hours had transpired, and she had selected nothing. She couldn't go back home empty-handed. She quickly selected a couple of insignificant items for her hair. As she approached to pay, Juan insisted she accept them as a gift. María declined, coquettishly stating, "What if I come back next week and take my time looking around? I saw some items that I might be interested in buying."

Juan wore a huge grin on his face at the prospect of seeing María again. "I will be here anxiously awaiting your return."

Thus began their weekly meetings. María found herself growing closer to and fonder of Juan as time passed. She could not identify what made her so comfortable around him.

Yes, Juan was much older than her other suitors, and maybe that was why she felt so comfortable around him. With Juan, she did not have to pretend or conform. He let her be herself, and he never tried to control her. She loved spending time with Juan. For the first time in her life, she felt free to be herself without feeling judged. Similar to the synchronization of their first dance, so was their relationship. It was as if she had known him her entire life. Juan was unlike any other person she had ever met. She could talk to Juan for hours and never get bored.

Unfortunately, she had limited time with Juan, spending only the brief moments she could get away from her parents' watchful eyes with him. María had fallen in love with Juan but struggled with her parents' expectations of the perfect mate. They would not accept a married man. They would not understand how much she loved him or how comfortable he made her feel.

She did not feel good about sneaking around, involved in an adulterous affair with Juan. Most of all, she hated lying to her parents to do so. But when she was with Juan, she did not feel that their relationship was inappropriate. Arranging her weekly visits with Juan was complicated, as her parents asked many questions, and she was running out of excuses for her absences.

After six months of sneaking around and ignoring the threat of inevitable wrath of her family and friends, María decided to follow her heart, regardless of the consequences and price she would ultimately have to pay. Juan was willing to take care of her and had offered to set her up in her own house. But according to her parents, this would be living in sin.

Falling in love with Juan was not something she had planned or expected. If she did not follow through with her feelings, she might regret sacrificing herself, her desires, for her family's and Dionisia's sakes. She had to be true to herself and what she wanted in life rather than trying to please her parents and surrender to societal norms.

She did not care that Juan was a married man and that their society considered their relationship a sin. Dionisia Batista was a lovely lady, but María could do nothing for her. Unfortunately, she had met Juan as a married man, so Señora Batista would have to get over it and forgive them both.

She didn't want to continue lying to her parents but struggled with how to let her parents know about her relationship without losing their respect and support.

Regardless of what they'd say, she wouldn't allow her parents to make her give up her relationship with Juan, even if their love and relationship were considered sinful, and even though she would never be considered Señora Batista. María had never fallen in love before and was not about to give it up now that she had found it.

Maybe this was selfish of her, but she didn't feel guilty about the prospect of living with a married man. Was she supposed to feel sorry for his wife? Perhaps she should have been feeling guilty about the shame, disrespect, and other consequences this might bring to Juan's wife and children and her own family. Maybe that was what having a moral compass meant.

Did this lack of guilt make her a bad person? Maybe it did. What other explanation could there be for her selfishness and indifference? She sat in her room, contemplating what she was doing, waiting for the remorse to set in, but it never came.

She fully understood the ramifications of her affair and what this union would mean for her and her future. Juan had made it clear that he did not intend to leave his wife and children. She loved Juan and was willing to live with the social stigma that being a mistress had imposed.

Those damned double standards in her society were at play. Society permitted men to have as many mistresses as they could afford, with no adverse consequences. However, those same women had to suffer social stigma and the ramifications of society's disapproval. These were the norms of their hypocritical society.

No, she was not one of those women who entered into a relationship with a married man expecting that someday he would come to his senses and leave his wife and marry her. She was entering the relationship with eyes wide open. By entering into this relationship with Juan, she agreed to be the "other woman." But at this point in her life, she was willing to accept those terms.

She expected that her family, friends, and neighbors might shame and scorn her, especially in her town, where everyone was so nosy and stuck up. She was not going to waste her time worrying about what her neighbors may say.

In María's mind, she had three choices: she could live the rest of her life as a spinster, trying to please her parents and society; she could marry someone she did not love, or she could be true to herself and follow her dreams. María chose to follow her inner guidance, regardless of her parents or societal norms.

After sneaking around for six months, María summoned the courage to tell her parents about her affair. The news that their daughter was having an affair with a married man mortified her parents. Her father yelled, screamed, and threatened to kill someone. He forbade her relationship with Juan. Her mother, in her dramatic fashion, cried and then fainted.

María's flair for individuality erupted when she failed to step in line with her parents' values by going against societal norms and eloping with Juan.

Telling her parents that she was planning to elope with a married man was extremely difficult and painful for María. It pained her to hurt her family deliberately.

She moved out of her childhood home and into a house that Juan had purchased and fully furnished that same day. She could not bear to witness the pain, disappointment, and disapproval in her parents' eyes.

The transition was much easier than she had expected. She was not surprised that she and Juan quickly flowed into a routine, given their great relationship. Juan spent most of his free time with María, with his two children in tow. They spent so much time together that María did not feel like the "other woman." María loved Juan's children as if they were her own. In turn, the children loved María as much as they loved their mother.

After four glorious years of living a blissful life as a couple, María and Juan had their first child, followed by three other children born between 1920 and 1927 (Lucia, Carmelo, Emilia, and Marcia).

Juan's six children loved each other as brothers and sisters with no differentiation. There were no secrets about the complicated relationships involved. María and the six children accepted and thrived in their blended family.

Dionisia, on the other hand, did not interact with María's children. Dionisia's opposition to the union was so fierce that she refused to permit Juan to give María's children the Batista name. To appease Dionisia, Juan complied by never legally recognizing the children as his own. It was the least Juan could do for his wife, even if it came at the expense of his biological children. María's children had her last name, Acosta.

Juan's actions to appease Dionisia were the beginning of the end of Juan and María's relationship. By failing to recognize their children before the law and society as his biological children, Juan had let her down in the most profound way. Though Juan had made no promises to her, she had not expected him to turn his back on their children. He had condemned them to the legal and societal discrimination of living with the stigma of being illegitimate bastards. Without Juan's last name, her children did not have a legitimate right to any inheritance. Her children relied on her, and she had to provide for them.

Juan's lack of courage was extremely disappointing. Why punish the children to appease Dionisia? Unforgivable. Not standing up for the children was one of the primary causes of the erosion of the love and respect she once had for Juan.

Although María and Juan were in love, they each had a significant problem with the other's most prominent characteristics.

María was the love of Juan's life, but her independence and willingness to get involved in his business made him uncomfortable. She stressed him out with her questions and her constant suggestions regarding new investment opportunities and the running and managing of his current businesses. She constantly questioned his policies and how he managed his businesses.

Juan had expressed his desire for her to be more docile, letting him take charge of her life. Juan wanted to pamper María and treat her like a queen. No matter how hard he tried, she was unwilling to sit back and let him take the lead.

From María's vantage point, Juan was a kind, honest, and generous man, and she loved him dearly. Nevertheless, he was a man with a weak character, who always fell for a sad story at the expense of losing money. On many occasions, Juan gave merchandise on credit and never enforced the collection of the debt. It drove María crazy to see how some people took advantage of his kind demeanor.

This lack of gumption was the source of the problem for the independent, business-minded María. Juan was too weak for her strong character. He was thin-skinned, too sensitive, softhearted, and easily offended. His weaknesses frustrated her to no end. She wanted to be in charge of their relationship, and that was a problem for both of them.

In María's mind, she could not afford to sit back and depend on Juan. Her survival and her children's welfare depended on her. She had to take charge of her destiny. She had too much pride to seek her parents' help. Seeking their support would be admitting defeat. She had to resolve her financial situation on her own. Although her parents accepted and loved the children, they had not gotten over her decision to live with Juan out of wedlock.

When María learned that the cantina and boarding house that served the workers of the sugar mill were for sale, she immediately approached Juan. María convincingly argued: "Juan, think about it. Boca Chica has an established sugar mill in the Town of Andrés. The town depends on the sugar mill, which should be operating for years to come. The boarding house and cantina are businesses with an established and captive clientele. The tenants and cantina patrons work at the sugar mill."

"María, I agree that this business with established customers and revenue would be a good investment. However, you know running a boarding house with a cantina is not the type of business I'm interested in managing or owning."

María said, "But that is the beauty of my proposal. You do not have to do anything. Once you make the initial investment, I will manage the business and any future required investment. I would like this to be my business venture."

Juan shook his head as he said, "I don't know about this. We had agreed that it would be best if you stayed home with the children."

María knew from previous discussions that Juan was using the children as an excuse for not granting her financial freedom. He foolishly believed that she would somehow leave him if she did not need his financial support. He had once teased her, saying, "María, you are like a thoroughbred horse looking for an opening to break from the pack, which would be the beginning of the end of our relationship." Despite his insecurity, María knew that if she persisted, Juan would eventually grant her request.

After much cajoling, Juan reluctantly agreed to finance and establish the business, with María as the sole proprietor.

María accepted Juan's help with the caveat that he would not interfere in the management of the business. The venture would be her business, and she would run it her way.

Juan selflessly agreed to help María set up her own business.

Chapter 10
EMBRACING NEW BEGINNINGS

María stood in the middle of the cantina reveling in her accomplishments of the last year. Yes, purchasing the business was a good idea. As she proudly stood amid her business, she had to smile at the realization of what had enabled her success. Yes, Juan had provided the initial investment but, ironically, the other skills required to run the business came from her mother.

She had to thank her mother for insisting on that daily routine that had left María feeling claustrophobic and trapped. Those daily lessons in the skills necessary to manage a home and domestic staff. Learning to bake pastries, cakes, and other desserts; the lessons that taught her how to cook many different foods, knowing how to set the table for any occasion, and her mother's insistence that she learn the basics of simple math, reading, and writing had served her well. The years of training had prepared her for the successful management of the boarding house and cantina.

María recalled the day José Fernández had strutted into the boardinghouse, looking for a room. He was slightly over five feet tall, but his attitude, confidence, and self-assurance were larger than life. What José lacked in stature, he made up in demeanor and looks.

He was a handsome man with distinct European features. José had dark hair, fair skin, thick eyebrows, and eyes the color of golden honey. She could not deny the instant attraction. However, having a personal relationship with her tenants was one rule María had made a point never to break.

But José had refused to be ignored and was persistent in his courting. He had offered to help with work around the boarding house. He assisted in the cantina by cooking Galician dishes for the patrons. He even helped with the children, and this, in particular, was endearing to María. Many men ran away from women with children. Not José. He embraced her children and loved them as his own.

José was steadfast in his quest to win her affection and that of her four children. José quickly made himself an indispensable part of María's daily life.

María was suspicious. She questioned José's motives. After all, she had four children, was six years his senior, and was not a glamorous woman by any stretch of the imagination. She was not rich, but she had a business and a comfortable lifestyle. He, on the other hand, had nothing more than the personal belongings in his room. What were his intentions? What did he want from her?

María was still committed to Juan Batista, and she did not want to be unfaithful to him, but she struggled with their relationship. Juan was a married man with a family and other commitments. Juan made no promises, and she fully understood the rules of their relationship. But after twelve years, she wanted more for herself and her children.

She'd hoped that Juan would commit one way or the other, but he would ever have the courage to listen to his heart and divorce his wife or legally recognize her children. As much as she loved Juan, she could not get past his weak character and lack of gumption.

María would have been willing to live with Juan as his mistress. What she found troubling and could not get over was his lack of commitment to the children. They did not deserve such disregard. Without legal recognition, her children's futures were not secure.

In her mind, María compared the characters of the two men. She had to admit that she preferred José's bullheaded, outspoken spunk to

Juan's weakness. Unlike Juan, José loved and encouraged her brainstorming sessions to improve the business. Also, José was single, and she had the option to marry him if she chose to do so. José and María were similar in their entrepreneurial spirits, and this attracted one to the other.

With their daily interactions, María was slowly opening up to José. But she had a hard time identifying her feelings for José. She admitted there was some chemistry between them but wasn't sure it was a sufficient reason to enter into a relationship with him. She did not want to rush into anything. She preferred to take her time and not share her feelings prematurely with José. She was upfront with him about her relationship with Juan.

Nonetheless, the more time they spent together, the more María let down her guard. Soon, they were inseparable.

In 1928, twelve years after she had eloped, María ended her relationship with Juan Batista. Juan was not surprised by María's decision. But still, her decision devastated him. His greatest fear had come to fruition. He had secretly feared that giving María her financial freedom would lead to her complete independence.

Juan also understood her decision to move on. Juan was not willing to leave his wife and family. María had the right to settle down into a life of her own. He also understood that he could not give María what she wanted the most. For years, María had begged him to recognize the children legally, but that was something he could not do. He had given Dionisia his word.

He now regretted having given in to Dionisia's demands and letting her hold him as an emotional hostage. Acquiescing to Dionisia's demands strained his relationship with the children now that María was no longer around. Dionisia did not permit open contact with María's children. In essence, he had not only lost his relationship with María but also, to some extent, with his children.

María decided to give her relationship with José a chance, and the two became an official couple in late 1929. José wanted to marry immediately, but María refused to give up control of her finances to any man. It had taken her over ten years to achieve her economic freedom.

The business was her sole source of support for her children. Also, in the back of her mind, she was still unsure and did not fully trust José's motives.

During the first three months of living together, José and María developed a routine that was quite beneficial for both. José took complete charge of managing the cantina, while María focused on everything associated with the boarding house, their home, and the children. This arrangement allowed María to discharge some of the staff, and José could quit his job at the sugar mill.

José now had a business and a family of his own, even though María would not marry him. María was everything he had hoped she would be. He admired her independent nature and did not rely on him for minor decisions. She was smart and interested in events outside of her family. They discussed business, politics, and other personal concerns about the future of their family and the country.

When socializing, Maria was a lot of fun and the life of the party. He loved to watch her dance, although he could never keep up with her on the dance floor.

They were both delighted with their relationship, their personal lives, and business arrangements. Their life together was off to a perfect start.

When he learned they were expecting their first child, their life shifted from perfect to ideal. José's life was complete. He had an exceptional woman by his side, a business, and now a child of his own. How he wished his parents were alive to share his good fortune.

José finally had what he had longed for many years—financial freedom, security, and a loving family. Having a family gave him a unique sense of purpose. His mother would have been so proud to see how he had turned his life around. José doubted he would have achieved this level of stability back in Cuba, with the temptation of its exotic and permissive environment.

CHAPTER 11
THE GOUGING OF HER SOUL

One day in 1930, María's youngest child, Marcia, developed a high fever and diarrhea. Initially, María believed this was a passing childhood illness. She left her daughter in the care of the housekeeper and proceeded with her daily routine at the boarding house. After Marcia's symptoms grew worse on the second day, María stayed home and took Marcia to the doctor.

After examining the child, the doctor said, "Marcia is weak and dehydrated from the long bout of diarrhea. I believe this is likely a bacterial infection, and there is little I can do. I recommend you keep her fever down with cool sponge baths and keep her hydrated with plenty of fluids."

María stayed home with Marcia, following the doctor's instructions. Marcia's symptoms were not improving. María took Marcia back to see the doctor, but to no avail. The diagnosis and advice were the same.

After seven days of fever and acute diarrhea, at three years of age, Marcia died of dehydration in María's arms. María was in shock and disbelief. How could her lively, vibrant three-year-old be dead? María was inconsolable.

She was angry. Although she directed her anger and outrage to no one in particular, it affected her closest relationships, as they suffered the brunt of her anger.

María experienced the classic stages of grief with depression the worst of the stages. María's depression was a tangible force that dominated her life and the lives of those in her household. Her family had a difficult time dealing with her mood swings and unpredictable behavior.

The ferocious pain of losing Marcia reached the depths of her being. Losing her daughter was the most profound, overwhelming, and inconsolable pain she had ever experienced.

The sound of her alarm clock awakened María. She was annoyed at being stirred back to consciousness. She reluctantly woke up to face her day. María was determined to triumph over her pain, loss, and suffering. She had three other children who needed her, and another one on the way. She had to remain strong, work through her emotions, and, hopefully, come out to the other end relatively unscathed.

María worked hard to overcome her pain and loss. But she was unsure how she was supposed to function in her old world with the burden of a new perspective that included fear, anger, sadness, and depression. These emotions were foreign to her, and she had a difficult time grappling with them. María could not describe the depth of her grief.

María was pregnant, and although the birth of one child could not possibly make up for the death of another, she was thankful for the life growing inside of her. The unborn child helped María get over the depression and despair she was living in, as it gave her a sense of purpose. Fortunately, José had taken over the management of the boarding house and cantina while María recovered from her grief.

Five months after Marcia's death, María gave birth to a baby girl they named Joséfina. Joséfina was a beautiful, spunky baby. María cherished Joséfina as she helped to fill the void Marcia's death had left in her heart and arms. She brought much-needed joy to the grief-stricken household and strengthened her relationship with José. His support during her time of grieving eradicated any doubt she may have had about his motives. He genuinely loved her and her children.

A few months after Joséfina was born, José suggested that they sell the business and move out of Boca Chica. They had saved some money, and with the proceeds of the sale of the cantina and boarding house, they could buy another house and invest in another venture.

María agreed that the house had an eerie feeling. Marcia's death had muted the daily hustle and bustle of the house, somehow unplugging it from its day-to-day emotions. Even the children were extra quiet, not sure how they were supposed to act. There were too many memories, and the couple agreed that the change would help María's outlook.

In 1930, María and José made a fresh start. They sold the boarding house and cantina business and moved out of Boca Chica and closer to the Colonial City, built by the Spaniards during their heyday. They bought a home and established a successful charcoal business.

On September 3, 1930, shortly after their move, Hurricane San Zenon, the fifth deadliest Atlantic hurricane on record, hit the island. The storm was an intense Category 4 that killed approximately eight thousand people when it crossed the Dominican Republic. The deadly storm, with its gale-force winds, flattened the boarding house and adjacent cantina in Boca Chica.

They could not believe how fortunate they had been to have moved out of the Boca Chica beach area, and that their current home and business in the Colonial City remained relatively intact after the hurricane.

In 1932, María discovered that she was once again pregnant. The dark cloud that had hung over her and the fog of depression had finally dissipated. They had sold the lucrative charcoal business and moved to Santo Domingo, where they had purchased a middle-class home and established a successful restaurant, which they named Avenida España.

The restaurant business was thriving, her relationship with José was better than ever, and she would now have two little darlings to help ease the pain of losing Marcia. They were one happy and growing family.

Until she was eighteen months old, Joséfina was a healthy, happy child. Then, one day, María noticed that Joséfina was lethargic and running a low-grade fever. María monitored the fever, keeping it down with cold baths. Despite María's efforts, Joséfina's temperature continued to rise and then followed by a bout of diarrhea. It had been five days, and Joséfina was only getting weaker.

María panicked as she recalled Marcia's illness. These same symptoms had caused Marcia's death. She suddenly felt faint and short of breath. María laid Joséfina on her bed and braced herself.

Once she had recovered, María gathered Joséfina in a blanket and rushed to the family doctor. As soon as she arrived at the clinic, she demanded that the doctor see her daughter immediately.

María explained to the doctor that her daughter Marcia had died of these same symptoms and that he needed to do something to help Joséfina. Unfortunately, there was little the doctor could do to help. Joséfina was weak. Her health quickly deteriorated until she succumbed to her illness. Joséfina died that same afternoon at the clinic.

The doctor tried to console María by telling her, "The three most common fatal diseases for children are tuberculosis, pneumonia, and diarrhea. Together, these three diseases cause about one-third of childhood deaths."

María sat stoically and thought to herself, "What good is this information? Why is this man trying to justify the death of my two daughters?" She was angry with the doctor for being so cold and clinical. María gave him a cold blank stare, stood up from her seat, and left the room without saying a word.

Once again, the universe had dealt María a severe blow. The familiar, inconsolable wave of pain engulfed her. She did not know how she was going to survive the cycle of pain brought on by the grieving process. She had barely started accepting Marcia's death when the same childhood illness claimed the life of her beautiful Joséfina.

Her well-intentioned friends and family could not help. Nothing and no one could make her feel better. Their kind words and actions fell short.

Facing her day-to-day responsibilities was extremely difficult, but her other three children needed her. She had to do her best to move on. Once again, she took comfort in the life that was growing inside of her, even though this baby could not replace Marcia and Joséfina. She would always remember her two little girls and keep their memories alive in her heart and mind.

Jesús was born six months after Joséfina's passing. He was a handsome boy at eight pounds and twenty inches, with a full head of straight black hair that stood up at the crown like a porcupine's quills.

Jesús brought much-needed joy into the household. As he grew and developed, María continually checked his temperature and took him to the doctor. She was overly vigilant of his health and welfare. He was a healthy boy with a ferocious appetite.

Once again, María was able to work through and overcome the grieving, loss, and depression. Their restaurant business was thriving. The other children were happy, healthy, and enjoying their childhood.

The family settled into a familiar and comfortable routine. José was out of the door by five in the morning headed to the restaurant to prepare for the breakfast and lunch crowds. María prepared the children for school, made breakfast for Jesús, and gave the housekeeper and sitter instructions for the day.

On a typical morning in 1934, María was scurrying around the house, giving orders for the day to the housekeeper and her older daughters, Lucia and Emilia. Jesús was at his table, eating his breakfast, which consisted of bread with scrambled eggs.

As María and the older children were about to walk out of the door, María heard a gasping, wheezing sound. As she turned toward the sound, she saw Jesús was choking. María dropped her bags and in an instant, reached Jesús and scooped him out of his chair.

As soon as she picked him up, she panicked at the realization that she did not know what to do. Nothing could have ever prepared María for the sheer panic and fear-provoking stress of watching her toddler in distress, choking and struggling to breathe, and not knowing what to do.

Jesús was not coughing, breathing, or crying, and she had to do something to help him. He was scared and could do nothing more than look into his mother's face with his eyes pleading for help.

María frantically turned Jesús over and tried to clear his airway with back blows. When that didn't work, she placed him on her lap and looked inside his mouth. She saw a piece of bread and attempted to dislodge it from his airway with her finger. However, that had the opposite effect as it pushed the obstruction deeper into his airway. She did everything she could think of to clear his airway, but nothing worked.

She did not have to be a doctor to know that Jesús was not getting oxygen into his lungs. His face turned pink, then red, then a crimson color. Then there was no sound coming from Jesús before going limp. She tried not to panic as she recognized that her child was in danger.

By this time, the house staff and the other children had gathered around María. María ordered one of her housekeepers to hail a public transportation car so she could rush Jesús to the family doctor. During the harrowing three-mile ride, María bargained with God to save her child as she yelled at the driver to go faster.

When she arrived at the doctor's office, she flew out of the car and handed the limp child to the nurse. The nurse recognized the urgency of the situation and rushed the child back to the doctor's office with María nipping at her heels.

Ignoring the blue coloring of Jesús's skin around his face, lips, and fingernail beds, the doctor closely examined the child. He studied the child's airway, checked for vital signs of life, and attempted to resuscitate Jesús to no avail.

After ten minutes, the doctor turned to María and escorted her to his office, leaving Jesús in the examination room with the nurse. He sat María down, and he explained, "Jesús has suffered an unfortunate accident. In the back of the mouth, there are two openings. One is the esophagus, the pathway for food that leads to the stomach. The other is the trachea, which is the opening where air must pass through to get to the lungs. When swallowing occurs, a flap called the epiglottis covers the trachea, which prevents food from entering the lungs. Anything that lodges in the upper airway will become stuck as the airway narrows. The brain is susceptible to this lack of oxygen and begins to die within four to six minutes, and irreversible brain death occurs in as little as ten minutes."

María sat in a daze, in shock, and barely heard the doctor's explanation of what had caused the death of her twenty-month-old child. In response to María's defiant, blank stare, the doctor said, "María, I want you to understand how choking occurs so that you can understand that Jesús's death was a horrible accident."

María looked at the doctor in disbelief. Why was he telling her this? Was it going to bring her baby back? Again, this same doctor believed that the clinical explanation would somehow make her feel better about the death of her child.

María was inconsolable. María stood up from her seat and walked out of the doctor's office without acknowledging the doctor's words and without her baby in her arms. The doctor's office contacted José so he could make final arrangements for Jesús's body.

Losing three children in four years was so much more than she could bear. Jesús death on top of the deaths of Marcia and Joséfina had shattered her life into a million pieces. How could she put those pieces back together without showing the cracks? The cracks represented the destruction of her life, hopes, and dreams, and those of her three dead children. María was tired of the constant adjustment required by her ever-changing world, trying to carry on despite the numbing pain. She was tired of being the reliable, strong, and independent person everyone relied on to keep the family and business afloat.

Jesús's death was a crushing blow for María. She could barely put one foot in front of the other. At times she would stay in her bed for days not wanting to eat. Drenched in sorrow, María spiraled into a deep depression.

The deaths of her three children violated the natural cycle of life. Her children were not supposed to die before her. Recalling the deaths of her three dead children evoked a rage in her at the injustice of it all. She was not only grieving the death of Jesús but also reliving and grieving the deaths of Marcia and Joséfina as well.

María took responsibility for Jesús's death, even though the doctor had ruled his death as an accidental choking. It was her responsibility to keep him safe, and she had failed to protect him and save his life. The look in his eyes pleading for her to help him haunted her. José tried to convince her that the blame was not justified, but she didn't want to hear it.

In lashing out at the injustice of her loss, María accused José of not loving the children sufficiently. Why was he not hurting like she was? In her grief, María could not see that people grieve in different ways. She interpreted José's actions, motives, reactions, and feelings as not caring because they differed from her own. María looked to José for support, understanding, and sympathy. José's lack of emotion and compassion disturbed her.

Instead of dwelling on the situation and his feelings, José focused on his day-to-day activities. While María was falling apart, José was making funeral arrangements, contacting friends and relatives, striving to take care of the rest of the family, and managing a bustling restaurant.

José grieved the loss of his children differently. Joséfina's death, similar to his mother's, blindsided him. He had finally been living the ideal life. He'd had the perfect mate, a child, a home, and a successful business. Then, when he had been feeling the euphoria of his accomplishments, he'd had to endure the death of his only biological child. It was as if the universe had waited for him to feel good about himself and his accomplishments to knock him off of his pedestal. He hadn't gotten over Joséfina's death when Jesús died. He was numb. And although he would not mention it to María, he was not optimistic about their future, since the universe's message was clearly saying, "There will be no true happiness for you."

He quietly accepted his fate and kept forging ahead. Someone had to. María had unraveled entirely, so he did not have the luxury of grieving openly. They could not afford for both of them to fall apart; one of them had to stay strong and take care of the family. He had to provide the strength his family needed to get through these challenging times.

José was the stereotypical strong protector who did not freely show his emotions. He held his grief inside, hiding his vulnerability. He fell back on familiar and comfortable behavior. He spent more time playing poker while visiting and bonding with his fellow compatriots. When the pain became more than he could bear, he shed his tears in silence.

Two months after Jesús's death, María learned that she was once again pregnant. But this time, she did not take any consolation in the child growing inside of her. She dreaded the idea of having another child. Life had taught her a ferocious lesson: getting emotionally attached to any child would cause his or her demise. She had to maintain her emotional distance.

María lived through the ensuing months of pregnancy in a fog of depression. She barely ate and rarely attempted to get out of bed and ignored her physical appearance. José was concerned about her welfare and that of his unborn child. However, no amount of coaxing could bring María back to life. María was numb. She had given up on life.

Her soul's sorrow was a tangible force that engulfed her. This time, she would not come out of this despair unscathed or a better person.

CHAPTER 12
A MARTYR OF LIFE

On September 21, 1934, María gave birth to a two-and-a-half pound, eight-inch-long, premature Carla.

Once again, the family doctor offered a clinical explanation. He said to both José and María, "Depression in pregnancy can be a cause of premature birth. High levels of stress hormones can trigger premature delivery. You should know babies born before thirty-seven weeks of pregnancy are more likely to die in the first weeks of life and are also at risk of developing a host of health problems."

For María, the doctor's warning confirmed her belief that this child would not survive. She convinced herself that it was a matter of time before Carla would join her siblings. Except, this time, María was ready and waiting for the next blow life would deliver.

María found it difficult to free herself from the mental hold the deaths of her children had imposed. Consequently, she became addicted to alcohol and bitterness.

She would no longer lull herself into a false sense of security and optimism. It took losing three children, but she learned her lesson. The universe was not going to catch her unprepared ever again.

María could not put Carla back into the womb to finish developing, so for the first two months of baby Carla's life, she lived inside her mother's blouse, sleeping on her chest, comforted by the rhythmic beating of her mother's heart.

To María's amazement, the child continued to grow and flourish. Even though Carla grew stronger by the day, María continued to care for her daughter from afar, in a cold, detached, and unemotional manner. She did not believe that Carla was going to live, and she remained reluctant to get attached to the child.

José and Lucia gave the child most of the nurturing she needed. While it wasn't fair to ask Lucia to take on responsibilities far beyond her years, José was grateful for her willingness to help, especially that first year.

From the age of fourteen, Lucia played the role of mother for Carla, taking care of all of her needs. She also took control of the management of their household. Despite the enormous burden of responsibility, it was a role Lucia cherished. Lucia loved baby Carla and wanted to protect her as their home life was far from peaceful with María's alcoholism and depression.

Lucia was patient with María as she had been a good mother to her and her other siblings. María patiently taught her the art of baking, cooking, sewing, knitting, and needlepoint. By age fourteen, Lucia was developing into a master chef and seamstress thanks to her mother's tutelage.

To Lucia, María was ill and needed her help. So, she gladly took charge of maintaining the household and caring for Carla.

Unfortunately for José and Carla, Lucia married and moved out of the family home at the tender age of fifteen. Nevertheless, she continued to help by taking Carla to her home when María was in the midst of one of her binges, and José was busy at the cantina and boarding house.

The uncontrollable crying and sleepless nights came with the anniversary of each child's death. When depression set in, María pushed José and her children away. María continually let her family down, which only added to the destructive, self-indulgent behavior. Her anguish took a toll on her family.

The universe dealt María three severe blows, one after the other. The deaths of her children were the most profound, overwhelming, and inconsolable losses, regardless of their ages and circumstances. One of the most prominent parts of her struggle was dealing with the guilt over the accident and illnesses of the children. What could she have done differently? Why had she been unable to protect her children?

She heard constant advice about letting go of her resentment and forgiving. But in her case, letting go and forgiving was not clear. Who was she to forgive? Herself? God? The universe? How was she supposed to survive one crushing blow and misfortune after another? How does a person continue to live after life has crushed and pummeled their hopes and dreams?

Life had been unfair to María and her family. Under these circumstances, shaking off the bitterness was extremely difficult for her. María became an emotional hostage to her situation, and it consumed her energy, enthusiasm, and effectiveness. Her ego told her it would be safer to remember and hold on to the past. She let the death of her children define her.

Although María received a lot of attention and sympathy because life had been unfair, it did nothing for her personal growth. She could not feel optimistic about her future or enjoy the present moments with her family. She even stopped working at the restaurant.

The pain and the hurt became part of her being. The pain was the badge she wore in honor of her children. How could she let it go?

Many criticized her alcoholism and depression. How could they understand? Had they lost a child, let alone three? No one could understand her pain, grief, and loss, not even José. How could they even start to fathom the depths of her despair? Did her so-called friends and family not know her by now? Did they not know that she rejected societal norms, with their faceless, critical, hypocritical, and unwritten rules of behavior? They had to recognize that she was resilient to shame and would allow no one to dictate how long she should grieve the deaths of her children.

Emotional and chemical toxins were destroying her body and mental effectiveness. The more she tried to dull the pain with alcohol, the more entrenched her memories became. María was stuck in a never-ending abyss of grief and sadness, shamelessly and unapologetically displaying her raw emotions.

She kept the memory of her children alive by replaying the beautiful memories and celebrating their birthdays in her heart and mind. She spent a lot of time talking to others about her children.

In 1936, when Carla was two years old, José once again suggested to María that they marry. José said, "María, I love you and want to find a way to help you out of this depression. I think that marriage will legitimize our relationship, which may give you a different outlook on life."

María, who had always rejected the idea of marriage throughout her relationship with José, said yes. Her older children were grown and out of the house. Carla would inevitably die soon, and she no longer had any interest in running a business. By agreeing to the marriage, she had effectively turned over their financial future to José, at least in her mind. She did not care about or want the responsibility of running a business or managing their finances. Marriage gave Carla something her other children had not had—a legitimate family.

The marriage had been a good idea, as it solidified their relationship and gave María a new outlook on life. Depression still dominated María's life as it ebbed and flowed for the first five years of their marriage. But María was slowly recuperating. José patiently and lovingly supported her and did not pressure her into doing anything she was not ready to do. As she healed emotionally, she slowly started going to work with José at the restaurant. The atmosphere around the home was less stressful and tense.

Glimmers of the old Maria were resurfacing as she reengaged in the business and Carla had turned seven years old, three years beyond Marcia's age. María was a bit more relaxed and began entertaining the notion that Carla might survive. Was Carla safe from the grips of death?

As the episodes of depression diminished, and María was recovering, life was preparing to clobber María once again. On December 7, 1941, fate delivered another crushing blow: her twenty-year-old son, Carmelo, died of tuberculosis.

María had not seen Carmelo's death coming. She had not prepared for or protected herself against the demise of one of her older children. She had talked herself into a false sense of security concerning the welfare of her older children. María once again spiraled into a deep depression.

Having an older child pass away was not much different from losing a toddler. The house was laden with memories of her handsome son, who looked so much like his father, Juan Batista. To María, Carmelo's death was a continuation of her grieving and one more anniversary to add to the list of days and children to mourn.

In her crushing grief, María turned to alcohol to drench her sorrows. Her depression and dependency on alcohol took a toll on her relationship with José and led to the disintegration of their marriage.

A major tragedy such as the one they had suffered could either strengthen a couple's relationship or tear them apart. José and María had had a stable relationship, marriage, and business venture, but the deaths of four children, combined with her alcoholism and depression, were more than they could handle as a couple.

José was stunned at María's transformation. The deaths of her children had pummeled her spirit and zest for life. Where was the stoic, optimistic woman he had once known? The woman he had never seen upset or hurt, even when business was not doing well or when her parents passed away? She was no longer the outgoing, goal-setting woman he had met years ago. She had surrendered to bouts of depression and alcoholism.

Despite not wanting to turn his back on María, he refused to stay in an unhappy marriage. José could no longer tolerate coming home to a drunk and depressed wife. He no longer recognized the woman that had captivated his heart.

María's depression and dependence on alcohol disabled her. During her binges, she was out of touch with the world around her. She constantly cried, which he found draining after managing the business all day. She was beyond his ability to help. She was committed to her distress, and no matter how hard José tried, María refused to be supported and guided.

He had run out of options and finally understood that the best way to help María was to leave her alone. With each of José's attempts to help her, María became more combative and defiant. The only person permitted to pierce the veil of her despair and depression was her oldest daughter, Lucia.

José also had to think of his young daughter's well-being. Both José and María had their reasons, but they agreed it was in everyone's best interest for them to part ways.

María believed that José had been unsympathetic to her suffering and loss, and she refused to live under the same roof with him. Also, she did not want to witness Carla's death; it was a matter of time. Carmelo's death convinced her that none of her children were safe from the grips of death. By the end of 1942, María had moved out of her family home to live with Lucia and her family.

María had pushed José and Carla out of her life, barely acknowledging their existence. She had dedicated herself to losing them by shutting herself into her world.

María and José divorced in 1944. The divorce was a tough decision for José to make, as he wanted to keep the family intact for the sake of his ten-year-old daughter. But María had emotionally abandoned them long ago. Carla's primary home would be with her father, as he could provide a more stable environment.

Shortly after the divorce, José sold the restaurant and divided the proceeds with María. With his share of the profits, José established a bodega, Central de España, that sold bulk and individual foods and other items catering to the needs of the town's residents. José could finally make one of his earlier dreams come true—to own a bodega like the one owned by Señor Lopez. José became a prosperous merchant and business owner who owned several rental properties. José could give his only daughter, Carla, an upper-middle-class upbringing.

María remained entrenched in her alcoholism and depression. The final devastating blow to María's life occurred in 1949, when her twenty-eight-year-old daughter, Emilia, whom she lovingly referred to as Milita, died of uterine cancer.

María had never imagined that for her, letting go would mean witnessing the deaths of her children. The deaths of her children left María disoriented. She had two living daughters, but it was difficult not to think about when, not if, they would be taken from her, too.

From 1930 until the day she died, María stayed adrift in a sea of pain. She lived with the devastating loss of one child after the next until she had lost five of her seven children. The constant grieving took a toll on María's health and her outlook on life.

Many people plan for their demise, but few, if any, prepare for the death of a child, let alone five of them. Parents expect to see their children grow, mature, and give them grandchildren because this is the natural cycle of life.

Losing five children left María emotionally pulverized, and she was unable or unwilling to stay conscious through such pain. In the beginning, she had accepted the good and the bad with composure. But even María's fighting spirit could not accept the deaths of five children with serenity and equanimity. Nothing and no one could ease her pain, for a fraction of her soul died each time she had to bear the unbearable pain of losing a child.

As the years passed, María tried to focus on the beautiful memories rather than the horrific ending of each child's life. Not a day passed that she did not think of each one of them. With each birthday, she imagined what they would be doing or how they would look. Her children kept living in her heart and mind.

María focused on children or adults who would be the same age as the particular child she remembered. She then used those observations as a gauge for her dead children. She did not want to let go of that connection. How could she abandon the only link she had with her children?

María died of a sudden heart attack on July 30, 1956, at the age of sixty-four. Throughout her life, she had said that she wanted a sudden passing. She would say, "*Me quiero morir como un pajarito*" ("I want to die like a parakeet"). She believed parakeets keeled over and died suddenly and unexpectedly no fuss no muss. That was how she wanted to pass. She also wanted her tombstone to read, "*Aquí descansa una martyr de la vida*" ("Here rests a martyr of life").

Through it all, María was a vulnerable woman with a feminine side. She was a strong, self-assured woman who witnessed the death of five of her seven children. She had to endure the greatest tragedy a parent can face fivefold. The deaths of her children reduced the once successful, confident woman to a martyr of life.

María had been a woman who shunned societal norms and lived her life according to her values. She had owned and managed a thriving local business during an era and in a country where women had few rights and were expected to provide their husbands with a clean home and food on the table and to raise their children. María had bucked these notions and refused to conform to society's definition of how she should live her life.

Rosa María Acosta was a woman far ahead of her time.

PART III
CARLA FERNÁNDEZ ACOSTA

A LIFE OF FALSE DICHOTOMY

CHAPTER 13
DADDY'S LITTLE GIRL

Carla sat on the edge of her seat, anxiously waiting for the school's dismissal bell to ring. She checked the time on the clock. There was still half an hour left to the school day. The clock did not appear to be moving. Why was the last hour of class the longest?

She could not wait to go home to share her noon meal with her father. It was their special time. Her father had been her constant source of love and affection. She loved her father more than anything in the world. She was daddy's little girl.

Her father made her feel grown-up when he talked to her about her family in Spain and his life in Galicia. She imagined herself strolling the interior of Galicia, with its hilly landscape, mountain ranges, and rural lifestyle.

He'd told her about his village in Nocedo. Life in Nocedo was not complicated. Few people lived there, and most of the news they heard was about the people who lived in their village. Hearing bad news was rare and was usually of a significant occurrence, like the sinking of that boat where many people died. Work and family interactions had consumed his daily life in Nocedo.

Despite living thousands of miles away from his family for twenty-four years, her father had his family at the forefront of his mind. He impressed upon Carla the need to always keep in touch with family. He talked about having learned his lesson about not keeping in touch with his family after losing his mother to a sudden illness. He also wanted Carla to know about her family roots and the family farm in Nocedo. He wanted his family to know about his special little girl, the only surviving child of his fifteen-year relationship with María.

José had told her stories about her grandparents and the sacrifices they had made to help him avoid joining the military and fighting in a senseless and irrational war. She could never imagine having to live away from her father. She would never want to move to another country.

Carla had learned that Uncle Juan had bravely joined the military, even if it was at his father's suggestion. At first, things had not gone well for Uncle Juan, and he hated the army and the war. Then, after his first leave, Grandpa Salvador had given him some advice that had helped him change his attitude. After his honorable discharge, he joined the local law enforcement, married, and had two children of his own.

Uncle Miguel was the youngest of the three boys. Unlike his brothers, at the time of his eighteenth birthday, Uncle Miguel had enlisted in the military for his two-year mandatory service. Later, when civil war broke out in Spain in 1936, he'd bravely fought in that war. Besides bravely serving in the military, he got a university degree majoring in education. He'd married, had a daughter, and had become a teacher in a school that taught elementary through middle school students.

Even though Carla had never met her Spanish family, she came to know each one of them through her father's stories. Even at her young age, she recognized these stories were an integral part of their family history. These stories were their connection to their Galician roots and family.

She could tell by the way her father's eyes lit up that these stories gave him a sense of belonging. They were his connection to his biological family and a way to include and integrate her into his family's history. Unfortunately, she never met her grandparents, as they had both passed away long before she was born. His stories brought her Spanish family and Galicia to life, making them a reality for Carla.

She wrote to her uncles to let them know how much she loved them and looked forward to meeting them someday. She had also told them she had the best Papa in the world. She was so lucky to have such a wonderful father who treated her like a princess.

She loved to hear the stories about her father's trip to Cuba, although she had to admit that they both saddened and scared her. She sensed her father's pain as he told her about leaving his family and living alone in Cuba. Most of all, she was saddened as her father's eyes welled with tears when he spoke of his mother's death.

The voyage from Spain to Cuba had been a scary one on a boat. She could not imagine having to spend one day in such a frightening boat. She made her father promise that if they ever traveled to Spain, they would not get on that nasty boat.

Carla's favorite story was how her father had ended up in the Dominican Republic. Losing his money and his passage in a poker game had forced him to stay in the Dominican Republic. Her father called them synchronistic events. Carla wasn't sure what that meant, but it must be something good since he had remained in the Dominican Republic and become her papa.

She was awestruck by her father's worldly adventures, Uncle Juan's bravery, and Uncle Miguel's intellect. She never tired of hearing stories about Galicia, Cuba, and the Dominican Republic. She continually asked him to retell stories of his life.

After the noon meal and siesta, Carla accompanied her father to his bodega. José had a housekeeper who took care of the home and meals and could have taken care of Carla, but Carla enjoyed helping at the bodega. Carla helped dust, stock shelves, and do light sweeping. Working by her father's side had been their daily routine since her mother had moved out of their family home.

Carla was the happiest and luckiest little girl in the world, with the greatest papa. Her life was perfect.

CHAPTER 14
THE BETRAYAL

It had been a typical school day. As usual, Carla anxiously waited for the dismissal bell. However, on this day, the clock was slower than ever. She anxiously sat on the edge of her seat with her books in hand, ready to dart out of the classroom, when the bell rang. Her father had told her he had news to share with her. She could not wait to get home and settle down at the dinner table to hear the news.

She had been distracted all day, speculating about what the news could be. Maybe her Papa would surprise her with the announcement of his Galician family visiting. Or maybe he would announce that they would be going to Galicia. What else could be so important for her father to make it a point to let her know that there was news? She could not think of anything that would be more pertinent to them than news about her Spanish family. Well, soon enough, she would know. As she looked up at the clock for the fourth time, she noted that there were another fifteen minutes before the dismissal bell.

At the sound of the bell, Carla darted out of her seat and ran the entire way home in the midday sun. She barged into the house breathless and sweaty. Carla was elated and surprised when she walked into the house and saw that her father was already home; this meant she would not have to wait long to hear the good news.

As she was catching her breath, her excitement quickly dissipated as she noted that a woman was standing by her father's side. Her father being home early was not her only surprise. He introduced Carla and the housekeeper to the stranger, Bienvenida. He added Bienvenida was someone special to him and they would be seeing a lot more of her.

Carla said a polite hello and immediately walked to her room to wash up before dinner. Although she had caught her breath, her heart was still pounding as she thought, "Was this the news? Who was this woman? What did she want? Why did her father bring this woman into their home? Why did her father think this woman was special? Really, who cared about this woman? What did he mean we would be seeing more of her?" Carla's mind was bombarded with questions she wanted to answer.

Ten minutes later, Carla sat at the dinner table and quietly studied Bienvenida, who sat immediately across from her at the dinner table. Not accustomed to seeing women so made up, Bienvenida looked fake with so much makeup. Her mother and sister did not wear makeup. Bienvenida had thick wavy hair, large square teeth, and long eyelashes. Were they even real? Carla hated to admit that Bienvenida had large, beautiful brown eyes.

Bringing a stranger to their dinner table was an intrusion of their time and space. This intrusion did not sit well with Carla. She quietly ate her meal, not hearing a word of what her father and Bienvenida were discussing. The chatter in her head was louder than their conversation. She was too distracted, thinking, "How long does this woman plan to visit? Hopefully, she will leave immediately after the meal."

After their meal, José asked Carla to go to her room for her siesta. Carla stepped away from the table without excusing herself. She did not say one word as she walked away from the table, suspicious of Bienvenida's motives. She walked at a snail's pace, looking at Bienvenida and her father from the corner of her eyes, hoping to get a gist of her father's conversation with Bienvenida.

When she was in her bed, she tossed and turned for the next thirty minutes. She finally gave up on sleeping, sat up on her bed, and listened intently to hear the goodbyes and the door closing behind Bienvenida as she left.

An hour later, Bienvenida was still at the house. Worse yet, when it was time to go to the bodega, Bienvenida joined them. Carla was not sure what was going on. She stayed at the bodega the entire time. When it was time to close up and go home, Bienvenida again joined them.

Carla was right to be suspicious. Bienvenida barged into their lives one day in 1944 and never left. Overnight, Carla's perfect world crumbled. Bienvenida invaded their lives and pierced the veil that had protected Carla's relationship with her father. Bienvenida changed their daily routine and brought a negative aura into their home.

Carla lost her special time with her father, as Bienvenida now sat at the dinner table and controlled the conversations. Carla was only to speak when spoken to because children were supposed to be seen but not heard.

On one occasion, when Carla tried to engage her father in conversation about her Galician family, Bienvenida said, "Children should only speak when hens pee. In case you didn't know, hens don't pee, which means you never speak at the table. There is nothing uglier than an opinionated child butting into adult conversations. It's a lack of respect."

Carla's face turned beet red as she looked at Bienvenida and then at her father as a large, painful lump was forming in her throat. Her father remained silent. His silence spoke volumes about how their home life had changed. The house no longer had that warm, welcoming atmosphere that Carla cherished. Her father no longer told her stories of his life in Galicia. Instead, he catered to and steered the conversation to please Bienvenida. Bienvenida was driving a wedge between father and daughter.

Three months after moving in, Bienvenida had taken complete control of the household. She had the last word on major household decisions.

Bienvenida was verbally abusive to Carla and complained when José spent too much money on or time with his daughter. Carla saw her father's mate as the epitome of the evil stepmother who had mastered the duplicitous blend of being kind to José and mean to her. Her father's relationship had become Carla's worst nightmare.

The first time Bienvenida suggested to José that Carla stay home with the housekeeper and not accompany him to the bodega, Carla refused to obey. One thing was not allowing her to speak unless spoken to at the dinner table. But not allowing her to go to the bodega with her father was a step too far.

Bienvenida claimed the bodega was no place for a child. She yelled at Bienvenida and told her how much she hated her intrusion into their family life.

Carla begged her father to take her to work with him, but her father told her she had to stay home with the housekeeper. In the meantime, Bienvenida accompanied José to the bodega. Carla was confused by her father's betrayal. She asked herself, "Why does he prefer to take Bienvenida to the bodega instead of me?"

Her father told her, "Carla, Bienvenida is not only my partner; she is now the lady of this house and your stepmother."

"But she hates me. She is mean and awful when you are not around."

"Carla, I will not permit you to disrespect and speak that way of Bienvenida. She does not hate you. She knows what is best for a little girl like you. You need to apologize to her," he said sternly.

Defiant, Carla retorted, "I will not apologize. Bienvenida is evil. Why can't you see that she is an evil witch who only wants your money?"

"Well, if you are not going to apologize, then I have no other choice than to send you to your room."

Carla darted out of the room in tears, puzzled by her father's reaction. Her father was taking Bienvenida's side. Why? Carla did not understand what she had done wrong to make her father like Bienvenida better.

Bienvenida made life as miserable as possible for Carla, escalating the verbal and physical attacks.

Carla tried hard not to be in the same room as Bienvenida so she could avoid her wrath. Sometimes, not even the sanctity of her bedroom saved her. Bienvenida ruled the house, storming into Carla's room at will.

One day, after one of Carla's outbursts, Bienvenida patiently waited for a moment when José was not home. She sent the housekeeper out to run errands so that she could have Carla to herself.

As Carla sat on her bed playing with her doll, she was startled as Bienvenida barged into her room and said, "Listen to me, little girl. I plan to marry your father someday, so you better get accustomed to the idea that I am here to stay whether you like it or not. If you don't like it, you can go live with your mother."

"This is my house, and you can't make me leave. You are an evil witch who wants my father's money. I hate you and don't want you living here."

Bienvenida lunged at Carla, grabbed her by the collar, slapped her, and tossed her on the bed.

"If anybody is going to leave this house, it's going to be you. I will not permit you to disrespect me. Who do you think you are? You are nobody around here, and you have no rights. The only rights you have are the ones I allow you to have — nothing more and nothing less. I do not want to see you at the dinner table today. You will stay in this room and then eat your meal with the housekeeper in the kitchen. And don't you dare tell your father anything about this. If you do, today will be like a mere swat on the butt compared to what I will do to you."

As Bienvenida triumphantly walked out of the room, Carla remained on her bed in shock. No one had ever talked to her in such a vile and hostile manner, let alone hit her.

Bienvenida's abusive treatment continued and escalated. Carla was defenseless against the evil witch. Blinded by love, her father did not see Bienvenida's duplicitous nature.

Bienvenida paced the floor, trying to understand why Carla did not live with her mother and sister. Carla's mere presence bothered Bienvenida. She had to come up with a way to remove the child from the house. It had been a year since she moved in with José, and she could no longer bear the child's presence, she gave José an ultimatum.

"José, Carla is disrespectful and does not listen to anything I say. I have tried to reason with her, to be nice to her, but she refuses to obey. Either you send her to live with her mother, or I will have to move out. I can't live this way anymore."

José had a bewildered look on his face as if he did not understand why Bienvenida was asking him to choose. "Bienvenida, you know that María is not emotionally stable and cannot take care of Carla," said José, trying to reason with her. "You are putting me in a painful and uncomfortable position by asking me to send Carla away."

She turned to José with her hands on her hips and insisted, "What about her sister, Lucia? She could take care of Carla."

"Lucia has a family of her own. I'm not going to burden Lucia with my responsibility."

Growing impatient with José and his weakness for Carla, Bienvenida snapped, "Well, you better think of something soon, because I'm no longer willing to live under these conditions."

José was having trouble processing what she was saying. He needed to go for a walk and clear his head. As he headed for the door, he said, "Bienvenida, your request is unrealistic. You dump a major issue that will affect my daughter's life on me and expect me to make an immediate decision and find a solution."

Bienvenida walked over to José with her hands on her hips and confidently commanded, "Let me help you. There is one other option that may be the best solution for the entire family. You could send Carla to a Catholic boarding school. You still have time to enroll her for the upcoming school year. She will not only get an exceptional education but also will get some discipline. God knows you have failed miserably in the disciplinary area. You have spoiled that child to the point where she thinks she is entitled to have everything her way. She is selfish and ungrateful and has no regard for the rules I set. If that is not bad enough, she is smart-mouthed and thinks she needs to be the center of everyone's attention."

José was disturbed and agitated by her suggestion. She adopted a softer, more seductive tone as she said, "With Carla out of the house, you and I can concentrate on our relationship and planning our wedding."

José did not respond as he headed out the door. Bienvenida trailed behind him. The thought of sending Carla away pained him. He had the first-hand experience of what it is like to live alone without the support of your family. He wasn't sure he could put his only child through the pain, loneliness, and displacement he had experienced when he had first left Galicia.

"You have put me in a tough position, and you can't expect me to decide on the spot. I need a few days to think about this."

With her arms flailing, Bienvenida shouted, "Quite frankly, José, I did expect that you would readily agree to send Carla away for the sake of our relationship. I am 100 percent committed to this relationship, but you are not. For God's sake, the child has a mother and sister who could take her in, and there is also the boarding school option. It's not like you are tossing her out into the street. Our relationship, on the other hand, needs time and space to flourish. That can only happen if Carla moves out of the house. The future of our relationship is in your hands. You decide what you want to do."

José pleaded, "Can't you give Carla a little more time to get comfortable with this relationship?"

"It's been a year, and Carla is still disrespectful and refuses to comply with my rules. If you do not make alternative arrangements, I will move out immediately, and this relationship is over."

Bienvenida returned to the house and slammed the door in his face. José walked away. Torn between his daughter and his girlfriend, he needed time and space to think.

He was not sure why Carla had developed a smart mouth or why she was behaving with such disrespect that he did not recognize her. She had been such a sweet, polite little girl. He could not understand what was happening to her. Maybe spending some time at the boarding school with the nuns could help her attitude and behavior.

The next few days were torturous for José. He could not sleep for several nights as he weighed his options. When he did get sleep, he was plagued with nightmares about his time in Cuba with no money, family, or permanent shelter. He wanted to do the best for his daughter.

By the third morning, José had convinced himself that the boarding school option was a good idea. He rationalized the decision to send Carla away by his desire to give his daughter the best education he could afford. Bienvenida was correct; it wasn't like he was tossing his child out into the world on her own. The boarding school would allow Carla to associate with girls from upper-middle-class families.

In 1945, right before the start of the school year, José enrolled Carla in Santa Clara, a Catholic boarding school that was also a convent.

One week before dropping Carla off at Santa Clara, José asked Bienvenida to spend a few days at her family's house. He wanted to break the news to Carla by himself. He also wanted to spend some time alone with her.

Carla beamed as she saw Bienvenida walk out of the house with a packed bag. Finally, the witch was moving out, and her home life could go back to being a warm and loving environment. She was so excited and hopeful that she would get back her special time with her father.

Looking forward to sharing their special time, she searched her memory for which story she wanted to hear first. It had been a long time; they had a lot of catching up to do. Maybe he would tell her more than one story.

That day, Carla put a bow in her hair and picked out her best outfit. She wanted to celebrate that the witch was gone. She asked the housekeeper to make her father's favorite meal of mashed potatoes, vegetables, and beef. Most Dominican households had rice and beans as their main dish, but today they would have mashed potatoes. That would make her father so happy.

Carla stood by the window, waiting to glimpse her father approaching the house. When she saw him coming up the road, she ran to the kitchen with a huge grin and twinkling eyes to advise the housekeeper that her father was on his way.

She ran back to the window to watch him walk up to the house. As her father approached the house, Carla noticed that his shoulders slumped, he looked down at the floor and walked slower than usual.

Maybe he had a bad day at the bodega. Sometimes he has problems with shoplifters. A shoplifter had once hit him in the face and broken his nose, which left it slightly crooked.

When José walked into the house and had settled down at the dinner table, Carla asked, "Papa, what is going on? You look strange."

"Carla, I am fine, just a little tired. It was a long morning at the bodega. Let's enjoy our meal."

Carla continued to talk, trying to engage her father in conversation; she could not get more than a few words out of him. Carla could not get her father to open up. He was not talking about his day at the bodega, nor was he telling her any stories. He ate in silence, which was not like him.

She was concerned. Her father barely looked up from his plate. She did not recall ever seeing her father so self-absorbed. Was he ill? Had he gotten some bad news? As they finished their meal, she asked again, "Papa, what is going on? Are you upset because Bienvenida left? You know that she is not good for you or me. She is evil and only wants your money. I hope she never comes back."

José sat back, cleared his throat, searching for the right way to say what he had to say. "Carla, listen to me carefully. Bienvenida is coming back. I love her very much and hope to marry her someday."

Carla swallowed hard, and blinked a few times, hoping to stop the oncoming lump in her throat and willing the tears away as she asked, "Do you love her more than you love me?"

"Of course not. I don't love Bienvenida more than I love you. You are my daughter, my little girl, and no one could ever take your place. But I love Bienvenida too. My love for her is not more or less; it's different."

"I don't understand. How different? What kind of love?"

Carla watched her father closely, waiting for him to respond. She wasn't sure why he struggled with a response to her questions.

"Carla, it's an adult kind of love. You are my daughter, and I love you because you are my special little girl."

Carla was confused. She did not understand how he could love them both.

"If you love me so much, why do you let Bienvenida live here? She hates me and beats me, and I do not want her to live here anymore. How could you love anything about her?"

José's calm tone and demeanor changed at Carla's accusations.

"Carla, stop making up stories about Bienvenida. I will not have you slander and disrespect her. She does not hate you, and I know for sure that she does not beat you. She is a loving and kind person who wants to do what is best for you. You should stop fighting with Bienvenida and try being her friend. You are getting older, and there are female issues that you should be learning about and discussing with another woman. Bienvenida could be a friend and a great stepmother if you let her."

Carla pressed her palms over her eyes, willing the tears to stop flowing down her cheeks. When she was able to control her tears, she dropped her hands to the table. Her hands were shaky, so she clasped her hands and interlaced her fingers squeezing as hard as she could until her knuckles turned white. She looked at her hands and then at her father's face as she exclaimed, "I have a mother and a sister. I don't need to learn anything from that witch. I certainly don't want to be her friend or talk to Bienvenida about anything."

Carla's confrontational tone must have infuriated José, who snapped, "This attitude of yours is what has been causing the discord in the house. Bienvenida was right. Your smart mouth and storytelling are unacceptable."

Incredulous, Carla grew impatient with her father. It was difficult to understand how he could be so blind. How could he not see Bienvenida for what she was? "I can't believe you're taking her side on this. Why don't you believe me?"

"Listen, Carla. Bienvenida and I have made a decision for this family. I want you to understand that this is the best outcome for us, especially you. We have enrolled you at Santa Clara for the upcoming school year. At Santa Clara, you will get the best education money can buy."

Carla furiously pushed away from the table, which caused her glass of milk to spill to the floor. Her father's betrayal was like a punch in the gut. She stared at her father with wide eyes and raised eyebrows, not recognizing the man sitting before her.

For the first time in her life, she yelled at her father. "Santa Clara? Isn't that a boarding school? Are you planning to send me away? Why? So, Bienvenida can have you and the house to herself? The best decision for who? Me or Bienvenida?"

Tears streamed down her face. She was waiting for her father to respond—waiting for him to say something, anything. These were rhetorical questions, but she expected a better explanation. She wanted him to say that he was kidding, that he did not want to send her away, and that Bienvenida was never coming back. Instead, her father looked at her with sorrowful eyes.

After a long, reflective pause, José responded in a reassuring tone. "Carla, you need to understand that going to Santa Clara is in your best interest. You will be with other girls your age. You will receive the best and most exclusive education. Boarding schools are prestigious, highly coveted institutions that few people can afford. Not many little girls are as lucky as you are."

Carla was furious with her father's rationalizations. "Prestigious? Highly coveted? Lucky? I don't even understand what you are saying. What I know is that I do not feel lucky. You are punishing me; except I do not know what I have done wrong to deserve this punishment."

Before José could reach out and comfort his daughter, she stormed to her room with a heavy heart, closed the door, and cried herself to sleep. The next few days were a blur for both father and daughter. The housekeeper packed Carla's bag, only including items the boarding school listed as permissible personal items.

Carla was in a daze as Bienvenida's words echoed in her mind: "If anybody is going to leave this house, it's going to be you, Carla." The day of her departure, Carla was glad not to have to face Bienvenida— glad she did not have to see the triumphant smirk on Bienvenida's face as José carted her away.

Carla was eleven years old when she arrived at the Santa Clara boarding school. Carla clung to her father as she begged him not to leave her. José gently separated himself, looked Carla in the eyes, and explained: "Carla, now that you are older, it is in your best interest to have a more structured form of education. Look around you. There are so many other girls your age. Think of the fun you'll have and the new friends you'll make."

Carla was not convinced this had to be Bienvenida's doing. Bienvenida had warned her this would happen. Carla refused to believe that her father would have sent her away without coaxing.

After José left, Carla stood by the window of the reception hall, sobbing and trembling against the windowpane as she tried to glimpse her father walking away. She was hoping he would look back so she could wave. She continued to stare out of the window until he disappeared, never looking back.

Carla had never been away from her father. For the first time in her life, Carla felt like an orphan. She had never been close to her mother, but her father had more than made up for the lack of her mother's attention. Now, she did not have a father or mother. How could he dump her here with these strangers?

Carla stood by the window in the reception parlor, frozen in place. She crossed her arms, trying to control her trembling. She watched as the other girls mingled around, waiting for further instructions from the nuns. They were happy, carefree, and comfortable in their surroundings.

Carla stood petrified as two nuns dressed in billowing black-and-white habits sternly took roll call and inventoried personal items.

After roll call, the girls filed into an assembly-like hall, where the nuns segregated them by age group. Carla was in the ten-to-twelve-year-old age group. The sisters then took each group to their respective dormitory, where they were assigned beds and roommates.

Carla's roommate, Alicia, was also eleven years old. She was visibly concerned about Carla and asked, "Carla, why are you crying?"

Carla was so distraught that she could barely get the words out, "I've never been away from home or away from my father. Enrolling me in this boarding school is a way of punishing me. But I do not know what I did wrong to deserve this punishment."

"Well, you will get used to this place in no time."

"Alicia, why did your parents send you away?"

Alicia was chipper as she corrected Carla. "I was not sent away. Both of my parents attended boarding schools and think this is the best education anyone can get. I have been attending Santa Clara since I was six years old."

"Is this okay with you?" Carla asked in disbelief.

"Sure. My older sister is also here. She is with the thirteen-to-fifteen-year-old girls' group."

Alicia moved over to Carla's bed and put her arm around Carla's shoulders. "I will show you around and help you adjust. But I have to say that the one thing I'll never get used to is the nuns pulling my ears or swatting me on the butt or pulling my hair. You need to be on your best behavior around the nuns, or they will hit you."

The girls were expected to uphold the highest standards of personal hygiene, presentation, and behavior. The dress code required a conservative uniform, including a pleated skirt or dress and knee-high socks.

The students were required to make their beds first thing in the morning. As the girls were eating breakfast, the nuns inspected the rooms and rated the neatness of their beds and the dresser drawers. Those girls who did not pass inspection would get back to their rooms to find their beds stripped and their dressers' drawers dumped for the girls to reorganize.

The sisters ran Santa Clara with unparalleled cruelty and tyranny. Within their system, Santa Clara tolerated a high number of pathological abusers. Some nuns used corporal punishment, not only as an acceptable tool for discipline, but because they enjoyed the violence and power it gave them over the girls. Corporal punishment was the culture, and, for most of the nuns, an occasional hand slap, pulled ear, or a swat on the behind was the way to get the attention of the offending student. A few of the nuns were not violent, but they did nothing to stop the violence.

During Carla's stay at the boarding school, she witnessed and suffered many incidents of abuse. The nuns marched the girls out into the hall and swatted their legs or hands with yardsticks. Hearing girls cry out in pain as the sisters dragged them by the ear from one end of the room to the other was commonplace.

The nuns taught Carla about personal hygiene and the changes that would transform her body into a señorita. She should learn about being a señorita from her mother or sister, not total strangers.

Carla found it difficult to assimilate into the boarding school environment and did not make many close friends. Santa Clara became Carla's home for five years, except for the rare visits to her sister's house. The five years at the boarding school were the most miserable years of her life. She constantly reminisced about her time at home.

During that first year, she rarely smiled, and when she did, it was a weak smile without that twinkle in her eye. She had lost her family, home, and everything familiar to her. Carla had a difficult time reconciling her despair with her peers' comfort. Those around her tried to convince her she was homesick and would soon get over it. But she never did. *Homesickness* did not describe nor do justice to the deep sense of bereavement she experienced during that first year.

As time transpired, she hurt less, but still grieved the loss of her home life with her father. Carla could never get acclimated to living with the cold, indifferent environment that Santa Clara offered.

Contrary to her bereavement, her father had told her that boarding schools were exclusive, prestigious, highly coveted institutions and that she was lucky to be there. So, who was right, and who was wrong? Was she an ungrateful, selfish child? Was it wrong for her to complain? Even though she learned to live in her new environment, she could never reconcile her feelings with what her father and others were telling her.

The boarding school experience was an unhappy one for Carla as she spent her formative years in an austere, strict, and abusive environment. This experience and her father's relationship changed her happy, confident demeanor. She had developed a tough exterior as a protective armor to protect the vulnerable child, and cope with the reality of having to live away from her emotional support system. The once happy, bright, bubbly little girl was gone.

She was also vigilant, expecting that at any moment, she would be rejected or betrayed by those around her. After all, the one person she had trusted and idolized—her father, had betrayed her.

In 1951, three months short of her seventeenth birthday, Carla had had enough of the nuns' abusive treatment and refused to return to Santa Clara after the summer vacation.

Her best friend, Alicia, decided to elope with her boyfriend that summer and would not be returning to Santa Clara the following school year. Alicia had helped Carla get through the first few months of her enrollment. She had been her constant companion, only friend, and support. She couldn't survive in Santa Clara without her best friend, Alicia.

CHAPTER 15
UNMASKING THE WITCH

Unbeknownst to Carla, during her five-year stint at the boarding school, José and Bienvenida had married. Carla could not believe that her father had excluded her from such a momentous event in his life. In hindsight, it may have been the right decision, as she was not sure how she would have reacted.

During those five years, Bienvenida had manipulated José's time so that he would not visit Carla at the boarding school, nor had she permitted Carla to visit her home. During the summer vacations and holidays, when the other girls visited their families, Carla had stayed behind with the nuns. The onetime Carla had visited, Bienvenida had made sure Carla understood that she could not stay or return. She had made Carla's visit a living hell, and Carla had left after the first few days, spending the rest of the time at her sister's house.

Bienvenida was not happy about Carla's decision to leave the boarding school and live with her father. Her intolerance for Carla grew to unprecedented levels, especially since she could no longer control or manipulate her.

Carla was older and could see through Bienvenida's duplicitous ways. More importantly, she could now defend herself from Bienvenida's threats. Carla had finally figured out this wicked stepmother. Bienvenida exhibited the classic characteristics of a sociopath. She was superficially charming, smooth, and engaging. She was arrogant, believing herself better than those around her. She was cruel to the household staff, yelling and threatening to cut their pay for minor infractions.

Carla suspected that Bienvenida did not love José. She was a gold-digger who had married José for the comfortable lifestyle his income provided. Carla set out to prove that the selfish and self-centered Bienvenida was only concerned with her welfare.

During the summer of 1951, Carla noticed Bienvenida behaving strangely. She no longer accompanied José to the bodega, opting to be a housewife instead. Ironically, there was nothing domestic about Bienvenida, and this decision to be a housewife sounded somewhat suspicious. In Carla's mind, Bienvenida was more like a lady of leisure and not a housewife. Carla observed Bienvenida's actions and movements from afar.

While José worked at the bodega, Bienvenida would go to the salon to have her hair and nails done. She was also a member of the social club and spent most of her days and afternoons at the club. At least, that was what she claimed.

Bienvenida would make it home fifteen to twenty minutes before José arrived, cutting it as close as five minutes. Carla was glad Bienvenida spent most of her time out of the house. But she did not like that Bienvenida was taking advantage of her father.

One day, Carla followed Bienvenida as far as possible on foot. About a quarter of a mile from their house, she saw Bienvenida get into the back seat of a car. The car could have been one that served as public transportation, but Carla could not be sure. Carla walked back home to await Bienvenida's return.

At 11:20 a.m., when Carla noted Bienvenida was not home, she hurried to the spot where she had witnessed Bienvenida boarding the car. She waited for twenty minutes. There was no sign of Bienvenida or the vehicle. The scorching sun was hotter than ever on that day. Carla was hot, hungry, and tired. As she was about to head home, she noticed a car coming up the road. She hid behind a wall and watched to see if it was Bienvenida.

Sure enough, the witch was sitting in the front seat of the same car. Granted, sitting in the front seat of a public vehicle was common. Carla waited to see where the car would stop. It stopped at the same location where Bienvenida had boarded that morning. Bienvenida walked out of the car, but not before leaning over and giving the driver a hug and a passionate kiss.

Carla was incredulous. Her eyes had to be playing tricks on her under the sweltering midday sun. She refocused and noticed Bienvenida getting out and walking around to the driver's side and giving him a peck on the lips before turning and waving goodbye. Carla ran as fast as possible to make it home before Bienvenida. She cut through a couple of alleys and neighbors' backyards. Bienvenida would never walk that route in her high-heeled shoes.

Carla ran to her room and quickly washed up before her father came home. As Carla changed out of her sweaty blouse, she pondered what to do with this information. She could tell her father. But would he believe her and finally see Bienvenida for who she was? No, he would not. She needed to have concrete evidence to present to her father. She preferred to sit on the information for the time. She would continue to watch Bienvenida from afar and see what other information she could gather.

When they sat down to eat their meal, Carla watched the dynamics of the conversation and Bienvenida's behavior. Bienvenida fawned over José, asking how his day went, making believe she cared about his welfare. José ate this up. He loved the way Bienvenida catered to him and made him feel special and loved.

When he asked Bienvenida about her day, she replied that it was uneventful. She had gone to the salon to wash and set her hair before getting together with a couple of her friends at the club.

Wow! She was good a liar.

Carla sat quietly, taking it in. Her poor father worked hard at the bodega during the day and could not see that this woman was playing him like a fiddle. What an idiot.

José interrupted her analysis of the dynamics at the table as he asked, "Carla, your food is getting cold. Why are you not eating?"

"I'm a little tired." Carla then turned to Bienvenida. "So, Bienvenida, how many times per week do you get your hair and nails done? I counted at least three times this week. Is it necessary to get your hair and nails done that many times per week? I have to say that your hairdresser is not doing a good job. Your hair looks the same as it did this morning. Papa, what do you think? How does Bienvenida's hair look to you?"

"Bienvenida looks beautiful. I think her hairdresser did a fabulous job."

Men. What would they know about hair and nails?

Carla noticed Bienvenida giving her a suspicious look, clearly trying to figure out what Carla was implying. Carla enjoyed keeping Bienvenida guessing.

"Well, Carla, if you must know, I like to wash my hair three or four times per week and prefer to have it done at the salon. After all, your father can afford to spoil me. Isn't that right, José?"

"Yes, dear. You deserve that, and so much more."

Carla's stomach churned as she witnessed the exaggerated display of affection. How she wished she could blurt out what she had seen. But she had to wait for the right time.

The next day, after José had gone to work, Bienvenida approached Carla.

"What are you trying to prove by questioning my whereabouts and routine?"

"I'm not trying to prove anything. I'm curious as to how you spend my father's money and what you do during the day when my father is working."

"What I do with my time is my business, and you should not butt in if you know what is good for you. Let me remind you that I am José's wife. As such, it's not your father's money. It's our money."

"Listen to me carefully. I'm no longer eleven years old, and if you even try to lay a hand on me, I will hit you back."

"No! You listen to me. You are still a nobody in this house, and I'll be damned if you are going to come here and try to stick your nose into my business. You had better stay out of my way, or you will be out on your ass."

"Is that a fact? We'll see who ends up leaving this time."

"Are you threatening me?"

"No, it's not a threat. It's simply a fact. I will no longer tolerate your physical abuse."

"What are you going to do? Go to your father? If you recall, that did not work so well for you the last time. Your father will never take your word over mine. Besides, this is now my house. If you don't like it, you are welcome to leave at any time."

"We will see about that."

Carla confidently walked away, leaving Bienvenida to wonder what she could know. It was so much fun to watch her squirm. Good to keep her guessing. Bienvenida stayed home the next few days, constantly watching Carla. Carla ignored Bienvenida, acting as if nothing was going on.

Bienvenida staying home was not good for anyone. She was a real tyrant. On the third day, Carla saw her getting ready to go out. She said to Bienvenida, "Another day at the salon?"

"My whereabouts are none of your business."

Carla ignored her comment. She gave Bienvenida a five-minute head start before she left the house. As she was following Bienvenida, she stopped abruptly, thinking to herself, "What am I doing? Bienvenida is right; my father will never take my word over hers." She slowly turned around and headed home.

She had to get away from the drama her father was living with his wife; this was his problem to solve, not hers. At that moment, thirty days after her return from Santa Clara, she made a conscious decision to move out of her father's home. Moving back had been a mistake. She now understood that it was no longer her home. It was Bienvenida's house and her rules.

Bienvenida was no longer physically abusive, but she was still verbally abusive. Bienvenida dismissed the lady who did the housework, demanding that Carla do it instead. In her opinion, now that Carla was older, she needed to contribute to the upkeep of the house. Why should she pay someone to do the housework when Carla could do it herself?

That afternoon after their noon meal, Carla advised her father that she would be moving in with Lucia and her mother.

"Carla, but Lucia's house is crowded with the children and María living in the house. You will be much more comfortable here."

"Papa, now that I am older and can make my own decisions, I refuse to put up with your wife's narcissistic behavior. The woman lacks a conscience."

Carla don't tell me you are going to accuse Bienvenida falsely of beating and berating you. I see you haven't outgrown that childish behavior. Why do you insist on maligning Bienvenida?"

Carla was tempted to blurt out what she had witnessed but did not have the heart to hurt her father deliberately. She chose instead to keep the information to herself.

"Papa, when Bienvenida moved in, she hit our house like a bomb that shattered our peaceful home life. My idyllic world was in direct contrast with the hell she brought into our home. Her negativity bombarded the beautiful, happy, loving world we enjoyed. This house is no longer my home; it is now Bienvenida's house, and I refuse to live in her house under her rules. Lucia's house, though crowded, is a loving home."

"Carla, you are unbelievable. You've been back a little less than a month, and already you are causing problems with Bienvenida. If you wanted to go live with Lucia, you should have said so. There was no need to malign Bienvenida."

"Papa, I do not expect you to believe me. Someday, you will see her for the evil witch she truly is and discover the depths of her deception."

Bienvenida quietly witnessed the discussion between father and daughter from behind her bedroom door, thinking, "what is Carla implying? That girl knew something. But how?" She had to find out.

After José had gone back to the bodega for the afternoon shift, Bienvenida barged into Carla's room and slammed the door.

"What the hell do you mean by telling your father that he will someday discover the depths of my deception? What are you implying?"

"Bienvenida, I'm not implying anything. What I stated was a fact, and you know it. You may be fooling my father, who walks around like a lovesick puppy, but you are not fooling me. I know what you've been up to."

"You don't know a goddamn thing. You are a spoiled brat that is jealous José has found happiness without her; and because you can't handle it, you want to spoil his happiness by making up stories."

"Because I chose not to say anything to my father doesn't mean I won't tell him what I know. If you think you can come in here and intimidate me, you are mistaken. The only reason I didn't say anything to him is that, unlike you, I care about my father and don't want to hurt him deliberately."

"Firstly, I don't think you know a damn thing. Secondly, no matter what you say, your father will not believe you. You saw how your father didn't believe anything you were saying earlier today."

"You're awfully concerned for someone who doesn't believe I know anything. Let's say I know you like to sit in the front seat of a public vehicle. Let's be clear; I don't like you. You are the worst thing that happened to this family. Unfortunately, my father is too blind to see you for who you are, and I don't want to be part of this drama."

"Carla, you're a stupid girl. You give yourself too much credit. No matter what you tell your father, he will never take your word over mine. So, what if I like to sit in the front seat of a public vehicle? My cousin often gives me rides. Nothing wrong with that," said Bienvenida as she confidently walked out of Carla's room.

Carla found herself in an awkward position. She loved her father and preferred to live with him. But she refused to stand by and watch her father make a fool of himself, walking around like a lovesick puppy. Most of all, she refused to deal with his evil wife. Carla did not want to admit it, but Bienvenida was right. Her father was so blindly in love with Bienvenida that he would believe any explanation she gave him.

Her mother was another story. Carla was not as close to her mother as she was with her father. Her mother had been there for her basic needs, but always at an emotional distance. Carla had learned early in her life that she could not rely on her mother. Carla accepted her mother's indifference as a fact. Regardless, Carla loved her mother, and it was difficult to witness the depression and alcoholic binges that could last up to ten days.

Since 1942, when her parents had separated, it had been Carla and her father taking care of each other. Lucia had already been married, but her father had made sure he met Carla's material and emotional needs.

Carla had been eight years old when her mother had moved out of their family home after Carmelo's death. After one too many of María's binges, her father had had enough of María's drinking. The marriage was over. They'd fought, and María had moved into Lucia's house.

Although he never mentioned it, she could tell her father had been relieved not to have to deal with her mother's mood swings and drinking. Carla had had to admit to herself that she was relieved as well. Even though she was not a violent drunk, her mother's dramatic mood changes made everything unpredictable, chaotic, and depressing. The minute her mother walked out of the door, the atmosphere, and energy around their home had immediately lightened…only to be dampened two years later when Bienvenida had moved in.

Regardless of how much it pained her to see her mother destroy herself with alcohol, she moved out of her father's house and in with her sister and mother. She shouldn't have to put up with an abusive stepmother. She had suffered five years of abuse from the nuns and refused to take it anymore. The abusive behavior she'd had to endure since the age of ten was terrible, but her father's failure to see what was right in front of him devasted her.

For the second time in her life, Carla felt like an orphan. She was fortunate to have her sister, Lucia, who was always there to support her. Lucia was the one person who she could always count on to support her. She was her sister, mother, best friend, and role model. Carla and Lucia were closer than any two sisters could be. Carla settled in with her sister, her sister's family, and her mother.

A LIFE OF FALSE DICHOTOMY

Carla enrolled in and attended the local public school and then attended and graduated from the local institute with a bookkeeping degree.

In 1953, when she was nineteen years old, Carla met Sam Rosa, who frequented José's bodega and other local shops in the neighborhood.

Sam was about six feet tall, had olive skin, and was quite debonair. Carla immediately fell in love with him. But soon after they met, Carla learned that Sam was married and had three children. Sam swore that he and his wife were separated. Nevertheless, Carla refused to entertain the idea of a relationship with him until he had resolved his marital status.

They started dating in 1954; once Sam was able to prove he had resolved his marital situation. He visited Carla at her sister's home under the watchful eyes of her family.

No one in Carla's family liked Sam. He was a divorcé, ten years her senior, and a bit too streetwise for the naïve Carla.

Sam was not the type of mate José had envisioned for Carla. He had hoped that Carla would marry a professional man. Carla was an educated young lady with a middle-class upbringing. Sam, on the other hand, was an illiterate divorcé with three children. To make matters worse, he was one of Trujillo's henchmen. He could not be trusted. What kind of future would she have with such a man?

The Dominican Republic attained independence in 1844 but mostly suffered political turmoil and tyranny and a brief return to Spanish rule over the following seventy-two years. The United States' occupation from 1916 to 1924 and a subsequent calm six-year period was followed by the military dictatorship of Rafael Leónidas Trujillo Molina until 1961.

During the time of the United States' occupation, the quartermaster (the officer responsible for supplies, including arms and food) of the new Dominican Army was a former telegraph clerk by the name of Rafael Leónidas Trujillo. Trujillo was an unscrupulous strongman. He used his powerful position as quartermaster to amass an enormous personal fortune. He engaged in embezzlement activities, initially involving the procurement of military supplies.

In March 1930, rebels initiated a coup ousting sitting president Horacio Vásquez, and the rebel leader became the provisional president for five months. During the five-month provisional period, Trujillo ran for president. His supporters killed opposition leaders, ransacked opponents' homes, and kidnapped anti-Trujillo newspaper reporters. Trujillo's campaign of terror and intimidation enabled him to block any government reform actions by his opposition. Trujillo killed his way to the presidency and ruthlessly destroyed anyone and anything in his way.

Trujillo took complete control of the country's political power. The dictator grossly abused his power, considered himself a godly figure, and demanded to be treated as such. It was mandatory to have a picture of Trujillo hanging in a prominent spot in the home. He even changed the name of the capital city from Santo Domingo to Ciudad Trujillo. People who spoke against his government were jailed and tortured, disappeared, or their bodies dumped in ditches with their tongues cut off.

His tyranny, historically known as La Era de Trujillo (the Trujillo Era) is considered one of the bloodiest of the twentieth century, as well as a time of a classic personality cult when monuments to Rafael Trujillo were in abundance.

Although cast in the mold of previous caudillos, Trujillo surpassed them in efficiency, greediness, and utter ruthlessness. The Trujillo regime brought economic stability to the country but allowed the people no political freedom whatsoever. Generally speaking, the quality of life improved for the average Dominican. Poverty persisted, but the economy expanded, the foreign debt disappeared, the currency remained stable, and the middle class grew. Public works projects enhanced the road system and improved port facilities, airports, and public buildings constructed, the public education system grew, and the illiteracy rate significantly declined.

Trujillo was a ruthless dictator who ruled the country like it was his personal fiefdom. His thirty-year rule brought the country stability and prosperity at the cost of civil liberties and human rights.

Life was hard for young women during the forties and fifties. Trujillo was known for his sexual desire for young girls whose families could not protect them. If he saw a beautiful young woman he wanted, he had his henchmen kidnap her, and she would be forced to become his mistress. Other times, young women were invited to parties, drugged, raped by Trujillo, and then sent back home.

Carla grew up during Trujillo's merciless, dictatorial reign over the people. Fortunately, Carla never came across Trujillo.

CHAPTER 16
SAM ROSA: HUMBLE BEGINNINGS

Life was hard for the Rosa family. The family lived in poverty, only able to afford the bare necessities. They struggled for each meal, not knowing how they would provide the next meal.

They had little in the way of what they considered vanity items, such as clothes, shoes, or other accessories. They were poor, but the children did not know they were poor. The children played and entertained themselves with the little they had available. Poverty was what they knew.

Sam was born on October 7, 1924, in the agricultural village of Los Llanos, San Pedro de Macorís, Dominican Republic. He was the oldest of fourteen children born to Aurelio Rosa and Andrea Sosa.

Aurelio Rosa had been born in Bayaguana, Dominican Republic, on July 26, 1899, and died at the age of eighty-four of cirrhosis of the liver. He was the second child of Manuela Hernandez and Juan Rosa Benitez.

Manuela and Juan were born, raised, and married in Puerto Rico. In the mid-1890s, they had struggled financially. Unable to find work in their hometown in Puerto Rico, the couple boarded a boat and sailed to the Dominican Republic, where they had settled in Bayaguana and worked on the sugar plantations. The couple had eight children (six boys and two girls).

Aurelio had taken after his mother's Spanish side of the family, with blond hair, fair skin, and a hard, angular jawline. Clint Eastwood could have been Aurelio's twin. His height of six feet, two inches, he'd gotten from his father, who had been six feet, three inches tall, with an olive complexion.

Andrea Margarita Sosa Ramírez had been born in 1910 in San José de los Llanos, San Pedro de Macorís. She died of a heart attack at the age of forty-two on February 7, 1952. She was the daughter of Joséfa Ramirez and Abelardo Mejia Sosa. The couple had had three daughters and one son.

Andrea had been an elegant woman with a voluptuous, curvaceous hourglass figure. She had been a statuesque five feet, seven inches tall, with a twenty-eight-inch waist, full hips, thick, shapely legs, and dark wavy hair.

Aurelio and Andrea had married in 1923 and had fourteen children. Both were illiterate and, with difficulty, scrawled awkward *X*s to sign their names on documents.

The family's first home had been in Los Llanos, San Pedro de Macorís, where the first three children had been born. Most of the town's residents had lived below the poverty level. The roads had been unpaved, and many of the homes had been dilapidated shacks with dirt floors. Only the most fortunate homeowners had cement floors. The furniture had been cheaply made stick furniture, with most families calling a mattress on the floor their beds. The sewage system had been practically nonexistent and required the use of latrines.

Because they were illiterate, Aurelio and Andrea could not recognize the errors made in several of their children's birth certificates. The family name was Rosa; however, some children had "De La Rosa" recorded as the family name on their birth certificates instead.

After five years, Aurelio could afford to move the family to Yerba Buena, a rural area in Hato Mayor, where they had purchased land and had a farm. Though their lifestyle was impoverished, the farm ensured they always had plenty to eat.

Their house was made of plywood and had a tin roof and a dirt floor. It had a living room, one bedroom with four beds, and a kitchen toward the back of the house. There was a bed for the parents, and the children slept five to a bed. There was no running water, which required that the older children retrieve well water for cooking and bathing.

Each morning, Sam worked the fields before he attended school because that was the family's only source of income and meals. Sam and the other older children helped milk the cows, pick the crops, feed the animals, and deliver crops and milk to their customers. As the oldest, Sam worked to help support the rest. Education was a luxury his parents could not afford. Sam could only get a third-grade education.

In 1932, after four years on the farm and nine children, Aurelio and Andrea lost the farm. Aurelio had paid cash, and the purchase and sales agreement for the land had been a handshake. When the landowner died in 1932, his family reclaimed the land, and the Rosas had no recourse. The Rosas lost their land, farm, home, and sole source of income. Having no title or legal purchase agreement, Aurelio had to move his family off of the farm and closer to town.

The family was destitute. The older children were forced to quit school and work during the day. Aurelio was not skilled in anything other than farming and living off the land. Swallowing his pride and putting his ego aside, Aurelio had no alternative but to work on someone else's farm.

The older boys shined shoes to help feed the family. When they collected five cents, they took the money home to their mother, and she bought the rice, beans, and meat for the one main meal of the day. Certain foods and other items sold for half a penny of this or a penny of that, and this enabled the family to put food on the table. In effect, the three older children contributed to supporting their large family. The oldest girls worked at the wealthier homes in domestic capacities.

At fourteen, Sam was hired to work at the coffee warehouse, storing, stocking, and preparing merchandise for shipment to Santo Domingo, the capital city.

In 1941, at the age of seventeen, Sam left his boyhood home and joined the military under the leadership of Trujillo for a monthly salary of seventeen pesos. As a military recruit, Sam worked undercover for the Trujillo regime. One of his primary duties was working at a nightclub owned by one of Trujillo's brothers.

Under the Trujillo regime, there were no police officers, only army recruits. Trujillo converted the recruits to police officers. When Sam became a police officer, his salary increased to fifty pesos (equivalent to one US dollar today) per month. The average salary in the Dominican Republic during the late forties and early fifties was approximately 1.50 pesos per day (approximately twenty cents in US dollars today).

CHAPTER 17
FLEEING AN UNSTABLE POLITICAL ENVIRONMENT

Carla's father was not pleased with her choice of a husband. José viewed Carla's marriage to an uneducated police officer as a step down the social ladder. José had always hoped Carla would marry someone from a higher socioeconomic status or, at the least, one equivalent to theirs.

Although José was also uneducated, he had improved his economic status and overcome some of the challenges of his rural upbringing. That his daughter would start her adult life at such a low social standing worried him.

José eventually relented and gave his blessings. Carla married in a civil ceremony on August 28, 1955, at the age of twenty-one, to a man ten years her senior and a divorcé with three children.

In the Dominican Republic, there were and still are three accepted forms of marriage: civil, religious, and free union. Both monogamous and polygamous unions were socially accepted. Since annulments and divorces were difficult to get through the Roman Catholic Church, many couples were reluctant to commit themselves to a religious marriage. Civil marriages, on the other hand, readily permitted divorce, and many couples opted for this uncomplicated union.

Social class also played a role; middle-class and upper-class groups favored a religious marriage, and it thus indicated a higher socioeconomic status. The ideal marriage involved a formal engagement and a religious wedding followed by an elaborate fiesta. However, because Sam was a divorcé, he and Carla were not permitted a religious ceremony, so they opted for a civil union.

When the couple first married, they could not afford their own home and lived with Lucia's family. The house was cramped; it had no bathroom and little privacy.

Once José had gotten over his disappointment, he reached out to his daughter and let the newlywed couple move into one of his rental properties, where they paid a nominal amount in rent. The rental property was an upgrade for them, as they now lived in a house constructed from cement and concrete blocks, with running water and the luxury of a full bathroom.

As a military police officer, Sam's fifty pesos per month could not support two families. Besides the subsidized rent, Carla was a resourceful homemaker who found ways to supplement the family income. She had learned the arts of sewing, knitting, and baking from Lucia, who was an accomplished seamstress and bakery chef. Carla made her clothes and those of her children as well.

By 1958, Carla and Sam had three children of their own: two girls and one boy. They worked hard to get ahead as a family, but living on one salary that had to provide for two families was complicated.

Even though Sam only had a third-grade education, he was street smart. He had a knack for hustling to supplement his income. He had a way with people and the gift of gab. He knew how to work the streets of Santo Domingo to his advantage. Yes, hustling was an acceptable way of life in the Dominican Republic, where you had to do whatever it took to feed your family.

In the Dominican Republic, money talked. As a police officer, Sam had ample opportunity to make an extra buck by working security details and, at times, looking the other way for minor infractions.

~❖~

On the night of May 30, 1961, Rafael Trujillo, the victim of an ambush, was assassinated by rebel military leaders on San Cristobal Avenue, Santo Domingo. But the Trujillo reign was not over, as his sadistic son and heir apparent, Ramfis, took over the presidency.

Trujillo's death left a power vacuum, and the country began to unravel as various groups, including the military, jostled for political power. Under the pressure of the opposition and an uncertain future, Ramfis looted the government coffers and fled the country in 1961 with millions of dollars. Fortunately, Ramfis's presidency was short-lived.

Trujillo's funeral and burial were that of a statesman, with the long procession ending in his hometown of San Cristóbal. The then-president, Joaquín Balaguer, gave the eulogy. After this, the people voted for the Trujillo family to leave the country, so his son, Ramfis Trujillo, came back to relocate his father's body outside of the country. Trujillo was buried in Paris in Père Lachaise Cemetery, at the request of his relatives.

The unstable political environment and constant rioting were unsafe. Sam was not sure what was going to happen, but he was determined to move out of the Dominican Republic and get his family to safety. Sam was quietly working on a plan and saving his money to move out of the city.

By 1962, Sam's assignment was that of traffic duty at the intersection of the US consulate's office. This assignment gave him the unique opportunity to have daily interactions with the personnel of the consulate. Also, to make extra money, Sam worked security detail at some of the consulate personnel's private parties.

With his usual charm and savvy, Sam took advantage of the access he had to some of the personnel. Sam consulted them on the best way to move his family out of the Dominican Republic.

They advised Sam that one of the fastest ways to get approval would be through an offer of employment by a US business. Fortunately, one of his younger sisters had taken the bold step of moving to New York City the previous year, and she could get the required letter of employment for Sam's application. The experts also advised that before he traveled to the US, Sam should file the petition for his family to join him at a later date.

Sam followed the advice the professionals gave him. Having expert advice and information on what paperwork was needed helped him get through the visa and green card application process easily.

Sam received his visa and green card by the end of 1962, by which time he had saved enough money for a one-way ticket to travel to New York City in search of a better life.

Sam arrived in New York City in January 1963, where he worked in a factory in the garment district. He saved as much of his salary as was realistically possible. After four months in New York City, the US Consulate granted his family visas and green cards. Carla and the children received permanent residency status and traveled on a Pan Am flight to John F. Kennedy Airport in May 1963.

For Carla, the move to New York City was bittersweet. She was going to reunite with her husband, but she was leaving the only life she had ever known. She cried incessantly as she said goodbye to her father and sister. Carla was going to miss the two people that had been her sole emotional support since the day she was born.

CHAPTER 18
ADAPTING TO LIFE IN NEW YORK CITY

In the early sixties, Latinos represented approximately 4.5 percent of the total US population. The mode of communication, written and oral, was English only. There were no bodegas or other shops geared to meet ethnic needs.

There was no Latino community to help newcomers adapt and grow within the dominant English-speaking culture. There was no one to help ease the difficulties of transition or the alienating experience of being an immigrant.

The school curriculum was also in English, with no bilingual or English as a second language program. Total immersion was the only option. Carla could not help her children during the adaptation process, as she was also striving to survive.

The entire family struggled to learn the language and adapt to the new environment and culture.

In 1963, Sam and Carla had left the Dominican Republic to escape the political turmoil and escalating violence of a government trying to redefine itself after Trujillo's assassination. Two years after their departure, their homeland was still struggling to find its way. This instability resulted in the Dominican Civil War from April 24 to September 3,

1965, in the capital city of Santo Domingo. Fearing another Cuban revolution, President Johnson ordered US intervention.

The Dominican Civil War was a bloody one. Over three thousand Dominicans and thirty-one Americans lost their lives. Joaquín Balaguer was elected and took office as president in 1966 under US occupation and intervention. Later that same year, international troops departed from the country.

It had taken approximately five long years after the assassination of Trujillo for the nation to begin stabilizing its government. Fortunately, Sam had had the foresight to get his family out of harm's way and into the safety of the US.

In the US, Sam and Carla found a nation that was prosperous, calm, and predictable, with a stable government. The country was also on the cusp of social and cultural changes, with numerous movements and protests clamoring for attention. Social and political movements ranged from the counterculture and social revolution to anti-war movements to the feminist movements to civil rights movements for blacks, Hispanics, and gay people. It was the cultural revolution of the 1960s.

The quagmire in Vietnam escalated and expanded its scope in the late sixties. Many Americans protested against a war that involved a faceless enemy thousands of miles from America. They did not understand why the United States was involved in Vietnam's internal conflicts and political battles, as these did not directly affect Americans. Countless young American men had to mature quickly as they had been high school and college students one day and soldiers the next.

The role of women in society was also beginning to change, and female activists demanded more rights for women. The birth control pill and other contraceptives had been introduced, giving women the ability to plan their families and careers better.

The assassination of famous leaders devastated American politics. John F. Kennedy, who had become the first Catholic president in American history, was gunned down in Dallas, Texas, in 1963. Kennedy became the fourth sitting president to be assassinated while in office. When his brother Robert ran for president in 1968, an assassin's bullet killed him in California. Civil rights leader Martin Luther King, who had done more for African Americans than any other person before him, was assassinated in Memphis, Tennessee, on April 4, 1968.

As a culmination of the era, the world witnessed the first manned moon landing in 1969.

The 1960s was a decade of protest. On the one hand, the numerous protests represented a revolution against the current culture and social norms around clothing, music, drugs, dress, sexuality, formalities, and schooling. On the other, some denounced the numerous movements as ones of irresponsible excess, flamboyance, the decay of social order, and a reckless abandon of societal norms.

During the sixties, Manhattan's garment district manufactured approximately 90 percent of garments in the country, and factory work was abundant. Most of the work involved monotonous assembly line work that required workers to perform one specific task during the workday. The minimum hourly wage in 1960 was $1.25, increasing to $1.60 in 1969.

Both Carla and Sam faced long hours and poor working conditions as factory workers. The constant supervision and watchful eyes of the foremen made for a stifling environment. Fifteen-minute breaks and half-hour lunches were predetermined and strictly timed. The turnover rate was high.

The lack of ventilation in the factories led to an unhealthy work environment. Workers responded to poor conditions by quitting their jobs and seeking work in neighboring factories. There were labor unions, but most of the factory workers had no other alternative given their limited understanding of the language and their lack of skills. They had to endure the hardships of factory work to put food on the table and clothes on their backs.

This type of work and its environment were difficult for both Sam and Carla. Sam had worked outdoors as a police officer, and Carla was working outside of the home for the first time in her life.

Sam earned approximately $46 per week, and Carla earned $40 per week. Their family income had increased from 50 pesos per month to $344 per month, for a combined $4,472 per year. They were sitting pretty; they would have never achieved that in the Dominican Republic.

No matter how hard or bad their finances became, they refused to seek the handouts that many low-income families were taking advantage of at the time. They were healthy, hardworking people who vowed not to seek public assistance programs. Come hell or high water, they were going to make it on their own.

Sam, who had started working at the age of seven, would say that his family would only get what he could afford to provide by the sweat of his brow. He could not fathom depending on the welfare program offered at the time. There had been no welfare program in the Dominican Republic, and they had managed to survive. In the Dominican Republic, if you did not work, you did not eat. He had grown accustomed to working hard for his food. The extent of the help he was willing to accept was living in public housing and attending the local free clinic.

Having grown up in poverty, Sam was aware that what they were experiencing in the US was not poverty—it was earnest striving. He could keep a roof over their heads and put food on the table. Anything above the basic needs was considered a luxury. It may not have always been comfortable or easy, but overall, it was a good life.

Best of all, they were living in a country with a stable, democratic government. The trade-off was giving up some advantages the Caribbean lifestyle offered. They exchanged their more relaxed Caribbean lifestyle for a peaceful nation with a stable government and a hectic lifestyle. They replaced their family noon meals and siestas for thirty-minute lunches in an unhealthy factory environment.

In the Dominican Republic, they'd had domestic help to assist with the children and housework—even the domestic help had had domestic help of their own. With approximately 40 percent of citizens in the Dominican Republic living below the poverty level, there had always been someone with a greater need looking to make an honest living. Life in the Dominican Republic, although politically unstable, had been much simpler, laid back, and organic. However, the peace and stability the US offered enabled them to focus on getting ahead as a family instead of focusing on safety and security issues.

In the US, they could not afford to hire a housekeeper or other domestic staff to help with the chores and care for the children. The irony did not escape Carla that in the US, the roles reversed; she was now in the position to work in a domestic capacity at someone else's home.

Carla worked hard during the day, took care of the home in the evening, and attended school a couple of nights per week. She was determined to fend for herself and not have to depend on anyone, not even for a simple translation. Carla was true to her word and received her GED certification, which is equivalent to completing high school. Her English was not perfect, but it was enough to get by and enabled her to understand what was going on around her without assistance.

Sam, on the other hand, only *thought* he could speak English. No matter how hard Sam tried, his tongue would not cooperate in formulating the English words. Only Sam could understand what he was trying to say. But he, too, was able to hold his own.

Sam worked in a factory until 1969, when he secured a job with better working conditions as a porter in the local Jewish nursing home. He no longer had to commute downtown to the garment district, contend with a foreman breathing down his neck, or be exposed to the dim, cramped space and poor ventilation of the factory environment.

Carla worked in a coat factory, Milton & Posner, until 1978, when she developed glaucoma and severe allergies to minks, dander, and the entire factory environment. She traded factory work for a simpler lifestyle and routine. Carla worked from home, babysitting, baking, and performing other miscellaneous work. She was back on familiar ground, being a resourceful homemaker and supplementing their monthly income with her work-from-home ingenuity.

Later that year, Carla's father suffered a stroke, and she had to make arrangements to take him in and become his primary caretaker. She was now an adult with children of her own, yet the anticipation and excitement she experienced when waiting for the school dismissal bell to ring overwhelmed her. She was going to have special one-on-one time with her father again. At 44 years of age, she felt foolish to have the feelings she had when he was ten years old.

She was awash in the nostalgia of the times when she and her father had shared their meals while he had told her stories of his life. She couldn't get enough of those stories. She even shared her father's stories with her children. Like her father, she wanted her family to know their Spanish family. As her father had advised, she always kept in touch with her family, updating them on her life and inquiring about their wellbeing.

CHAPTER 19
COMING FULL CIRCLE

After hastily leaving Galicia in 1916 to avoid compulsory military service, José returned home on September 1, 1965. He arrived in the Port of Vigo at six o'clock in the evening on the passenger ship *Antillas*. The exhilarating anticipation of seeing his family and walking on Spanish soil made him nervous.

As he stood at the top of the gangway, he scanned the sea of people below, looking for the familiar face of his brother Miguel. José squinted his eyes as he slowly searched the crowd. To no avail, he could not find or recognize him among the many faces. Nevertheless, he forged ahead, hoping he would see his brother among the people below.

As he walked down the gangway, José recalled the naïve sixteen-year-old that had boarded a similar ship destined for Cuba forty-nine years earlier. He remembered the youthful drive and self-confidence he had possessed during his younger years. Lost in reverie, José did not notice that a gentleman had come up to him.

As José walked away from the landing, a gentleman he did not recognize approached him. He studied the stranger, who could have been about ten years his junior. Why was this man staring at him? After a few seconds of staring, the man said to him, "Hola."

José responded aloofly and dismissively as he continued to scan the crowd for his brother, "Hola, amigo."

"Not amigo, brother."

José had to step back and recall the recent photos his brothers had sent to him. Yes, of course, this had to be Miguel.

"My brother Miguel?"

"Yes, your brother Miguel."

As they hugged, tears flowed down their faces. They recalled the last time they had seen each other, forty-nine years earlier. Any initial trepidation José may have had about seeing his family vanished immediately.

Until that moment in time, Miguel had lived in José's mind as a nine-year-old boy. But now he was standing before José, a fifty-eight-year-old man. Though they had exchanged letters and pictures, José had had a hard time associating the person in the images with his brother Miguel.

The brothers traveled to Orense and visited their childhood home in the village of Nocedo. His parents' home, the place he had once called home, was still standing. As José walked through the house, the fields, and the other places that had made up the landscape of the first sixteen years of his life, he was mentally transported back in time and flooded with many childhood memories and emotions.

The depth and intensity of the emotional connections he felt with his childhood home and his village surprised him. Tears flooded his eyes and streamed down his cheeks as he visualized his interactions with his parents, his brothers, and that fateful day he had left Spain. He returned to that place and time when his family had been intact, and he'd had their full support.

He saw that strong young man going through his daily routine of working the fields, tending the livestock, planting, gathering firewood, bartering with his neighbors, and preparing the produce and livestock for sale.

He visualized his mother's illness, imagining her bedridden and her sudden death. He relived the profound guilt over his silence for the first year and his inability to be with his family. He felt guilty for having left Spain. Guilty for being unavailable to his brothers during those stressful days and time of need.

As the three brothers talked about their childhood and the events that had transpired over the last forty-nine years, Juan proposed that they settle their father's estate, sell their father's property, and split the proceeds to include José and his daughter, Carla. Spanish law entitled José to a third of their father's estate. José appreciated the generous offer made by Juan, but he could not, in good conscience, accept any inheritance. José told Juan that he would relinquish his rights to any inheritance, as Juan had taken care of his parents, had taken Miguel in after their father's death, and had taken on the family's responsibilities.

The brothers' lives were intertwined but dramatically different because of their individual life experiences. Although José was proud of his brothers' accomplishments, he would not have traded one day of his adventurous life on the move for Juan's law enforcement career or Miguel's intellect and professorial career.

It was an emotional month of reflection, getting reacquainted with his brothers and meeting his niece and nephews. He told his brothers about his eight-year nomadic and impulsive lifestyle in Cuba. Living life with reckless abandon had perhaps been his way of expressing his liberation from the arduous work at the farm and their father's totalitarian rule of the family. However, that lifestyle was not conducive to settling down and getting ahead. As José matured, he recognized that he needed to change his lifestyle. So, he moved out of Cuba and ended up in the Dominican Republic.

As he reflected on his life and on the pivotal moments that had transformed him, he acknowledged he had been the happiest when he'd had the least. At the height of his wealth and material possessions, he believed himself to be happy and living a fulfilling life. But in reality, those were the times his egotistical arrogance led him to make poor decisions. He had allowed himself to be bamboozled by two women who had demanded a lifestyle that was above his means.

His life with María had been about getting ahead as a family, growing the business, and their savings. However, after his divorce, he turned to a different type of woman.

His second wife, Bienvenida, had been a conniving, manipulative gold-digger whose lifestyle had led him to financial losses. In 1954, José had finally seen Bienvenida for what she was and confronted her. He had unmasked her affairs, stealing, and squandering his money. He struggled with his finances as he had allowed Bienvenida to live beyond their means.

When Bienvenida had seen that José was serious and that she was not going to save the marriage, she had falsely accused him of physical abuse and having an incestuous relationship with his daughter, reporting him to the local police.

It was only then that José recognized the depths of her deception and duplicitous nature. How could it be that he had never noticed? Fortunately, Orlando, Lucia's husband, had a high-ranking position in the police department. Orlando, who was familiar with the family dynamics, had advocated on José's behalf and got the charges dropped.

José sadly admitted to his brothers that Carla had been right about Bienvenida. He regretted not investigating his daughter's claims. He lamented he had allowed himself to be convinced to send his only child away to a boarding school, and he had left Carla to contend with God only knew what else when he was not around.

He had been blind to the events happening in his household and, thus, had failed to protect his daughter. The worst part was that Carla had interpreted his blindness and silence as an endorsement of Bienvenida's cruel behavior. He had failed to see how everyone in the household had tiptoed around Bienvenida's wrath.

Fortunately, he had developed a strong bond with his daughter, and no long-lasting damage to their relationship had resulted from Bienvenida's behavior.

After his divorce from Bienvenida, he had met but had not married Candida, another gold digger who had further depleted his finances. Eventually, he had been forced to sell his bodega to get out of the mountain of debt. He had squandered much of the wealth he had amassed while married to María.

After five years of living together, she left him for a younger man. She had moved to Puerto Rico, leaving him with a one-year-old daughter whom many of his friends had questioned whether he had fathered. He had refused to believe that Joséfina was not his daughter. He loved her and did not care whether or not she was his biological child. In his heart, she was his daughter.

After Candida's departure, he met and married Eudosia in 1962, who had been closer to his age and was a lot like María. With Eudosia, he could get back on track with his business and grow his savings. They combined their resources and established a Fonda they named Casa España. Casa España was a restaurant that sold Gallegan dishes. He also had a section where they sold used furniture and other odds and ends. They also built a small apartment as an addition to their home, which they rented to supplement their income.

Eudosia was a hard-working woman who took great care of their home, him, and his daughter. This time, he paid attention. He was hypervigilant and confident that his home, his business, and his four-year-old daughter were in good hands while he was in Spain.

The time he spent in Galicia was therapeutic. His visit to his parents' graves and his childhood home enabled him to come full circle with his emotions. He healed some old wounds and came to terms with his past. Though he had made virtual peace with his parents at the time of their deaths, it felt good to visit their graves. Finally, he could close the Spain chapter of his life.

He reflected on his life's journey and the unique and exciting twists, turns, and synchronistic events that had shaped his life. He appreciated the opportunity to go back to the beginning of his journey, where he had come from, the roads he had traveled, and where he planned to go in the future.

When he left Galicia, he felt freer, liberated from the old demons that had haunted him for so many years. He had finally settled the unfinished business he'd had with his family, his hometown of Nocedo, and Spain. He returned to Santo Domingo invigorated and excited about his future and raising his young daughter.

By 1965, José had experienced some health issues. Fortunately, the Fonda was less work than the bodega. It was also less profitable, so he heavily relied on the rental property to supplement his income. He no longer had the strength or stamina of his younger years, but he had a daughter to raise and forged ahead. He could not afford private education, but he encouraged her education, nevertheless.

In 1975, his wife, Eudosia, passed away. He did his best to manage a home and raise his teenaged daughter on his own. He had done it once before, albeit at a younger age. He was determined to do the best he could for his daughter.

In late 1977, José had a debilitating stroke. He could no longer work. Living expenses and medical bills depleted his savings. His sixteen-year-old daughter, being a typical teenager, had no interest in being a caretaker. Carla immediately intervened and planned for José to travel to New York City to live with her. Joséfina contacted her mother to make arrangements to live with her in Puerto Rico. They agreed that Joséfina and José would leave Santo Domingo at the same time.

In 1978, at seventeen, Joséfina left the Dominican Republic to join her mother in Puerto Rico, leaving José to fend for himself. The timing of her departure was questionable, as she knew her father could not fend for himself, and she selfishly left him alone. José never heard from her again. Not a letter; not a phone call. Nothing. She disappeared from his life.

José agonized over her well-being. Was this what his parents had experienced when he had left Spain and had not communicated with them for a year? The guilt over his mother's illness and subsequent death overwhelmed him. But only then, when he did not hear from Joséfina, did he fully understand the magnitude of what he had inadvertently put his parents through.

He gave his daughter the benefit of the doubt for the first year. After all, she was only seventeen years old, similar to the same age he had been when he had left home. She might have had a compelling reason for not contacting him. Joséfina's memory consumed him during the first two years. He didn't give up hope that someday she would reach out to him. Each day he hoped that "Today may be the day I receive a letter or telephone call," but the letter never arrived, and the phone never rang.

As another year passed, followed by another, José finally came to accept that, most likely, Joséfina was not his biological child. What other reason could there be for her silence? He was the only father she had known until that time, and he had been a good father to her. Had her mother confirmed that he was not her biological father? And had she, therefore, chosen to ignore him? As much as he missed and loved Joséfina, he accepted she was out of his life permanently. He found it hard to function, but he had to wish her well and get on with his life.

The universe had given him children and then taken them away, leaving him with only one child out of four. The deaths of the younger children constituted a closure, a sense of finality, as he knew what had happened to them and where they were. Joséfina's absence was that of a missing child. The not knowing was the worst. Was she even alive? He suppressed that notion and refused to entertain the possibility that harm had come to his youngest daughter. He preferred to believe she was safe, and that she had made a conscious decision not to communicate with him. As much as that pained him, it hurt much less than believing harm had come to his youngest child.

CHAPTER 20
THE END OF A LONG JOURNEY

A new adventure! Who would have predicted it? It was 1979, and José was a long way from his native Spain.

Even at the age of seventy-nine, after three marriages and two divorces, being widowed once, and having four strokes, José was looking forward to these new beginnings. After growing up on a farm in rural Galicia, then living in the Caribbean, New York City was going to be unlike anything he had ever experienced. New York constituted his third major move.

Living in New York City, an urban lifestyle was shocking to his system. He loved being able to spend time with Carla, but the confines of an apartment and his limited mobility because of several strokes were not conducive to walking out in nature whenever he wanted.

Aside from the confinement of apartment living, he was grateful for the opportunity to witness the impact and domino effect of the migration process started by Christopher Columbus in 1492 in North America. Having lived in the Caribbean, José had witnessed the long-lasting impact that the Spanish conquistadors' and settler's actions centuries ago had had on the Caribbean islands. Now he would get a glimpse of the impact on the Americas.

~✦~

Christopher Columbus: hero or villain, friend or foe? It depends on whom you ask. What is indisputable is that his voyage in 1492 was the catalyst for the opening and transformation of the Western Hemisphere. His actions and those of other conquistadors and subsequent settlers resulted in the collision of three distinct cultures (the Europeans, Africans, and indigenous populations) that gave the Americas and the Caribbean a distinctly blended culture.

Spain, a country barely the size of Texas, had enormous ambitions to conquer the world. Although it did not manage to do this, it played a unique and pivotal role in shaping Western civilization, from religion to trade. For over two hundred years, over seven hundred fifty thousand Spaniards immigrated to the New World, and this influence reshaped the Western Hemisphere, leaving Spanish as the world's second most widely spoken language, following Chinese.

In large part, Spain's never-ending thirst for conquering the world and engaging in wars helped shape the world into what it is today. Over five centuries, Spain discovered continents, formed one of the biggest empires in modern history, lived through revolutions and civil wars—and, in the end, lost it all.

At the beginning of the nineteenth century, Spain was a multinational, global empire with colonies around the world. However, the Napoleonic Wars, combined with the worldwide spread of nationalism, marked the beginning of the end of the Spanish Empire.

The Napoleonic Empire was brief but extremely violent. It posed severe ideological and geopolitical challenges to the existing monarchies, confronting them in a series of wars that sent the continent into turmoil until Napoleon's defeat at Waterloo.

Napoleon overthrew the Spanish king, Ferdinand VII, and placed his brother Joseph on the throne as ruler. Dethroning the Spanish king fractured the bond between the Spanish colonies and Spain. Spanish colonies around the world sought their sovereignty and independence, insisting that the absence of a legitimate Spanish king freed the colonies from Spain's rule and economic and political burdens.

British colonies had successfully achieved their independence and emboldened other colonists around the world. If the English colonies could successfully rid themselves of the British monarchy, then why could others not rid themselves of the Spanish monarchy?

Thousands of Spaniards had immigrated to the colonies as sailors, soldiers, settlers, and government officials. Although many returned to their native Spain, many stayed and intermarried with the local population. Their descendants saw themselves as belonging to their new land with no loyalty to Spain. When the native-born Creoles began to outnumber the European-born settlers, loyalty to Spain weakened severely. The native-born Creoles wanted to forge new countries, cultures, and national identities, free of Spanish rule.

Simón Bolívar, El Libertador (the Liberator), was the most instrumental figure in the planning, launching, and execution of Latin America's independence movement. Bolívar, an icon in South America, is considered one of the great heroes of the Latin American independence movements of the early nineteenth century.

Bolívar was a Venezuelan military and political leader, educated in Europe, who was inspired by the revolutions in North America and France. Bolívar and his men played a leading role in freeing South America from Spanish rule. By 1825, Bolívar and his men had liberated most of the lands in South America from Spain.

By 1830, Spain's remaining colonies were Cuba, Puerto Rico, and the Philippines. With the help of the US, these three nations were able to gain their independence. By the end of the nineteenth century, Spain had lost the last remnants of its global empire.

Spain had heavily depended on the revenue derived from sugar, tobacco, cocoa, and coffee grown in the Caribbean Islands and the Americas. The loss of income from the colonies was financially devastating to Spain's economy.

José was glad to witness the positive impact that Spanish descendants had made and continued to make to the US. After all, Spanish descendants had been in the Americas longer than other European descendants.

To envision the US untouched by Latinos is to imagine a country without much of its folklore. Woven into the many facets of US history are the contributions of Hispanics to the development and success of North America.

Bernardo de Gálvez, the Spanish governor of Louisiana in 1777, played a key role in General George Washington's battles against British soldiers. A quarter-million Hispanics served in World War II. Tejano leaders such as José Antonio Navarro and Francisco Ruiz joined the independence movement at the Alamo against the Mexican Army to help win Texas Independence. Sylvia Mendez, of Mexican-Puerto Rican heritage, paved the way for integration (Mendez v. Westminster—desegregation case of 1946. At age eight, she was denied enrollment to a "whites-only" school). Cesar Chavez, who led a national boycott of grape growers in California, forever changed the migrant labor movement; and the enduring legend of the Western cowboy, which originated from the Hispanic culture to name a few.

For decades, Latin Americans have been leaving their imprint on the tapestry of the US, influencing US culture from shore to shore, from the names of some of US cities and states to the Latin food.

Though the many accomplishments were good and well, José could not ignore the ugly side of the Spanish contribution—the unintended consequences of extinguishing the indigenous population and contributing to African slavery.

The conquistadors had hit the Caribbean islands like a Category 5 hurricane, destroying everything and everyone in their path, leaving death, destruction, and devastation in their wake. They had sailed across the Caribbean and into the Americas, conquering and annihilating the indigenous population. The conquistadors had had no respect or understanding for the relationship the indigenous people had had with nature and the land.

The mortality rate of the indigenous population in the Caribbean islands was tremendous. About six million people had lived in the Caribbean islands when the conquistadors landed in 1492. Fifty years later, the population numbered in the few thousands because of the careless and inconsiderate actions of the new arrivals against the people and the land.

Bartolomé de las Casas, a sixteenth-century Spanish historian, social reformer, and Dominican friar, had been one of the first European settlers in the Americas. He had arrived in 1502 in search of riches and fortune, like so many others of his time. In the first few years, Bartolomé had participated in the atrocities against the indigenous people. After some reflection, he had changed his viewpoint, recognizing that the barbaric actions against the Native American population were wrong. He had given up his slaves and vigorously advocated on behalf of the native's civil rights.

Unfortunately, in his quest to protect the native population, Bartolomé had advocated for the use of African slaves instead of the native population, whose numbers continued to decline to the point of extinction. The conquistadors had believed Africans to be much more resilient than the native population, thus starting the migration of Africans to the New World. Later in life, Bartolomé had advocated that any type of slavery was wrong.

In the 360 years between 1500 and the end of the slave trade in the 1860s, approximately twelve million Africans had been forcibly transported to the Americas and the Caribbean islands. The slave trade represented one of the largest forced migrations in human history, relocating members of approximately fifty ethnic and linguistic groups from their native African nations. South America and the Caribbean Islands received the majority of the African slaves, with less than half a million, taken to North America.

Cristóbal Colón, the conquistadors, the early settlers, the indigenous population, the slave trade, and slavery in North America were in the past. However, as a Spaniard, José was disturbed by the atrocities. He could not help but blame the Spaniards for the actions and atrocities against the African slaves in North America. After all, it had been a Spaniard that recommended the use of African slaves instead. Although the Spaniards were not directly involved, the British settlers immediately followed the actions of the conquistadors in how they had treated the Native population and the importation of African slaves.

As he looked out of the window of his bedroom in New York City, José acknowledged how fortunate he had been throughout his entire life. After starting in Cuba by himself, with no familial support, little money, few personal belongings, and many great memories of his life in Galicia, now he was in New York City with his daughter and her family, with little money and stupendous memories of a life well-lived.

José lived in New York City with his daughter Carla for four years before he died of a bleeding ulcer on June 22, 1983, two months short of his eighty-third birthday.

Carla took José's remains back to the Dominican Republic, the land that he had loved and called "home sweet home." Carla had José buried next to his first wife, her mother, Rosa María Acosta.

His had been an adventurous life on the move since he had left his hometown of Nocedo. In Cuba, he had lived a lonely nomadic life, stopping long enough to make money and then keep on moving. Throughout the years, there had been an ebb and flow of his luck and fortune.

The one constant in his life had been hard work, starting at the age of seven and ending at the age of seventy-seven, when he'd had a debilitating stroke. His strong work ethic had enabled him to own several businesses and rental properties. He had transformed himself from a penniless rural Galician immigrant into an upper-middle-class businessman in the Caribbean. But in the end, he had lost it all, like the Spaniards had lost their empire.

José had lived his life in harmony with his enthusiasm, passion, and adventurous spirit, refusing to be burdened by material things. For the most part, he had lived a carefree lifestyle. Yes, at times he had been reckless and irresponsible, but what a fulfilling life it had been.

José Fernández ended life as he had begun it, as a penniless adventurer.

CHAPTER 21
GONE WITH THE WIND

They didn't know it yet, but the Rosa family's life was about to change dramatically. The ensuing trauma would produce massive positive and negative changes in the lives of each family member, shaping and influencing their paths in life. Overnight, the life they had been living and enjoying would be gone with the wind.

The diagnosis was stage four uterine cancer, with a 15 percent chance of survival. Carla cried, and Lucia, the mother, and nurturer assured her that everything was going to be okay. In 1970, even in the face of one of the most devastating news a woman could receive, Lucia felt compelled to console Carla.

In April 1972, Lucia called Carla and conveyed the news that her chances of survival were not great and wanted to spend some time with her. Carla immediately traveled to Santo Domingo to spend a month caring for her sister. During her stay in Santo Domingo, Carla spent day and night at the hospital, tending to Lucia's needs, only leaving her side to shower and ensure that Lucia had home-cooked meals.

During that month, she witnessed the deterioration of Lucia's body. The family figured Lucia's death was a matter of time and continued to do what they could to make her comfortable. Carla agonized over, leaving Lucia's side. But she had been in Santo Domingo for a month and had to get back to New York to check on her family.

The day before Carla's departure, she stood at the threshold of Lucia's room and found her sister sitting up, smiling, and happily waving her into the room. Lucia was radiant and back to her old self. She talked the entire day, made jokes, and spoke about going home soon. She even requested a special meal of guinea hen and rice with gandules.

Seeing that Lucia was doing so well, Carla felt comfortable leaving her for a few weeks. Lucia's upbeat demeanor gave her hope and comfort.

Carla returned to New York on Monday, May 1, confident that Lucia would be getting better and vowing to see her in a few weeks. Later that week, she telephoned her family in Santo Domingo to inquire about Lucia's health. According to her family, she was doing well.

On May 6, 1972, Carla received the fateful telephone call from Santo Domingo. Lucia had passed away at the age of fifty-two. Carla was shocked and confused by Lucia's sudden passing. When Carla had left Lucia's side, she had been doing well—so much so that they had hoped for a miraculous recovery. Why the deceptive improvement when Carla had been present? Had it been a farewell to the family?

Carla was devastated by her sister's passing. To add to her devastation, she could not attend her sister's funeral. Lucia died on a Saturday and buried the following Monday. Unfortunately, Carla did not have the resources to fly back to Santo Domingo on such short notice.

Since childhood, Lucia had been her role model. Despite the fourteen-year gap in their ages, they had always been close. Lucia had stepped in and assumed the mother role when María, incapacitated by alcohol, could not care for Carla. She had also supported Carla during her darkest days of having to deal with Bienvenida and boarding school. After their mother's passing, they had felt the overwhelming need, as the only surviving offspring of María Acosta, to take care of each other. Now that Lucia was gone, Carla was alone. She could not shake the utter feeling of abandonment. She was going to miss Lucia, her best friend, mother, and confidant.

Lucia's death was a significant turning point for Carla and her family. The life they had known before Lucia's death disappeared overnight. Carla's devastating loss turned out to be life-altering for the entire family.

Carla and her family had claimed to be Catholic before Lucia's death. She had attended a Catholic boarding school; the family had attended Sunday mass, and the children had attended parochial school for a portion of their elementary school years. However, at age thirty-eight, during her time of mourning and after she had been introduced to the Jehovah's Witnesses by a coworker, Carla questioned her religious beliefs and affiliation.

She was inconsolable after the death of her sister, and the message of the Jehovah's Witnesses was comforting to Carla. Their philosophy uplifted and inspired her. She attended the weekly meetings and took Bible study classes with a personal mentor until she was baptized and became an official member of the congregation. Her sister's death left an emotional support vacuum, which Carla replaced with the Jehovah's Witnesses.

The control of the Jehovah's Witness elders limits the freedom of their members based on their particular belief system. The congregation instills a strict shunning of former members and also family members who are not part of their society. Some members choose to disengage from their families altogether.

Many members, if asked to choose between the religion and the family, would easily choose the religion, with the congregation's sense of moral right and wrong being stronger than family bonds. The congregation's influence and dogma on its members lead their family members feeling ostracized for not conforming to the moral standards of the Jehovah's Witnesses.

This "us" (Witnesses) versus "them" (worldly people) attitude creates physical and emotional isolation from the general population. A worldly person includes non-Witness, whether family, acquaintance, neighbor or coworker. The members are cautioned continuously about the evils of the world and the worldly people who live in it.

The members are conditioned not to trust their thinking and are indoctrinated to suppress questioning and reasoning abilities to exercise unity and control. They cease to evaluate information through research or further investigation. This suppression, based on mindlessly following internal Jehovah's Witness publications and sermons, creates unity among the members.

Overnight, the household changed: all celebrations came to a complete halt. There were no more birthdays, Christmases, or observances of any other holiday. Dogma was introduced into their daily lives. Carla turned away from "worldly" events, including those celebrated by her immediate family members. She remained present to meet their basic needs, but in an emotionally conflicted manner.

Carla tried to integrate her family by encouraging them to take Bible studies and attend the reunions at the Kingdom Hall. They tried, but eventually, everyone declined to take part and incorporate into the religion of the Jehovah's Witnesses.

Religion, clubs, and other organizations provide a positive service to those aligned with their message. But the message will not resonate with everyone. It's a personal and individual decision. Everyone must follow their hearts and stick to what works for them and their personal growth and development.

If any of her family members had doubts about religion when only exposed to the Catholic faith, they had even greater doubt after spending time with the Jehovah's Witnesses. The indoctrination, suppression, and control within the religion only pushed her family away from organized religion altogether.

The abrupt change in the family pattern was disconcerting to the family. For the most part, the family rejected the drastic changes and continued their prior activities outside of the home. The conservative religious faith negatively affected the cohesiveness of the family, as each member associated with other families or friends during major holidays, birthdays, and holiday weekends.

The Rosas did not engage in the events that tend to bring families together. They did not have close family ties. There were no family outings, vacations, or family traditions to speak of or pass on.

Before the Jehovah's Witnesses, Carla and Sam had been a fun-loving couple that frequently socialized at parties, visited friends, hosted dinner parties in their home, and spent the occasional Saturday night at the club for a fun evening of dancing with friends. All such socializing abruptly ended.

Sam found this drastic change difficult to manage. He did not know how to compete with the influential, mind-controlling religious group. In essence, he had lost his wife to the Jehovah's Witness religion and elders, who now influenced her thinking and decisions.

Whether it was genetics, the environment, or the Jehovah's Witnesses was hard to tell, but by 1975, Sam had developed a severe alcohol addiction. Current evidence indicates that alcoholism is 50–60 percent genetically determined, leaving 40–50 percent to environmental influences. Most of Sam's brothers were also alcoholic, even though their father did not drink alcohol.

Sam had been a functioning alcoholic for many years, which had been a significant source of anxiety for Carla. His alcoholism brought back the memories of her childhood of contending with an alcoholic mother.

Carla had shunned an alcoholic mother and had ended up with an alcoholic husband. His alcoholism was a constant reminder of the failures of her mother, and it compounded her shame in front of her religious brothers and sisters.

By the late seventies, the drinking had gotten out of control, as Sam was experiencing falls and blackouts. By the end of each shift, his hands would shake, and his vision would become blurry, so he started drinking on the job to calm his symptoms. Drinking at work became a survival issue for Sam, even more than the paycheck and benefits that the job afforded.

One day Sam was caught drinking on the job and was relieved of his employment. Fortunately, the labor union was able to save his position, claiming that alcoholism was a disease, as declared by the American

Medical Association in 1956. They further contended that Sam needed treatment, not punishment.

The union advocated for a thirty-day in-house treatment program, considering how tough it was for an alcoholic to fight the relentless craving for alcohol on his or her own. The employer agreed and made the treatment plan a condition for reinstating his employment.

After many years of drinking and excessive consumption, Sam had developed a physical dependence on alcohol and cirrhosis of the liver. Cirrhosis is a condition in which the liver slowly deteriorates and malfunctions; scar tissue replaces normal, healthy liver tissue, preventing the liver from working as it should. In the early stages of cirrhosis, many people have no symptoms, so they continue the behavior that is causing the damage. In Sam's case, the damage was because of heavy alcohol consumption.

Alcohol abuse had also scorched Sam's brain. During the last few years of his life, Sam no longer had mental acuity. He suffered from slurred speech, slow reaction times, and impaired memory and judgment. In his early sixties, doctors had warned him that if he did not stop drinking, he would not live another five years. Of course, he had not immediately heeded the doctors' advice. He stopped drinking about three years before he died, which was too little, too late. Sam had done irreparable damage to his liver.

Sam passed away on May 9, 1992, of cirrhosis of the liver, five months short of his sixty-eighth birthday. Sam lapsed into a coma at home and died in the hospital a couple of days later.

In his home, with his family, Sam had been a man of few words; not engaging with his family on a significant level. He had always appeared remote and preoccupied. It had been difficult to figure out what he was thinking. Sam cherished his freedom and spent an inordinate amount of time out of his home. No one knew where he went or how he spent his time, but it appeared that he was happier outside of the home. Sam was responsible and took care of his family. However, he appeared to be bothered by being tied down to responsibilities in the home front.

Outside of the home, Sam had been a different person. He was social, with many acquaintances and friends. He had been the life of the party. Everyone in the neighborhood had known and loved him. His standing in the community was clear during the viewing at his funeral; the room was overflowing with mourners. Many shared their stories of how generous and helpful Sam had been with them and their children.

Sam's immediate family members were glad to see the outpouring and support. They tried to reconcile the contrast of the man they knew with the one described by the mourners. It was as if they were talking about two different people.

Sam had been the type of person who meant well but did not always do well.

After Sam's passing, Carla was left alone in the three-bedroom apartment. Now that she was alone, her bond with her spiritual brothers and sisters grew stronger. She no longer had to choose between her family and her religion. Sam had passed, and the children were grown and on their own. She could now wholeheartedly dedicate herself to her congregation without the internal conflict.

When Carla joined the Jehovah's Witnesses, she had set boundaries by keeping her family at arm's length and choosing to focus her time and energy on her faith, pushing everything and everybody else aside. Because of this indoctrination, Carla had missed out on much of the life of her husband, children, grandchildren, as she would not partake with the worldly events her family continued to celebrate.

Her adult life had been one of a false dichotomy, living between the beliefs of her religion and the worldly life her family lived. The conflicting ideas of her religious beliefs and the outside world her biological family lived in had forced her to live on the periphery of her family's life.

But what makes up a family? You have a biological family and a spiritual family, which can be at odds. Sometimes your biological and spiritual families are aligned, and that certainly makes life easier.

However, you have to live the life you choose and align yourself with those who best meet your personal needs. You should not compromise your life to meet anyone's expectations, family, or not. You have to live the life you choose and let your family live theirs.

Carla dared to be true to herself and lived with integrity in her ideals. She identified and aligned with the people who made her feel safe, supported, and free to be herself. Her spiritual family was not within her biological family, and she chose to align herself with those who honored her true nature and her path in life.

She had inherited her dark hair, fair skin, and European features from her Spanish father. But only from life did Carla acquire the stern attitude, sharp tongue, need to be the center of attention, and insecurity she at times displayed.

Raised as an only child, she was the center of her father's attention for the first eleven years of her life. After she had lost her father's attention to marriage and enrolled in a boarding school, Carla had constantly striven to regain what she had lived the first eleven years of her life, but she had been unable to replicate it. As she had grown up, she had continued to reconstruct that same environment where she had been the center of attention.

Carla was a smart, educated woman and could have been successful in any career she chose. Unfortunately, Carla was the victim of the societal and cultural standards and indoctrination that took her from one controlling situation to the next.

It took her from the watchful eye of her father to the vigilant and ruthless austerity of the nuns to the controlling arms of her husband and, finally, to the intense control of a religion that forced its members to believe and behave in a particular manner. Maybe her years at the boarding school and the powerlessness she initially felt made her susceptible to following a group that exercised high control.

Carla had not inherited her mother's independent free spirit. Or, maybe, on some level, she rejected everything that represented her mother.

PART IV
BLANCA DE LA ROSA

A LIFE OF UNTOLD BLESSINGS AND OPPORTUNITIES

CHAPTER 22

NEW YORK CITY: THE EARLY YEARS

My father was so thrilled that I was born eleven months and three weeks after my sister that he did not even go to the hospital to see my mother and his fourth daughter in a row. Had I been a boy, maybe—just maybe—my arrival would have been somewhat acceptable.

My mother often mentioned that during the nine months of her pregnancy, the household atmosphere had been tense. My father had been less than thrilled about the pregnancy. His displeasure and hostility had been palpable. Maybe he had been reacting to the financial strain and frustration of having an additional mouth to feed.

I was born in an impoverished town called Villa Duarte in the city of Santo Domingo, Dominican Republic. I was my mother's second child and my father's fifth. My brother was born twenty months later. Fortunately, he was a boy, so my father was excited to have a son after four daughters in a row. He now had six children to support: two boys and four girls.

I have few memories of our years in Villa Duarte. The most vivid memory is of the dirt roads and dilapidated mint-green and aqua-blue shacks its residents called home. I do have a vague, distant memory of traveling from the Dominican Republic at six years of age. My mother, two siblings, a cousin who was going to join his mother in New York, and I traveled on a Pan Am flight in 1963.

My grandfather, José, and my Tía, Lucia, traveled with us to the airport to see my mother off. My mother cried as she said goodbye to her father, sister, and the only life she'd ever known. My young mind did not understand why she was not excited about the trip. As children, we viewed this as a fun adventure as we stood in awe of the size of the airplane and anxiously awaited our turn to board. At six years of age, I did not comprehend the magnitude of the impact that the trip would have on our lives.

During the 1960s, flying was akin to being at a cocktail party on wings. Everyone dressed up for the occasion. My mother had made new dresses for our trip, and my brother wore his best suit. The stewardesses looked like models and treated everyone on board the flight special—akin to first-class service today. For our family, the flight was indeed a special occasion. It was a magical and marvelous trip that transported us to a new land and life in New York City.

Our first home in the US, located in Manhattan on West 94th Street, was a furnished studio apartment. The apartment had no bedroom, bathroom, or a full kitchen. There was a shared bathroom on each floor for the tenants to use.

My siblings and I slept in a pseudo-living room on a sofa bed, head to toe. My parents had apportioned one side of the room to serve as a bedroom. We lived in that one-room apartment for a little over a year.

During that time, my sister and I attended Public School (PS) 75 on West End Avenue and 95th Street. My younger brother was only four years old, so my mother stayed home to take care of him and picked us up after school.

I can't name any of my elementary, middle, or high school teachers, except for my first-grade teacher, Mrs. LeBuff. She was a grandmotherly lady who was extremely kind and patient. Maybe she wasn't old enough to be a grandmother, but to a six-year-old who had never seen anybody who looked like her, she looked old to me.

As a six-year-old, it was scary to be dropped off in a place where I did not understand or speak the language. As I looked around the classroom for an ally, no one looked like me or spoke Spanish. It was likely that Mrs. LeBuff, as an experienced teacher, was able to detect that I was a scared child, so she did what she could to make me feel comfortable, easing the uncertainty of being in an unfamiliar environment.

I learned quickly that I had to decode my environment subconsciously in real-time as I was learning the language, custom, and culture. I had to discern intuitively what others could immediately understand from the spoken word.

In the early 1960s, total immersion was the only option for immigrants, as there was no such thing as bilingual education. Mrs. LeBuff was extremely patient in making sure I understood the lessons. I can honestly say that I do not remember when I learned to speak, read, and write English. But what I can say is that my kind first-grade teacher put me on the right path.

One day I came home from school disgusted because Mrs. LeBuff had announced that the class would be going on a picnic and that, among other foods, they would serve hot dogs. Well, that did not translate well in the mind of a six-year-old who did not understand the language and the culture. My mother had to explain to me that we would not be eating dog meat at the picnic.

One day, my mother was late to pick us up after school. When the other children were gone, and the two of us were the only students there, my sister boldly declared she knew the way home and led the charge. I lagged, in tears because I was not sure she knew where she was going.

It was a rainy day, and we had worn our yellow rain gear and boots. The gear had a separate hat that did not fit my head because of the way my mother combed my hair. My mother's preferred manner of taming my hair was to comb it into various buns.

I hated the unfashionable look of the buns, especially when she made three, with one on each side of the head and one on the back of my head. I called this hairdo the aviator, as it reminded me of an airplane. The buns, whether there were two or three, did not permit the hat to fit around my head, so the hat clumsily sat over the buns. I was a crying mess and looked hideous as I splashed up the street.

We met my mother halfway home, but that terrifying fifteen-minutes episode of sheer panic and abandonment in a place that was still foreign to me—where I did not understand the language—lingered for some time.

I attended PS 75 through the first grade. In 1964, our family's finances must have improved as we were able to afford a one-bedroom apartment.

Our family's second home, from 1964 to 1965, was a one-bedroom, fifth-floor walk-up apartment in a five-story brownstone at 225 West 105th Street between Broadway and Amsterdam Avenue. The apartment was a railroad apartment, where one room led into the other with no connecting hallway. We children still slept in the living room, head to toe on a sofa bed, but at least we did not have to share the bathroom with other tenants or go out to the corridor to use it. We had a full eat-in kitchen, and my parents had an actual bedroom.

Despite the benefits the larger apartment offered, there were two problems. The entire building had a severe rat and roach infestation. No amount of fumigation or number of traps extinguished the roaches and rodents. The rats and cockroaches ruled the apartment.

They came out from behind the walls when the lights were out. A trip to the bathroom or kitchen in the dark was a terrifying adventure, as you never knew what you were going to encounter. Sometimes, the brave roaches and rodents came out from behind the walls even when the lights were on.

For some reason, we walked around the apartment's linoleum floor barefoot, which required that we wash our feet before getting into bed each night. One night, as my brother and I were washing our feet, a rat joined us in the tub. To me, the rat appeared to be the size of a medium-sized cat. The rat hissed as it exposed its menacing razor-sharp teeth, ready for the attack. My brother and I screamed as we tried to get away from the rat that was intent on getting away with a piece of flesh. The louder we yelled and screamed, the more agitated the rat became.

At the sound of our screams, our father ran to the bathroom to investigate the commotion. At the discovery of the rat, he immediately scooped us out of the tub, grabbed a bat, and turned his attention to the rat. The rat scurried around the bathtub as my father swung the bat. It squeaked, hissed, and made chattering sounds as it frantically searched for an escape route. But there was no place to go. The smooth, wet surface of the tub made it impossible for the rat to escape. Finally, my father landed the fatal blow and killed the rat with the bat.

That harrowing experience still lives with me. I'm still petrified and disgusted by the sight of rodents. I can't even bear to see them on the big screen, and I refuse to visit or live in any place that shows any sign of them.

The one good thing about living in this apartment was its proximity to our elementary school, PS 145, located about one and a half city blocks from our family home. By this time, my mother had gotten employment outside of the home, and we became latchkey children. The term referred to the latchkey of a door to an apartment and commonly used to refer to children who returned home from school to an empty home because both parents had to work to make ends meet. We usually had a copy of the apartment key strung around our necks during the day.

After school, we attended a program at a community center called Grosvenor House, which was conveniently located immediately behind the elementary school. It was a lot of fun, and I always looked forward to the end of the school day. I have many fond memories of my afternoons in this after-school program. I believe the program was free or required a nominal fee for low-income families with children in the public school system.

At the end of each school day, we walked from PS 145 to the building next door, where the counselors had numerous indoor activities planned. We gave our names as we walked through the door, and the counselor assigned a specific activity for the afternoon.

Grosvenor House was an excellent program with activities ranging from cooking to music to activities in the gym to board games. You name the indoor activity, and they had it. The program even had access to the building's gated rooftop, which was set up like a playground. We played dodgeball, kickball, and other outdoor games.

In the mid-sixties, Grosvenor House employed a holistic approach to developing the youth in attendance. The counselors and staff were committed to developing the youth to their full potential. They treated us with the utmost respect, regardless of race, ethnicity, or cultural background.

Grosvenor House's approach was to view the program as an extended educational experience and not merely a holding place for children while their parents worked. The program provided a safe, structured environment for us to socialize with our peers, stay physically active, learn healthy habits, and have wholesome entertainment. The summer of my fourteenth birthday, Grosvenor House even offered me my first job as a junior counselor.

At Grosvenor House, I socialized with children and counselors who were fluent in English and familiar with the culture, which helped me assimilate to life in the US.

CHAPTER 23
THE CONCRETE JUNGLE

New York City—the concrete jungle where the primary mode of transportation is the iron horse (a.k.a. the subway—an underground rapid transit system) and children play in concrete playgrounds. A fall in one of those concrete play yards was no fun. But that was one of the growing pains as a kid in the concrete jungle.

In New York City, we grew up immersed in plenty of cultural diversity. School field trips took us to Broadway plays, the Radio City Music Hall to see the Rockettes and the Nutcracker, ice-skating at Rockefeller Plaza, the Empire State Building, museums on Fifth Avenue, and the Statute of Liberty, to name a few.

Central Park West and Riverside Park flanked our slice of the Big Apple. We spent most of our time from 94th Street and Riverside Drive to 110th Street and Central Park West, where we escaped the concrete jungle of the inner city. In Riverside Park, with a view of Jersey City, New Jersey, we witnessed spectacular fireworks over the Hudson River, picnicked, relaxed, and played in the park. In Central Park, we ice-skated in the winter and swam at the pool, rode our bicycles, and attended free concerts in the summers.

In 1965, our family moved to our third and last family home in one of the Housing and Urban Development buildings, also known as 'the projects.' The projects are government-subsidized housing complexes for low- to moderate-income families. The rent paid by the tenants is income-based and includes utilities. They are typically large complexes of buildings, but some are stand-alone.

830 Amsterdam Avenue (830 Amsterdam) was one of those stand-alone buildings that proudly stood between 100th and 101st Streets and Amsterdam Avenue. It was a twenty-story high-rise, had eight apartments on each floor, and accommodated one hundred sixty families.

It was conveniently located about one city block from the 24th Precinct, the public library, and the free clinic, and was three city blocks from the subway station. The building's location was across the street from the Frederick Douglass Houses, a complex of projects located between 100th and 104th Streets, to the east of Amsterdam Avenue and west of Manhattan Avenue.

Moving to 830 Amsterdam was exciting for our family. We had witnessed the construction of this high-rise building from the time they broke ground to the time they put up that last brick.

Since our family had lived on 105th Street, we walked by 100th Street on our way to visit family members, shop, go to the library, and go to appointments at the clinic. As children, we would usually run ahead of our parents and stop to play around the construction site. I do not recall there being a gate to wall off the property. The open space allowed us to run around and play.

We were fortunate to be one of the first families to occupy the building. When we moved into 830 Amsterdam in 1965, it was clean and safe. Unfortunately, it started to deteriorate shortly after that until it reached a point where the entire building was dirty and unsafe.

Despite attempts by the management office to keep the building clean and maintained, some tenants were not sufficiently motivated to help keep the common areas clean. The walls in the stairwells had graffiti, some of the hallways and stairwells were garbage-strewn, and some people even used the elevator and stairwell as their toilets. We believed that primary culprits for the garbage and using common areas as toilets were homeless and others that came in from the cold or rain during the night.

Our fifth-floor apartment had a great layout with an open-space concept. The living room area flowed into the dining area and the dining area into the kitchen.

There were three bedrooms—one for my parents, one for my brother, and one for my sister and me to share. For us, this apartment was the lap of luxury. It was spacious and comfortable. It afforded the best living conditions we had experienced in New York City by far. There was also an elevator—no more walking up to the fifth floor.

For me, the best thing about this apartment was that we did not have to deal with the rat and roach infestation that had existed at the 105th Street apartment.

For those of us who lived in apartments below the eighth floor on the northwest part of the building, there was not much of a view. Looking straight out of our living room window, we faced a brick wall that read "AAMCO Transmissions," which was part of a parking garage. Looking down, we could see the concrete play yard, divided into two sections. One section had concrete checkered tables and benches for playing checkers or chess. I must admit I do not recall ever seeing anyone play a game of chess or checkers. The other section was a play area with monkey bars, a concrete turtle, hopscotch, and concrete tubes and tunnels.

Some children played in the backyard, and others played on the sidewalk in front of the building. Where the children played was primarily driven by the parents' ability to keep a watchful eye from their apartment windows. We played in the backyard. I spent many happy days playing in that yard. There were scraped knees, a chipped tooth, and a sprained ankle, but even those experiences could not dampen the fun I had socializing and playing with my friends.

Two other family members lived in the same building, and plenty of friends became our extended family. We spent a lot of time running from one apartment to another, up and down the stairs. Although this was not a safe environment, we always took the safest routes, avoiding the landmines,

The projects, whether complexes or stand-alone buildings, evoke images of violence in the minds of many. When you tell someone that you lived in the projects, they immediately conjure up a neighborhood with drugs, violence, and gangs, where low-income families live. For the most part, which is what the projects were. Regardless of how outsiders viewed the projects, it was our home.

During the late sixties and seventies, the projects were a breeding ground for crime in some of the roughest neighborhoods. It was a harsh environment to grow up in, with a reputation for violence, drug use, prostitution, and juvenile crimes were commonplace.

Some of us who grew up in that environment were able to escape relatively unscathed. For others, the way out was being carted off to jail or out in a coffin, dying at a young age of a drug overdose, alcoholism, or gang-related violence. And some even stayed in the neighborhood under the same living conditions.

Most, if not all, of the children who grew up in the projects, developed survival instincts that made them indifferent to the violence and crime in their midst, acquiring a "don't mess with me or else" attitude. We always had to be ready for a fight—ready to duke it out with someone. I lost count of the number of fistfights I had to engage in to defend myself. It was an environment where fistfights resolved differences and conflicts.

This resilience was a matter of survival. We had to show a tough exterior because we knew inherently that displaying any sign of weakness could be detrimental to our physical welfare. We found ourselves on guard, in defensive mode, and not trusting anyone. It was the survival of the fittest in the concrete jungle.

The circumstances of their environments can force children into lives they would not have chosen for themselves. Sometimes, when you peel back some of the tough exteriors, you find a vulnerable and frightened child hidden underneath, one who doesn't know how she is going to survive another day. The need to survive overshadows and supersedes any thought of the future, getting ahead, or getting an education. Attaining the American dream is a distant and elusive concept.

Some children witnessed adult situations they should never have had to encounter or contend with as they were growing up. There were children whose parents were on drugs or living a life of crime, which forced them to assume caretaker roles for their younger siblings. At times, they had to become the head of their household when one or both parents were passed out from alcohol or drugs.

In the seventies, drugs and drug use were an everyday occurrence; it was a given in our environment. Bumping into an addict sleeping it off in a stairwell or some drug dealer conducting business during the day was commonplace. It was a negative environment in which people did the best they could to survive from one day to the next.

Many of the families were on welfare or were unemployed. No one talked about buying a home, investing, or planning for retirement. Drugs, gambling, and gossiping about the neighbors or the latest Telenovela playing on the Spanish network were the major topics of discussion. I can honestly say that I do not recall hearing much in the way of positive discussions.

Something or someone always prevented some from getting ahead. For some, the family inheritance was welfare, with many families claiming two or three generations of welfare recipients.

Many lived paycheck to paycheck, their income enough to pay for living expenses. If anything was left over, they put it toward something frivolous, such as drugs, alcohol, or gambling, which did not improve the value or quality of their lives.

For some, gambling—playing the numbers game—was their way of investing for the future. There was always the chance that someday they would hit it big. The numbers game was my father's favorite pastime. The numbers game was a form of unregulated gambling or lottery played in most poor and working-class neighborhoods in New York City. In the numbers game, the bettor attempted to pick three digits matching randomly drawn numbers the following day. The winning number was the last three digits of "the handle"—the amount racetrack bettors placed on race day at a major racetrack.

Few people had savings accounts, and those who did have some savings had nothing substantial. Retirement plans were social security or an employer-provided pension, for those lucky enough to have a job that offered a pension plan.

Growing up in the projects, I did not see any role models. For many minority and immigrant children, it's difficult to see success in their futures, especially if they look around and see no one they can emulate.

Despite the negative environment, many of these children are street smart and, when given the opportunity, can excel as well as any kid from the suburbs. When given a chance to display their resilience and talent, inner-city kids can make sense of their lives and excel in many different fields.

My mother always encouraged education, but she did not know how to help us achieve those educational goals. No one expected us to excel, and no one encouraged us to go to college. The highest expectation was to get a high school education and then go to work, and that is what I did.

During my middle and high school years, I wish someone had taken the time to look at my grades and give me some guidance about higher education. I had excellent grades in both elementary and high school, always making the honor roll.

In high school, I took Honors and Regents classes, graduating in the top 5 percent of my class. However, at that time, I did not know what any of that meant. I did not appreciate the value of my grades. I had no idea that my grades could open doors to higher education. No one ever told me that my excellent grades could qualify me for grants and scholarships that would enable me to go to college. The guidance counselors never encouraged me to look into financial aid, and they never told me about the value of the SAT and going to college. I was ignorant of the educational process in the US. I wanted to excel in school, but I did so without understanding the value of my accomplishments.

As a young teen, I had an innate ability to style hair. I could cut it, set it in curlers, and do the fancy updos of the late sixties and early seventies. You name it, and I could figure out how to do it. Therefore, I believed that this meant that I should be a hairdresser. When I expressed this to my mother, she said, "*Mi hija*, you are too smart; you need to do something that will require the use of your brain."

Minority and immigrant children need role models who can provide guidance and be beacons of light and inspiration. They need people to show them that the perceived obstacles of poverty, learning a new language, and acclimating to a new culture are not insurmountable and that they can excel in whatever they set their minds to do.

As a society, we tend to blame immigrant or low-income children for being unwilling to pursue an education, calling them lazy or lacking in ambition. The truth of the matter is that the rejection from schools, peers, and society as a whole are partially to blame. As a society, we tend to ignore the plight of some of the most vulnerable in our communities.

Society tends to place the blame on the children for not being able to adjust and perform academically, totally ignoring the impact of a culture that does not have the patience to work with some of them. For some of the kids in our neighborhood, this alienation resulted in behavioral problems, which led them to give up on their educational pursuits, dropping out of school. Children need to be inspired and given a reason to forge ahead, not cast aside because we do not understand them or know what to do with them.

Since our mother worked outside of the home, we had to take over the household chores at an early age. When we were no longer attending an after-school program, we had to take on more responsibility around the home, run errands, and complete specific assigned chores.

My older sister was always trying to get out of whatever duty had been assigned to her each week, especially going to the laundromat. Since our apartment building did not allow clothes dryers, we had to take our wet laundry to the local laundromat to use the coin-operated dryers. I usually did not mind, I brought a book and sat at the laundromat waiting for a machine to free up and for the clothes to dry.

My brother was too young to take on any chores. Also, he was a boy, which meant that he was the prince and did not have to do anything around the house. As a middle child, I felt burdened by additional chores. Maybe it was my imagination, but anything my sister did not want to do fell on me, the reliable middle child.

There is absolutely nothing special about being a middle child. The oldest, being the first, gets lots of attention. The youngest, of course, is the baby of the family and always gets preferential treatment. The middle child is the pillar that holds up the oldest and the youngest. If the three children are close in age, the middle child has to grow up quickly, since there can't be two babies.

My sister and I had to take turns between kitchen duty and cleaning the house. We were required to cook, set the table, and clean the kitchen immediately after dinner—I mean, strictly from the table straight to the sink. There were no excuses.

Whenever my mother attended her reunions at the Kingdom Hall, my sister and I had to take turns setting the table for my father. Although my mother would leave the food in the oven, one of us had to be there to set and place the food on the table, wait for him to finish eating, make coffee, and clean up afterward. My sister would be so pissed off about having to do this when it was her turn; she would say, "The king is coming home." And so it was.

My mother treated my father like a king and my brother like a prince. Culturally, the men of the house were treated with the utmost deference. I vowed never to cater to any man that way. I hated the way my mother made us tiptoe around my father. Our apartment had one bathroom. God forbid you happened to be in the bathroom when my father came home and wanted to take a shower. No matter what you were doing, you had to stop and get out immediately.

My mother demanded that we come straight home after school. We were not permitted to visit anyone or have company. One time, when I was about thirteen years old, I stayed after school to hang out with some friends, even though it was my turn to cook dinner that night. When I arrived and was about to take the elevator up to our apartment, I saw that there was a notice posted by the elevator advising the tenants that the water had been turned off in the entire building and would remain off from 4 p.m. to 7 p.m.

Well, if dinner wasn't ready by the time my mother came home from work, I would get not only the lecture of a lifetime but also an ass-whipping with a belt for not coming straight home. There was no way I was going to subject myself to a beating that night. So, I did what I had to do to save myself—I fetched water from the toilet tank. I boiled the water and made dinner for everyone. Hey, don't judge me; it was a matter of self-preservation.

Corporal punishment, using a belt, was my parents' favorite mode of discipline. In their minds, this was a valid and effective form of discipline. After all, that was how my father, his father, and his mother had been raised. In those days, no one questioned corporal punishment, and did not consider it child abuse; it was discipline—a good old-fashioned ass-whipping. Even the nuns in our Catholic school used corporal punishment. When we were much younger, we would have to kneel on the floor facing the wall. I don't recall how long we had to stay in that position, but it always seemed to last an eternity.

My father would usually dole out the lashings for major infractions at my mother's direction. She would evaluate the offense and decide the punishment and sentence. She would warn us, "Wait until your father gets home." The waiting gave us time to put on some protective padding to minimize the sting of the belt. But even the extra padding did not eliminate the bruises and welts left by the belt.

We were hit with the belt so often that after a while, I was numb to the lashings. I would be so pissed off about the unfair beating that I would stand defiantly, without flinching, waiting for it to stop. I would then walk away with an "is that all you've got" attitude.

Oddly enough, decades later, the sound of the unbuckling and swoosh of the belt traveling through the loops of the pants until it finally comes off triggers the memory of those dreadful beatings. It is difficult to explain what I feel when I hear those two sounds in sequence. I know that no one is going to beat me, but I immediately brace myself in fear.

Although my mother also used a belt, her preferred weapon of choice was her *chancletas* (house slippers), as they were readily available to her. She whacked us with one of her chancletas for major, minor, minuscule, and, at times, nonexistent infractions.

So, as you can see, I had no alternative. I had to use the water that was readily available to me. Besides, we all ate the food and didn't get sick. Phew!

What would you have done?

~❖~

As an immigrant, I struggled with learning a new language and acclimating to the weather, fashion, values, and customs of a new culture. At times, these changes were so overwhelming that I wasn't sure I'd ever fit in.

Our parents could not help, as they were also struggling to acclimate, and they did not understand or know what it took to get ahead in this new environment. Like many immigrants before them, they were busy trying to find their place in the land of opportunity.

In the 1960s, there was no supportive Latino Community to help with assimilation and ascension within the dominant English-speaking culture. With no one to help ease the difficulties of transition, there was ample opportunity to stumble linguistically and culturally. We made plenty of mistakes along the way.

Sometimes, I felt alienated in school and rejected by my peers because of my accent and different culture. Learning a new language and culture and trying to keep up with the curriculum was hard enough without having to deal with the cruelty of the other children.

In the early 1960s, there were white, black, and Puerto Rican people around us. Because we were Dominican, initially we were not accepted by any of these groups. To be rejected because I was perceived to be different was a lonely existence. At times, I wanted to stay in the haven of my bed and not go to school to face the cool kids, who could be so cruel.

My mother made most of our clothes, including her own. She dressed my sister, and I like twins, and we both hated it. We finally broke free of the twin look when I was about twelve, and my mother finally started respecting our individuality.

Homemade clothes saved my parents money, but it was a real nightmare for me. As I compared those homemade clothes to the "cool" girls' clothes, I admired their fashionable, stylish outfits with matching socks and other accessories. The beautiful outfits were the only good thing you could say about those girls, as they were rotten and ugly inside. They were cruel and mean-spirited. They made fun of my homemade, uncool clothes and bargain-brand shoes, as well as other students whom they perceived to be beneath them.

The concept of "cool" was foreign to my parents, who were working hard to make ends meet. As a low-income family, my parents were glad to be able to provide basic needs. Who cared that our clothes were not cool? What was wrong with those bargain brand shoes? Who cared that the outfits were not color-coordinated? Who cared that there weren't matching accessories? We had shelter, food on the table, and clothes on our backs. Anything else beyond the basics was a want, not a need.

My brother was lucky; he could wear store-bought clothes, even if they were the bargain brand. When my brother was about ten years old, he wanted some cool Converse sneakers instead of the bargain-brand shoes from the five-and-dime store. My parents would not hear of it, as this was an unnecessary expense. My brother was so determined to get the cool sneakers that he took a razor blade to his bargain-brand sneakers. In his young, naïve mind, this would justify new sneakers—hopefully, a cool pair. Not only did he get the same bargain-brand sneakers, but he also received an ass-whopping to go with the new shoes.

Kids are cruel. If you wear ugly, uncool clothes, they make fun of you. The kids direct this teasing toward the less fortunate who do not have the latest fashion in clothing and footwear. The experience can adversely affect a child's self-esteem and grades and can also cause depression and can make them feel inadequate.

Most children do not understand that it is what is inside of us that matters, as children and teens care what their peers think of them. During the teen years, appearances are at the highest level of importance. It is the time when some of the "cool" kids let their appearances go to their heads and abuse the perceived power it affords them.

Going from public school to parochial school in the fifth grade eased some of the teasing and bullying. Holy Name of Jesus required its students to wear uniforms every day except for Wednesdays when we could wear our street clothes.

The girls in the parochial school were primarily from middle-class households and were worse than the public-school students. These girls were mean spirited, snobbish, and cliquish. One girl was especially arrogant and cruel; we'll call her Annette.

One winter morning, as I stood among a group of students on the crowded sidewalk, awaiting the opening bell, I overheard Annette complaining that her nose was running, and she needed a tissue.

In our family, a box of tissues was a luxury—a want, not a need. My parents did not buy them. Instead, we used multipurpose toilet paper to wipe our noses. Nothing wrong with that. Right?

Well, I naively offered Annette the toilet paper I had in my coat pocket. Annette turned to me with a look on her face that said, "How dare you talk to me?" At that precise moment, I froze, recognizing I had made a grave mistake, but with my hand extended, I could not take back my offer. She then looked at the toilet paper in my hand with disgust and arrogantly said to me, "I want to wipe my nose, not my ass." Of course, this elicited laughter from her friends. I turned beet red and looked like a schmuck, and her nose continued to run until she was able to get inside the school.

Many years later, I saw her at the daycare when I was picking up my son. We recognized but did not acknowledge each other. Words were unnecessary. She looked shocked at my appearance. We were in our late twenties, and I was pleased to see that she was looking rather matronly for her young age. Somewhat vindicated, I walked away, physically fit, and in my professional business suit. Karma? Sweet Revenge!

Frank Sinatra once said, *"The best revenge is massive success."*

Bullies, regardless of age, tend to have domineering and controlling personalities and want to have the last word. And if you ask me, many even have some unaddressed psychological issues. Who knows what gets those people going? But in my experience bullies are selective about whom they bully. They are careful not to take on someone they perceive to be either emotionally or physically stronger than them, as the bully wants to maintain the upper hand.

Looking back, I did not have a happy home life, but I did have a good childhood—if that makes any sense.

My older sister was like mean Angelica from the children's animated show, *The Rugrats*. She made my life, and that of my brother's a living hell. My mere presence bothered her, and God forbid I crossed her path when she was in a foul mood. She may have wanted to be an only child. She was usually well-behaved around the adults but was notoriously mean to my brother and me, especially through lying and distorting the facts.

Growing up with a bully in the house made my life so miserable that I could not wait to leave the unhappy home and be on my own. I spent a lot of time either at friends' homes or in my bedroom, reading or doing my own thing. It is only by the pure grace of God that I did not grow up with a lack of confidence and self-esteem and require therapy. Some others that have suffered from bullying are not as fortunate. If a child is not sufficiently resilient, bullying can leave deep emotional scars that can last a lifetime.

I spent many days fantasizing about a grandmother I hadn't met, wishing that I could go live with her or visit for an extended stay. My best friend growing up lived with her grandmother. In my mind, she had the ideal situation. She would visit her mother's home for a few hours after school and on the weekends, then go to her grandmother's house. How I wished I had that option. The older I became, the less time I spent at home. It was school, work, or spending time with my friends. I filled my time at home fantasizing about when I could leave.

We have heard quotes such as, "Beauty is personified from the inside," and "Beauty is in the eye of the beholder," which are meant to make someone feel better about his or her appearance.

Within the family, I felt like an outsider, as if I did not belong in this family, questioning whether I was adopted. But since that was not the case, then I can only surmise that I must've been born into the wrong family.

My looks, demeanor, and personality were opposed to the rest. Not looking like the rest and having a bully to contend with compounded my feeling of being an outsider. At the time, this caused me to withdraw into my world, planning and plotting an exit strategy, patiently waiting for the right time.

My mother had European features, the Spanish señorita look, and was gorgeous as a young woman. My sister looked a lot like my mother—not as pretty, but you could tell where she had gotten her looks. My brother looked a lot like my paternal grandfather: fair-skinned, with blond hair and European features—a young Clint Eastwood look-alike. We called him Clint.

Then there was me. I was a shy, solemn child who rarely smiled. Any time anyone views my childhood pictures, they always ask, "Why were you so mad?" I swear I wasn't mad; it was the way I usually looked. In hindsight, I believe the pictures depict an unhappy child.

I had a flat nose, a huge ass, and buck teeth, and I wore thick coke-bottle glasses. To top it off, I had unruly curly hair with a mind of its own. Curly hair was not fashionable; it was either long straight hair or an afro. If ever I tried to straighten out the curls to appear more fashionable, my rebellious hair would frizz, refusing to be tamed. Yikes!

During those awkward adolescent years, I heard people—family and nonfamily alike—commenting on how unattractive I was and how I looked nothing like my sister. My sister reveled in making sure I was aware of how ugly I was with my fat lips and razorblade (flat) nose.

I came to believe and internalize that I was ugly, indeed. It was impossible for me to find anything beautiful about myself. After all, the adults around me had reinforced that sentiment, so it had to be true. Didn't it? I had to embrace it, accept it, and move on.

To this day, whenever anyone pays any semblance of a compliment on my looks or appearance, I feel as if the person is ridiculing me. I think, "Surely it can't be true. They are just trying to be polite." For a long time, the image I saw when I looked in the mirror was that of a hideous girl whose lips were too fat, and nose was too flat. To this day, that ugly girl appears in the mirror from time to time. They are just trying to be polite.

I sensed that my mother was troubled by my appearance. When we were taking our passport pictures in Santo Domingo, I recall my mother telling me to gather my lips. I had no idea how to do that. But I understood that my lips had to be positioned to look smaller. I sucked in my lips, which resulted in a pissed off look in our passport picture.

One other time when I was about eleven years old, my mother commented that you must be careful whom you marry, because you will get children who are not good-looking, and you will be embarrassed when you introduce them to your friends. I can't be 100 percent sure, but I had a feeling my mother was talking about me. After all, I was the ugly duckling of the family.

The first person to tell me that I was beautiful was my then-boyfriend and later husband when I was about fifteen years old. I would say to him, "The only reason you see me as beautiful is that you love me, and we all know that love is blind."

How could I go through years of programming and not be affected by it, whether I wanted to be or not? The experience had verbally and emotionally diminished me to a negative self-image. When someone came along and acknowledged my worth, beauty, and value, I did not believe them.

Through that experience, I learned that, whether intentional or not, some relationships shape and ingrain a negative reflection of self into our consciousness through years of verbal abuse and destructive criticism. As an adult, I can attest that these negative reflections tend to stay with us and develop our overall impressions of ourselves and life as a whole.

Fortunately, I have always been a practical and resilient person, even as a child. The comments were initially hurtful to me, but after a while, I learned to live with being comfortable in my skin. I had to accept my blended African/European/Native roots, my brown skin, curly hair, flat nose, and other imperfections with a sense of pride. I had to accept, respect, and love myself first before I could expect anyone else to do so.

I also know from personal experience that being overly concerned about what other people think of you can be psychologically and mentally exhausting and can affect your self-esteem. The best you can do is to be yourself, whatever that means to you, and everything else will fall into place. The constant worry about how you look and how others perceive you is a colossal waste of time and energy. There were more productive ways to spend my time.

At times, I look into the mirror and still see the ugly duckling, while other times I see the beautiful swan that the ugly duckling grew up to be.

Most children can't discern between constructive and destructive criticism and can be adversely affected by comments made by adults. *"It's easier to build up a child than to repair an adult. Your words and actions have power in your child's life, use them wisely."* — *Unknown*

CHAPTER 24
TOO YOUNG TO MARRY

I don't know about you, but as a teen, I was at the peak of my intelligence and knowledge. I was a know-it-all. I was invincible.

Since my teen years, I've learned that the various parts of my brain were not working together to fully evaluate choices and make sound decisions as the teenage brain is a work in progress.

Scientists have discovered that from early adolescence through their mid-twenties, a teen's brain develops from back to front, with the part of the brain that controls reasoning and impulses developing last. This lack of connection between the back and front parts of the brain may explain why, as teens, we make stupid decisions and engage in risky behavior.

Unfortunately, life does not have a rewind button, and even if we've made bad decisions because of faulty equipment, we still have to live with the consequences of our choices and actions.

At the tender age of eighteen, not only did I decide that getting married was a good idea, but I also decided that I would not be going to college. I wanted to move out on my own, get a job, and take charge of my life. The universe had put two options before me.

The first was one of my best friend's cousins. I met him when I was about twelve years old. We were good friends; it was puppy love, an innocent relationship. Although he was my "boyfriend," we did not date in the traditional sense. I was too young to date and could not have a boyfriend. We met outside in the backyard under watchful eyes from our living room window. We met among a group of friends in my friend's home where we played board games and socialized.

He was my "boyfriend" for about three years, and there was some chemistry between us. Was it love? Can one fall in love at that age? I don't know. He believed he loved me, and maybe he did.

He was three years older and would try to control where I went, what I wore, and what I did. I refused to comply, which made him angry. He was also about my same height, which meant that if I wore shoes with a heel, I would be taller than him. Unacceptable. I was not thrilled about that prospect. Do you think that was love, ego, or vanity?

One day, when I was about fifteen years old, we were in the backyard, sitting at one of the concrete tables, talking and hanging out, when out of nowhere my future with him flashed before my eyes. It was extraordinary as if in a trance and having an out-of-body experience while fully awake. A movie of my life with him played out in my head.

I saw myself living with a womanizer who would go out of his way to control me and not let me be my true self. I had seen his temper and frustration when I'd refused to let him tell me what to do. There was no doubt in my mind that the anger he had displayed would someday turn physically violent.

After that epiphany, I broke up with him. Breaking up was one of the hardest decisions of my fifteen years. It was a decision I had to make with my head and not my heart. I missed our friendship, but even at the young age of fifteen, I recognized he was not the right person for me.

Shortly after that, he enlisted in the army and was stationed overseas. Years later, I learned he had named his daughter after me. Maybe you should think twice about allowing your husband to name your daughter. Explore the meaning behind the name.

The second option was Danilo Céspedes. There was no way I was going to get around this relationship. The universe had ensured our relationship would happen. Or, at least, that we would meet.

As a teen, Danilo worked in the produce section of the supermarket where we shopped. I first noticed him when I was about thirteen years old, while at the supermarket with my mother. He was always trying to get my attention, and I hated it. I tried to avoid that section of the supermarket. You may think that thirteen is too young, but I was a mature-looking and acting thirteen-year-old.

He was the best friend and schoolmate of my first cousin's boyfriend. He once sent a message to me through my cousin, saying, "Tell her that if I don't marry her, I will never marry." My reply had been, "He should prepare for a life of bachelorhood."

He was friends with Sam from the local barbershop and from fixing cars in the parking lot of the building where I lived, although he did not know that Sam was my father.

Unbeknownst to me, his sister was my mother's hairdresser. He lived with his sister, half a city block from our apartment building. On more than one occasion, I had to pick up a wig that my mother had washed and styled at his sister's house.

Danilo was destined to enter my life one way or another. No matter how hard I fought it, it was a relationship we were meant to experience.

There were about two hundred people at our wedding reception. It was the party of the decade, which included a popular live band of the mid-seventies led by Santiago Cerón (a Dominican singer, musician, and composer). The reception took place in a warehouse-type building converted into party salons. The venue accommodated over two hundred people. Folks talked about the reception for years.

Despite being the party of the decade for the attendees, I have only vague memories of the reception. I was extremely nearsighted and did not wear my glasses on that day. I am sure that I missed a lot of the nuances and details of the evening. On a previous occasion, I had seen a bride with glasses and saw how unattractive and distracting the eyeglasses were.

From an outsider's viewpoint, it was the perfect ceremony and reception. But from an insider's perspective, the day was riddled with controversy.

Having been raised a Catholic for the first thirteen years of my life, I wanted a Catholic church wedding like many I had witnessed. For me, the ideal wedding ceremony would have been walking down the aisle to the beautiful altar of Holy Name of Jesus, the Catholic church we attended. Instead, I had to get married at the Kingdom Hall of Jehovah's Witnesses, the place of worship for the congregation my mother attended.

The Kingdom Hall was modest, with no religious symbols or elaborate structures. There was no long walk down the aisle past wooden pews decorated with bows as family and friends admired the procession of the wedding party. There was no elaborate marble altar where the groom waited for his bride and the wedding party to assemble.

Missing was the large interior of Holy Name of Jesus Church, with its hammer-beam ceiling, stained glass windows, and terrazzo floor. There would be no pictures in front of the Gothic architecture of the church or at the top of the stairs outside the grand wooden entrance of the church.

Instead, we had rows of drab, black plastic chairs with metal legs in a carpeted salon-style room. The wedding party congregated at the front of a room with a brown panel stage backdrop. The wedding pictures on the sidewalk outside the Kingdom Hall were in front of two white industrial-looking doors. It was not how I had envisioned my wedding. It was disappointing.

At the time of my wedding, my mother had been a Jehovah's Witness for about six years. As an active member of the congregation, she had refused to attend the ceremony if conducted in a Catholic church.

Jehovah's Witnesses believe that they are the only true religion directed by God and that other religions do not preach the truth. They also believe that the world is under Satan's rule, including other religions other than their own.

Because of these beliefs, they are adamant about not associating with worldly people. Because they think that other religions ultimately belong to Satan, entering a Catholic church or any other religious establishment means they are entering a building that belongs to Satan. To escape Satan's influence, they choose to isolate themselves from other religions and from the world itself.

Danilo and I struggled with the planning of our wedding because of a religious conflict. We were both Catholic, and so was his entire family. It was my mother's religious proclivity that caused the consternation. We wrestled with the idea of not having a Catholic wedding for the sole purpose of keeping my mother happy.

At that time, I was so confused about religion that I am not sure whether my desire to get married in the Catholic church had to do with religion, upbringing, the optics of the ceremony, or the resulting pictures. Danilo and his family were disappointed with the decision but graciously agreed.

Another controversy I had to contend with involved my sister, who refused to attend the ceremony because I did not make her the matron of honor. Instead, I had chosen my best friend.

Then there were my cold feet. As much as I wanted to get out of my childhood home, I had reservations before the wedding. It suddenly dawned on me that I was too young to get married and that I was probably making a mistake. My inner self was crying out against marriage.

About three weeks before the wedding, I wanted to call it off. Danilo would not hear of it. We had a fully furnished apartment in Queens, New York, and the preparations for the wedding were made and paid for, down to the last detail. How could I cancel at this stage of the game?

We both agreed that I was most likely suffering from cold feet. But at the age of eighteen, what does anyone know? Nothing! No one should make life-altering decisions at such a young age.

I graduated from high school on June 21 and married on June 28. Was I desperate or what? I was free at last, or so I thought. 1975 was a crucial turning point in my life.

In the Hispanic culture, at least in 1975, a bride did not wear her wedding gown for the entire reception. About one to two hours before leaving the reception, the bride would change into a formal gown, symbolizing the transition from a single young lady to a married woman. I wore an emerald-green gown.

The bride and groom were also expected to leave about one hour or so before everyone else. I did not want to leave the reception. I cried as I tried to hold on to my single, carefree life. Walking out of that door represented stepping into my new role in life as a married woman. At the age of eighteen, it was a scary prospect.

I cried for about three months after the wedding. Anytime friends or family members came to visit, I became melancholy and wanted to leave with them. My inner self was crying out as it adjusted to this new life. I did not want to go back to my family home, but I also did not want to be married. I had no place to turn.

I moved from one emotionally charged, stressful situation to another. I married too young and for the wrong reasons. I wanted out; I wanted my freedom; I wanted to take charge of my life, so I married. What alternative did I have?

Although we were living in the US, we still honored our cultural background and the customs from back home. As such, the only honorable way for a young lady to leave the family home was to get married in 1975. I was so unhappy at home that I wanted to get married at age sixteen. However, my mother had insisted that I at least graduate from high school before getting married. She was concerned that I would stop going to school if I married. Nothing could have been further from the truth. I loved going to school. I had perfect attendance for three out of my four years of high school.

I didn't even entertain the notion of going away to college, moving in with a roommate, moving in with my boyfriend, or getting my apartment. My only option was to get married.

Changing my last name after marriage was something that I naively and foolishly believed was a must-do. I perceived unseen societal pressures forcing me to change my name. I honestly struggled with this decision.

Changing my name thrust me into an emotional avalanche of doubt, unease, and confusion. Where had the old me gone? I had lost a part of myself, a piece of my identity, and my individuality. I had a difficult time identifying with the new name and the person it represented. Walking around with somebody else's name was strange. My birth name represented who I was born to be. I resented the fact that I had sacrificed my name, identity, and individuality to marriage. At the time, I believed that it was something I had to live with and accept.

Changing my name made matters worse. I now felt lost, besides regretting having gotten married so young. This combination was more than my developing brain could handle. I constantly questioned why I had gotten married and why I had changed my name. At eighteen, I do not think I knew what love was. So why had I gotten married?

After intense self-analysis and introspection, I discovered that other than not knowing my ass from my elbow at eighteen and wanting to move out of my childhood home, the simple answer was that we had gotten married because it was the way it was meant to be. The synchronistic events that culminated in our meeting could not have been coincidental—it must have been destiny.

Growing up in an emotionally charged environment caused me to retreat into my world, guarded and careful not to get too close to anyone. My relationship with Danilo forced me to come out of my shell and get close to another person, to love, and to share.

CHAPTER 25
MAJOR DECISIONS AND POINTS OF INFLEXION

That first year of marriage was tough for us. I was attending a co-op secretarial program where I worked part-time, earning $60 per week, and attended secretarial school the second half of the day. Danilo earned $185 per week. We made ends meet by eating at a different relative's house each day. When it was close to payday, we would have to sneak into the subway station with one token. But we persevered.

For the first three years of our marriage, we lived in Astoria, Queens, in three different apartments. The first apartment was in a single-family home, where the owners had the basement apartment. It was an affordable $185 per month rent, one-bedroom apartment in an area that was convenient for shopping and transportation. But the landlord did not believe in heating the house. The landlord and his family wore their coats while in the house. To keep warm, we resorted to spending time in the kitchen with the oven turned on. We did not spend a second winter in that apartment.

In my naïve eighteen-year-old mind, not only did I decide not to go to college, to get married, but also have a child. Wasn't that what I was supposed to do now that I was married?

Somehow, fate knew I was not ready for a child at eighteen years of age. Between the ages of eighteen and twenty-one, I had three miscarriages—or spontaneous abortions, as the doctors referred to them. I mourned the loss of my first pregnancy, as I miscarried at about twelve weeks of gestation.

The doctor told me that a spontaneous abortion was the uterus expelling a defective embryo/fetus. He emphasized the uterus expels the embryo or fetus approximately 50 percent of the time when it's not developing normally because of chromosomal, genetic, or other problems. The doctors performed a D&C (dilation and curettage); a procedure used to remove the contents of the uterus after a miscarriage.

After the D&C, I was empty; physically empty, because the doctors had removed the fetus, and mentally empty because there was "nothing" for me to mourn; there was no baby to bury. So, what was I grieving?

I was confused about the enormous grief I experienced over the death of a child I had not seen or held. I did not even know the sex of the child. All of my dreams and plans related to this unborn child and its role in our family life had died with the child.

Danilo also grieved, but he did not have the same connection with the unborn child. He did not understand the experience of having a life growing inside of you. Although some family and friends sympathized, they couldn't relate. After all, this child was not real to them. So, I understood how they could not comprehend how real my baby was to me. Even though I did not hold my baby in my arms, I had carried it in my uterus, under my heart, for three months.

The other two miscarriages were at four- and six-weeks' gestation, much earlier in the process, which did not phase me as much. After the third consecutive miscarriage, the doctors told me this was known as recurrent spontaneous miscarriage, and they ran some tests to determine possible causes. They found nothing.

By the age of twenty-one, I was a bit more mature than the naïve eighteen-year-old. I questioned my decision to have a child and evaluated what I wanted to do with my life.

After three years of working as a legal secretary, I looked around and took stock that there was no room for growth. My intuition was telling me that there was more to life than making a living. I was earning an excellent salary at the law firm, but it was a dead-end job. Unless one attended law school, the highest position one could hope to attain at the law firm was that of head secretary, office manager, or paralegal.

Why did I think I needed to have a child? Because that was what you did once you were married? Ridiculous! Instead, I recognized that I needed to continue my education. Working at the law firm had piqued a renewed interest in the law. Growing up, I'd watched the television show *Perry Mason* and had toyed with the idea of being a lawyer. I've always been fascinated by the law. I was seriously considering law school in my future. I was going to get on birth control and continue my education.

When I advised Danilo of my decision to further my education, he practically forbade me to go. What he failed to recognize was that I was not asking his permission; I was merely advising him of a decision I had already made. I was determined to go to college, with or without his support. He wasn't happy about my decision, nor was he ever 100 percent supportive. He could not understand why I had this need for more in my life.

After I had solidified the decision to go back to school, I discovered the fact that I couldn't afford the tuition. I was not going to let this minor issue deter me from my desire to get a college education.

I arranged a meeting with one of the senior partners and negotiated an agreement with the firm, whereby they would advance the money for tuition at the beginning of the semester, and I would repay the loan by working overtime. Working overtime was a necessity at the law firm, and sometimes the other secretaries were unwilling or unavailable to do so. By agreeing to serve as the overtime stand-in, I met one of the firm's needs in exchange for tuition advancement. I was incredibly grateful for the interest-free loan and the generosity extended by the partners.

As fate would have it, after I had made the decision that I did not want to have a child and wanted to go back to school instead, I learned that I was pregnant yet again. I had mixed emotions about this unplanned pregnancy, but abortion was out of the question. There was a lot of uncertainty during the first few months of the pregnancy, given my history of miscarriages.

Having a child would make achieving my educational goals that much more complicated, but I didn't waver in my plans to get a higher education. There was so much more I could accomplish in my life, but I couldn't do it without that little piece of paper that opens doors: a college diploma.

My first son was born in January 1978, and in 1979, I started to pursue my educational goals at a business school called Taylor Business Institute. However, after one semester, I recognized this was not the right program for me. So, in January 1980, I started my education with Pace University.

Once I started taking classes, I found that I needed to retrain myself in the art of studying and taking exams, as I had been out of high school for about five years. It was a slow start taking one or two courses, max per semester. Taking classes was made even tougher because I had a demanding full-time job, a family, and a home to keep. Thus began the busiest time of my life, the years 1980 to 1985.

Our second apartment in Queens was in a modern ten-story building in the same general location as the first apartment. Although the rent included utilities, the owner of the building had not been paying the utility bills. We came home one day to find a dark building and a utility bill for several thousand dollars, which we could not afford to pay. The law firm I worked for handled the matter, and I was able to break the lease and move out without paying the outstanding utility bill.

By that time, I was about eight months into my first pregnancy. We temporarily moved into my mother's home so we could be closer to St. Luke's Hospital in Manhattan. In the meantime, Danilo rented our third apartment in Queens.

The apartment was a first-floor railroad apartment in a four-story, somewhat run-down walk-up building, with the two bedrooms at opposite ends. I was concerned that the second bedroom was too far away from the master bedroom. It was not what I would have chosen.

Shortly after we moved in, I noticed some droppings that could have been from mice. I cleaned up and ignored it. As the days passed, I heard movement in the drop ceiling that sounded like mice moving around. I did not know how old the building was, but there was nothing modern about the structure or the apartment. In New York, the older the building, the more likely it is to have rodents. I mentioned it to Danilo, and he said I was making too much of it, so I let it go.

At night, when we were supposed to be sleeping, I could hear scurrying and scratching coming from the drop ceiling and from behind the panels on the wall. As soon as I shut my eyes and began to fall asleep, the scratching would start. Many nights, I lay awake, reliving my childhood nightmares. Again, I mentioned this to Danilo, but he said he could hear nothing. Maybe he did not want to admit it. To him, my complaints were ridiculous.

As the weeks passed, I grew more uncomfortable in the apartment. I recognized the night sounds of the critters and could not sleep. Although I also heard them in the kitchen during the day, rats are nocturnal, so they were much more disturbing at night. Danilo was able to sleep through the commotion. But for me, it brought back vivid memories of that apartment on 105th Street when I was eight years old.

One night, as we were watching television, I saw a mouse come out from behind the hamper. I told Danilo that I saw a mouse; he looked up and did not see anything. About twenty minutes later, the mouse came out from behind the hamper again. I pointed out the mouse that had been taunting me. I was so persistent that he finally walked over to look. Once again, he looked behind the hamper and, of course, did not see anything. At least, that is what he said.

For me, finally seeing what I had been hearing was the last straw. I told Danilo that I refused to stay in the apartment and that we had to move out. He refused, saying that it was ridiculous. I told him he could stay if he wanted to, but I was moving out the next day.

True to my word, the next day, I packed my bag and my baby and showed up at my mother's apartment unannounced. When she asked what happened and why I had left my apartment, I told her I had seen a mouse. Everyone found my encounter with a mouse hilarious. They did not let me live it down for a long time.

I did not care what they had to say; it was not funny to me. That mouse had parents that were much bigger than him. The scurrying I heard from the drop ceiling and behind the paneling on the walls was not from that tiny mouse. I recognized the droppings and the scurrying to be coming from a much larger critter. Potentially a rat.

I didn't return to that apartment, not even to pack up our personal belongings. It took Danilo two weeks to realize that I was serious about not living in that apartment and joined me at my mother's apartment.

This mouse, regardless of its size, was the catalyst that pushed me out of Queens and back to Manhattan, where I achieved one of my dreams. I secured an apartment in the building I had been eyeing for years; conveniently located on the corner of 96th Street and Amsterdam Avenue, four city blocks from our families' 830 Amsterdam apartment. It was a much more convenient location to commute to work and access childcare.

For years, we had frequently driven by this building on our way in and out of Manhattan. Each time I had passed that building, I had either made a mental note or verbalized that someday I was going to live in that building. I was obsessed with it. Like the 830 Amsterdam building, we had witnessed the construction of this 25+ story high-rise in the early 70s.

One day, as I was walking with my son in his stroller, scoping out the area for an apartment, I looked up at the building as I usually did. We desperately needed an apartment, so I walked into the leasing office to inquire about an application for leasing an apartment.

I spoke with the leasing agent on duty and told him my story. He had a good laugh at the reason I had left my previous apartment and gave me an application to fill out. He reviewed the application, looked at me and then at my six-month-old sitting in the stroller, and told me he had an apartment available, and it was mine if I wanted it. Of course, I accepted.

The apartment was on the sixth floor, had two bedrooms, and an open floor space concept with the kitchen flowing into the dining area and dining area into the living room that had a balcony. The area was convenient with everything we needed in one area: bank, supermarket, daycare, subway station. This luxury building also had 24/7 doorman and a laundry room in the basement.

When I had walked into that leasing office, I had intended to file a lease application and wait my turn on the waiting list, if any. I don't know how or why the leasing manager offered the apartment without requiring a waiting period. There was usually a waiting list a mile long for these rent-regulated apartments; especially in a modern building, located in a convenient area, with so many amenities. Although I had not been on a physical waiting list, I had been on a cosmic waiting list for years, as I had channeled and proclaimed my apartment each time I drove or walked by that building.

When I told Danilo later that evening, he did not believe me. No one believed me. I had been talking about living in this building for so long that no one believed me. We lived at 733 Amsterdam Avenue from 1979 through 1987, when we purchased a townhouse in Mount Vernon, New York.

By age twenty-three, I had a two-year-old son and had spent the first five years of my marriage regretting my decision to marry so young. It was then that I understood I had gotten married for the wrong reasons. There was no turning back; I had a child to rear. I stopped whining about having gotten married too young and committed to putting that energy into my marriage. I then decided to have a second child.

To say that 1980 was a tough and stressful year for us would be an understatement. Again, fate wanted to test my will and determination. Four months into my second pregnancy, Danilo lost his job. I was pregnant, working full-time, working overtime, and pursuing a college education. We were barely able to make ends meet on one salary.

My second son was born in 1981 by cesarean section. Not only was my son two and a half weeks overdue, but he was also breech. According to the doctors, I had developed a "lazy uterus," meaning the uterus would not contract to expel the baby.

Raising two children, working a full-time job, and pursuing my educational goals kept me busy. My oldest son was three years old, and my second was eleven months old when I made the decision not to have any more children. But destiny had a different plan for me.

It's difficult to concentrate on work and school if you do not have reliable childcare. A trustworthy and dependable childcare provider helps working parents financially and emotionally. Knowing that you have a person you can trust with your children without worrying about their well-being is priceless.

I was extremely fortunate when it came to childcare. From 1980 to 1987, I lived four city blocks from the projects where I had grown up. My mother, who was still in the same apartment, took care of my oldest son until he was ready to attend daycare. At that time, the daycares in New York City within my budget required that the child be potty-trained and at least thirty-three months old.

My mother also took care of my second son until October 1981, when she had a heart attack at the age of forty-seven. At the time of my mother's heart attack, my second son was nine months old, and I had to embark on finding a reliable and affordable sitter.

I found a woman in our building who was a good sitter. She took care of my second son for about four months. When she moved to Puerto Rico for an extended stay, I had to begin another search.

As if it weren't tough enough with work, school, keeping a home, and no sitter, fate again wanted to see if I could handle just one more responsibility in my life. In December 1981, I discovered I was about sixteen weeks pregnant. This pregnancy had sneaked up on us. At the time, I said to myself, "This child will either bring a lot of joy or a lot of turmoil into our lives, and only time would tell." The doctors advised against carrying the pregnancy to term because of the contraceptives I had been taking. As bad as our finances and stress were at the time, abortion was out of the question, especially at four months' gestation.

Studies at the time indicated that taking birth control pills while pregnant could result in an increased risk of congenital disabilities. My doctor performed the tests available at the time and said that the baby had suffered no adverse effects from the contraceptives. The only thing they could not determine was whether the baby's sight or hearing would be impaired. Thank God, my third son was born in 1982 with no congenital anomalies.

I searched for a sitter for about a month, during which time I had to take my one-year-old to work with me. I packed as much as I could carry on the subway to make him comfortable in the office. I would place a blanket under my desk when it was time to take a nap. The lawyers at the law firm were extremely flexible, but the situation was not sustainable. Especially since I was pregnant and had to carry my son in his stroller plus a packed baby bag and my pocketbook up and down the subway stairs. I had to find a sitter.

My neighbor, who was aware of my plight introduced me to a woman she believed would be a great sitter, who, coincidentally, conveniently lived in our building, one floor below our sixth-floor apartment.

When I first met **Doña** Ana, she had recently lost her son. The passing of her son was a most unfortunate situation; he fell out an eleventh-floor window. I did not know the exact details of the story, but the belief was that he was pushed out of the window by an accomplice or someone else while he or others were burglarizing the apartment. Unfortunately, he was addicted to heroin and, like many addicts at the time, stole from family and friends, robbed strangers, and burglarized homes and stores to support his habit.

She had gone through so much with her son when he'd been alive, dealing with him being in and out of jail, drug abuse, and the stealing. The final blow of his violent death was the hardest to bear. That he had brought so much pain and grief to her life had not stopped her from doing everything to support him and help him turn his life around. After all, he was her son, her flesh and blood, and she had refused to turn her back on him.

Children are not supposed to die before their parents. We expect to see our children grow, mature, and give us grandchildren because this is the natural cycle of life.

I'm sure that to many people, her son was one more derelict drug addict taken off of the streets of New York City and good riddance. But to her, this was her child, and she had always prayed that he would straighten his life out. As long as he'd been alive, she had held on to the hope that he would change and turn his life around.

When I first met her, she was so grief-stricken that the heaviness in her heart was palpable. Her apartment was a dark, grim, and depressing environment. We were both initially apprehensive. I was concerned about leaving my child in such a depressing atmosphere. In turn, she did not want to entertain the idea of taking care of children. However, the neighbor who had introduced us highly recommended this woman to me. She also advocated my plight to the kind lady by saying, "This is a hardworking young lady; she is working full time, goes to school at night, and could use your help."

I explained that I had lost my babysitter and that I had resorted to taking my son to work with me. I pleaded with her to help me until I could find another sitter. She agreed to help, took one look at my swollen abdomen, pointed, and stated, "I'm not taking care of that one, so you better find another sitter soon."

"I understand. I will do my best to find someone else as soon as possible."

It was a match made in heaven. She turned out to be a godsend for us, and we turned out to be the people who needed to enter her life to help her overcome her loss. Taking care of my children was the therapy she needed to get her through the mourning cycle. Having my son in the house forced her to deal with life. She opened the blinds and finally let the sunshine into her apartment.

Not only did she take care of my second son from the age of one, but she also took care of my third son until he was old enough to enter kindergarten in 1987 when we moved out of New York City.

She became a grandmother to my children. She was more of a grandmother to them than our flesh and blood. She helped us as much as we helped her. We helped her furnish and remodel her apartment so she could have comfortable furniture. She was so grateful for everything we were able to provide for her, and we were equally thankful to have found such a kind and caring person to create a loving environment for our children.

Having a reliable daycare provider helped me accomplish my educational and career goals. I could not have done it without **Doña** Ana, who became our sitter, grandmother, and mother for the seven years my children required in-home care.

Doña Ana was a kind, honest, and reliable sitter, and we loved her very much.

Getting a college education was one of my primary goals, but my family came first. I could not allow my educational pursuits and job encroach on my family's needs. I wanted my career and education to enhance our lives, not substitute them.

Tending to my young family's needs took priority to study time or attending class. I attended classes on the weekends, after work, during lunch breaks, or early in the morning before work ("early bird" classes). Fortunately for me, Pace University offered many different options, programs, and locations for me to choose from as I worked on my schedule for the semester. Pace University was even flexible enough to allow me to take a final exam while in the hospital recuperating from the cesarean after the delayed birth of my second son.

Family obligations made studying a challenge, and beyond that, on many nights before a midterm or final exam, I was in a hospital emergency room with my oldest son, who suffered from bronchitis with a touch of asthma and ran extremely high fevers.

I had to make some sacrifices. For example, from 1980 to 1985, my weekends were spent doing housework, homework, and spending time with the kids. I only attended family gatherings during holidays or other special occasions.

My hectic daily schedule required exceptional organization on my part so we could leave the house with sufficient time to get to our respective destinations. I did laundry on Sundays and set aside each child's outfits for the entire week. This way, there was one less thing to do as we frantically tried to leave the house each morning.

Fortunately, Danilo was way ahead of his time by being a Mr. Mom. During the early to mid-eighties, being a Mr. Mom was not common or popular, and taking care of children was considered a woman's job, especially in our Latino community. Fortunately for me, he was willing to take on some of the duties in the home and the responsibility for the day-to-day care of our family.

Danilo and I had an equitable distribution of responsibilities in the home. After work, Danilo picked our oldest son up but would leave the youngest with the sitter until I came home from school. Depending on our schedules, whoever came home first would make dinner while the other picked up the boys from a sporting event. We capitalized on each other's strengths and expertise when dividing these responsibilities.

It was not perfect, and there were times he was not as supportive of me going to school at night. Sometimes, I would get home at nine or ten o'clock at night to find him lying on the couch in front of the television, a sink full of dishes, dirty counters, kids running around unbathed, and messes throughout the entire apartment. Although we didn't speak about it, there were times when he believed that making it tough for me would get me to give up on my educational pursuits. It was psychological warfare. He was waiting for me to break, but—I never did. I did not let the mess bother me. I put the kids to bed, cleaned up the kitchen, and settled down to eat dinner.

As the kids grew older, it became easier as everyone was assigned chores. Even though I had been raised watching my mother and other women in our family treat the men in their lives like kings of the castle, I did not espouse that philosophy. I had a husband and three sons, and there was no way I was going to cater to four men. Instead, I preferred to be the queen bee. Everybody had to do their share of work around the house. In summary, it is important to recognize that the burden of child-rearing and household tasks should not disproportionately fall on women, particularly those who are employed.

I graduated from Pace University in 1985 with a degree in international business management. I was physically and mentally exhausted and did not even attend my graduation. I had little in common with the other graduates. Most of them were younger, single, and had no children. I, on the other hand, was twenty-eight years old, married, had three children, and was a full-time employee.

In hindsight, I did not give myself sufficient credit for what I had accomplished. I was glad to have obtained my bachelor's degree and grateful for the knowledge that I had gained. But I still felt as though I had more work to do and enrolled in Pace University's graduate program the following semester.

Looking back, I honestly do not know how I obtained an undergraduate degree. With three children, a demanding job, and the responsibilities of keeping a home, there were times I could barely make a C+ grade. My determination to get a college education enabled me to graduate with a B average and attend graduate school for an additional three years.

I took it one day at a time, one course at a time, one semester at a time, and came out the other end a much stronger person for having survived that grueling but rewarding experience. The desire to make a better life for my family gave me the strength and stamina to keep on going. From those challenging circumstances emerged a woman who had dreams of a successful professional life.

With Danilo's help, an excellent sitter, Pace University—an educational institution that met the needs of working students—and pure determination, I was able to achieve my career and educational goals.

CHAPTER 26
THE JOYS OF PARENTHOOD

In 1990, Danilo and I agreed to move from New York to Fairfax, Virginia, with my employer. We also agreed that my job would be our primary source of income in Virginia. Danilo would have a flexible working arrangement so he could be home for the kids and help our family adjust to our new environment.

When we moved to the suburbs, we believed the stereotypical view that most drug activities occurred in the rougher areas of the inner city. In the urban environment of New York City, we had known what to look for, how to recognize the "bad guy," the lingo, and where kids purchased drugs. In the suburbs, we were in foreign territory. We were ignorant about life in suburbia and what most kids did when unsupervised.

Fairfax County is one of the wealthiest counties in the nation, with an abundance of upscale homes and manicured lawns. There was no way these affluent kids were using and selling drugs. That Fairfax County Public Schools ranked high, and the kids had good grades did not mean there was no drug activity.

The fashionably dressed kids were polite, articulate, came from good families, attended good schools, and earned good grades. But this was a façade, as these kids had purchasing power. On the weekends, in empty houses or hotels, they had wild parties, during which they used drugs and drank too much alcohol.

We lulled ourselves into believing that the suburbs would be a less threatening environment than the city, so we let our guard down. By the time we discovered that kids from the suburbs are as likely, if not more so, to succumb to high-risk behaviors as their inner-city counterparts, it was too late. We were not as vigilant as we would have been had we still been living in New York.

We believed it would be a safe environment; it was why we moved from the city and paid a considerable mortgage. We wanted to insulate our children from the inner-city environment I had contended with growing up.

We attended and supported our children's schooling and sporting activities. We partook in plenty of family bonding activities, such as vacations and local outings to the beach, pool, zoo, circus, auto show, and other fun events. We had convinced ourselves into believing that because we had been supportive parents and raised them well, our children could not possibly succumb to risky behavior. Wrong! We did not factor into our equation forces and influences much greater than ours: peers and peer pressure.

Unlike the drug dealers of the inner city, who stood on street corners or sold from apartments to anyone who came calling, the drug dealers in the suburbs had a closed society, where they only sold to people known and trusted. It meant they could operate undetected for years.

We tried to protect our children from making some of the same mistakes we had seen many other teens make. We wanted to save them from themselves. But guess what? They had to make their own mistakes. They had to live the lives they were born to live per their individual life's journey, not ours.

Choosing to have children was an irreversible decision that changed our lives forever. Two of my three pregnancies sneaked up on me. Unfortunately, children come into this world without an instruction manual to help you navigate the challenges you will ultimately face while protecting your investment.

Pregnancy, for me, was an awe-filled time with the wonders of the creation of life. It was also a roller-coaster ride of emotional and physical experiences: the changes in one's body, mood swings, emotional outbursts, the first kick, constant wiggling, and listening to the baby's heartbeat, culminating in the miracle of birth.

Notwithstanding some of the unpleasant experiences, the fact that life was growing inside of me didn't cease to amaze me. That was a special time and experience that is difficult to explain to men or women who haven't had a child.

With the first pregnancy, there was the dread of labor and giving birth, given everything I had heard, seen, and read. Despite the dread and fear of childbirth, I recall thinking to myself, "The baby has to come out one way or the other. Besides, women have been delivering babies for eons. How bad could it be?"

With the second pregnancy, there was still the dreaded labor, but this time, I was keenly aware of what was coming, so in my opinion, the anticipation was worse. When the doctor told me she had to perform a cesarean section, I was not disappointed because this meant that I could forgo the pain of the contractions.

You can watch videos, take Lamaze classes, and get advice from others who have gone through the childbirth process, but until you have to go through the actual delivery, there is no way to grasp the magnitude of the experience adequately.

After the birth of the child, the reality of the situation finally hits you. Your life will never be the same. Your child depends utterly on you for its survival. The responsibility to tend to the child's needs can be a source of energy and stress, as the child has no one but you. You can't take a day off from being a parent; you can't call in sick. You must be there for your child no matter what is going on in the other areas of your life.

You may have many opinions about how to raise a child and what you would do in a given situation. You can also have experience in the world at babysitting, but you will not fully understand the responsibility of parenting until you have a child of your own.

I did not appreciate the meaning of the word *obsession* until my first pregnancy. I was so obsessed with having a girl that anyone who told me otherwise was in trouble. I would genuinely get upset if anyone told me I was carrying a boy. I was so sure that I was carrying a girl that I even promised Danilo that if it were a boy, he could name him whatever he wanted, and I would not interfere. In my mind, that was not going to happen, because I was carrying a girl.

Well, sure enough, I delivered a five-pound, eleven-ounce baby boy. It took me a couple of months to adjust to the fact that *he* was not a *she*. Delivering a boy was the first of my expectations that shattered.

As parents, we had many different expectations for our children. In reality, children rarely grow up to be how and what we want them to be. Throughout the years, I learned that part of being a parent is watching your kids grow, develop, and become independent.

It also dawned on me that those expectations we had were a form of trying to control their decisions and how they would ultimately turn out in life. But in many cases, children make decisions that parents do not and won't ever approve.

As parents, we fooled ourselves into believing that we could control the destinies of our children. In reality, the best we could do was give them advice and an excellent foundation to fall back on. Then we had to let them live their lives.

It took me a long time to drop the "if my child fails, I've failed" attitude. As parents, we did the best we could given the life experiences, resources, and information we had.

We had three children raised in the same household under the same conditions, and they each turned out to be different. Why? Because they each have their road to travel and path to walk. Nature or nurture? Or a combination of the two?

As a mother, I refuse to take credit for any of my children's accomplishments and successes, nor will I take the blame for any of their actions or failures. Children come into life with their agendas. As each snowflake and fingerprint is unique, so is a person's purpose in life. As parents, we are merely the catalyst that helps them enter the world.

In my opinion, parents get too much credit and too much blame for their children's accomplishments and failures. For the most part, parents do the best they can for their children. Despite the angst and the horror of those teenage years, your children are your flesh and blood, and you will do everything in your power to protect and help them along the way.

Notwithstanding the above, there is absolutely nothing rational about purposefully committing to an eighteen- to a twenty-one-year period of constant investment of capital and emotions, agreeing to an increased level of stress, and losing your free time and peace of mind with no guarantee of a positive return on your investment. You don't even get an instruction manual to help you navigate the challenges you will face. Think about it. As a business proposal, this proposal would not fly. If you asked a bank or an investor to back you on this venture, they would think you were crazy.

One thing you are guaranteed is the longest roller-coaster ride of emotions, from the sheer elation of your child's birth, the first step, first word, graduation, and wedding, to the grief and heartache they can inflict as teenagers.

Of the various stages of raising children, the tumultuous teen years were the toughest for me. It is a time when children start to assert their independence and push the boundaries you have set. A time when parents are trying to straddle the fine line of giving their teen independence while trying to steer him or her in the right direction without being overbearing. A time when parents and their teens are pushing and pulling in different directions.

You'll wake up one day to discover your car is missing. You think it has been stolen and call the police to report it missing, only to discover your child has taken the car for a joyride. You'll ask yourself, "When did he learn how to drive? Who taught him?"

Sneaking out of the bedroom window and taking your car for a joyride is one thing, but having to deal with a disrespectful teen is a different kind of nightmare.

Your child's sweet personality can last up to age thirteen, when he or she may then start acting up, culminating in a disrespectful teen and young adult.

Some teens can be extremely disrespectful, obnoxious, and abusive toward their family members. They can frustrate, exhaust, and overwhelm you with the constant arguing, pleading, and negotiating. By age fifteen, some teens turn into complete monsters.

Teenagers can be moody and stubborn, and their behavior usually gets worse before it gets better. But some teens can cross the line from being a teen trying to assert him- or herself and establish his or her independence to being rude and demeaning toward everyone around him or her.

Things get so bad that one day when you've had enough of your teens rude, disrespectful behavior, you uncharacteristically push your teen up against a wall and say, "One of us is going to die, and the other is going to spend the rest of their life in prison, and neither scenario has a pretty ending. So, I suggest that you clean up your act." You realize that your eyes must have been bulging, your tongue flickering, and your hair up on ends, because you smelled the fear on your teen's breath and saw fear in the eyes of your teen.

The experts say that you should not take this type of behavior personally, because other kids are doing the same thing two houses down. I would bet it probably has something to do with the teenage brain on drugs.

The reality is that some parents get a raw deal. Some silently wonder what happened to that sweet child they once knew and loved, bewildered as to how they produced a lemon from a beautiful apple orchard. Not only does the lemon fall far from the tree, but it somehow grew in an apple orchard. Go figure.

As hard as the teen years can be, it is difficult for those who have to deal with the illness of a child. I was fortunate that I had three healthy children, except for a short period of dealing with juvenile rheumatoid arthritis (JRA).

At age five, the doctors diagnosed one of my sons with JRA. The disease was progressing so rapidly that the doctors said he would be crippled and in a wheelchair by age twelve.

JRA is a common type of arthritis in children that attacks most the joints in the body. We discovered the disease when he woke up one day with hip pain and a severe limp. When the doctors took an X-ray, they discovered that he had JRA. For about six years, he had severe flare-ups that lasted up to a week and included joint pain, swelling, stiffness, limited range of motion, and warm red joints. Whenever he had a flare-up, depending on the joints affected, he could not walk, constantly falling because of weakness in the legs, or he would have trouble feeding himself.

As a parent, it is extremely difficult to see your child in pain and not be able to do anything about it. Sometimes he would lie on the floor, crying in pain, and we could not even touch him. Sometimes the swelling was so bad that his shoulders looked like he was wearing shoulder pads.

When he was ten years old, he expressed a desire to play football. I did not want to say no, but I did not think this was a good idea, given his condition. I said to him, "Let's make an appointment with the doctor and see what he has to say. If the doctor says it's okay, then we will sign you up."

In my mind, the doctor was going to say no, and that would be the end of that discussion. Well, to my horror, the doctor said it was okay. I couldn't believe it. It was like when I had told Danilo he could name our first son—I couldn't take it back.

He played football from age ten and through high school. Sometimes he had to take eight hundred milligrams of Motrin after the game, but he played. I could not understand why he subjected himself to that kind of torture.

Fortunately, he started outgrowing the JRA by age twelve. Maybe the conditioning for football helped strengthen his joints.

In 1995, at the height of dealing with those challenging teen years, my firstborn announced that his girlfriend was pregnant. Facing the parents of a teen who was carrying my grandchild was stressful; it was stressful for both families.

At the age of thirty-eight, I became a grandmother. I was in denial. It took me a long time to embrace the title.

Being and becoming a good parent means something different to everyone. No matter how much you think you know about babies and raising children, that knowledge may not keep you from being overwhelmed by your child. Even if you have experience with older children, each child is different and will come with his or her unique challenges. You will have to work on getting to know and understand the needs and wants of each child.

Having children is like "a box of chocolates; you never know what you're gonna get" or what kind of parent you are going to be.

Like everything in life, there were good and bad times, but overall, it was a rewarding experience. If you are lucky, by the time your child is about twenty-five, the required capital investments diminish significantly, your teens become humans, and you become smarter in their eyes and, hopefully, a friend for life.

If you are extremely lucky, you get grandchildren, as they are your "gift from God for not killing your children."

CHAPTER 27
RECLAIMING MY IDENTITY

Do you ever feel you need a reprieve from your day-to-day life? You want to unplug from your daily routine.

For forty-plus years, I had followed an orderly, goody-two-shoes kind of life, doing the right thing, and following the rules. There were no crazy stories, no unhealthy, lustful relationship. No secrets. No intrigue. I'm sure many would say, "What a boring life." And maybe that is so in the eyes of some. But it had been a busy and productive life thus far.

From 1975 to 1998, everything had been about school, work, raising children, maintaining a relationship, and keeping a home. I transitioned from being a daughter to being a wife, mother, student, and employee. There hadn't been a time when I focused on me—on what I wanted to do.

I was exhausted, and I wanted to take and make the time to focus on my wants and needs. I needed to nourish and energize my soul. But here's the thing: I had been taking care of so many people for so long that I did not know how to start to take care of "me." That "me" that I had sacrificed to marriage, motherhood, and work. That "me" that I hadn't had the chance to get to know.

I needed to get to know myself as an adult. Throughout the years, I hadn't stopped long enough to get acquainted with the adult "me." I was intimately acquainted with Blanca Céspedes the mother, wife, and employee. I did not know Blanca De La Rosa, the adult.

Some may argue, it's just a name, no big deal. Right? Some may even say that I'm overreacting and exaggerating the symbolic power of my name. But in reality, everyone recognizes themselves by their name, which represents their personal history.

The Céspedes name represented Danilo's history and heritage; it was his identity his life, not mine. I wanted to explore the powerful influence my birth name would wield over my life—the life I'd been born to live.

The first thing I had to do on the road to that reprieve was to ease the self-imposed burden of changing my name. I had to reclaim my identity. For twenty-three years, I had lived as someone I had had a difficult time accepting.

As the years transpired, using my married name became bothersome. I resorted to introducing myself by my first name only. A co-worker would tease me, saying, "What are you, like Pele and Madonna, known by your first name only?"

A name change after marriage is a personal decision that women make for different reasons. I, like so many other women, took it as a given as it was the tradition. Some husbands take it personally if their wives do not take their married names claiming: one family, one name. However, no one should feel guilty or pressured into one or the other.

For me, it was not the right decision. Even after twenty-three years of being a Céspedes, which was five years longer than I had been a De La Rosa, I still could not get accustomed to using someone else's name.

In 1998, I reverted to using my maiden name. Ahh, what a relief. It was the relief one experiences when taking off a tight garment. I could be me again. The name change had empowered and invigorated me. I was born a De La Rosa, and I intend to die a De La Rosa.

The paperwork required to change my name legally was tedious, but the hardest part of the entire process was the discussion I had with Danilo. It was tough, as he immediately took it personally. He could not understand that I felt I had lost my identity, that I felt disconnected from my roots, and that using his name felt unnatural to me. He was not happy, and it took him a while to acclimate to the name change. He eventually relented, accepting the name change with one caveat: he did not want anyone to call him Mr. De La Rosa.

The twenty-four years of marriage had been good. We'd had our differences, but for the most part, we had a good relationship. But in 1998, we experienced a lot of turmoil that drove a wedge between us.

Between 1997 and 1999, the position I held within the company required approximately 70 percent of business travel. This travel schedule, my wanting a reprieve, and the name issue put a real strain on my relationship with Danilo; and I precipitated a separation, which he reluctantly agreed to.

After the announcement of divorce, came the weaning. We had been together for twenty-four years of marriage plus three years of dating. After twenty-seven years, we had become codependent. Our lives were tightly intertwined, to the point of fusion. I needed him as much as he needed me. Neither one of us was ready to be independent.

We shared the house from the moment I announced the divorce in September 1998 to March 2000, when he purchased his condo and moved out. I wanted to give the entire family time to adjust to the changes. In hindsight, this was the best approach. It took longer, but we emerged from the experience relatively unscathed and were ready to face life on our own.

I was uncertain if our time apart would cause more damage, fortify our bond, or pave the way for a fresh start for us both. Either way, I was confident that everything we had shared over the years, and our friendship would find a way to make everything work out in both our best interests; whatever that may be.

Getting divorced had been a heart-wrenching experience. It was one of the most difficult periods of my life, but I knew in my heart that I was making the right decision for both of us. I had developed a plan for walking away, but that did not make it any easier.

I received little to no support from friends and family. My closest friends were less than supportive. Instead, they were judgmental. We were in our early forties. They had embraced religion and had settled into their matronly family lives. Then there I was, talking this nonsense about finding myself and getting divorced.

Since I had married so young, I had always been at the opposite end of the social spectrum compared to the lives of some of my friends. When they had been out partying, traveling, and socializing, I had been home with a husband and three children. When they had finally settled down, I was ready to explore the world.

I was surprised by how hard my children reacted to our divorce. They hated me for breaking up the family. They accused me of living a lie, claiming that the perfect world I had portrayed for them as they were growing up had not been real. How could I do this to them? How could I be so selfish? I was getting divorced for no apparent reason. I was a terrible mother. Of course, they sided with their father. No one wanted to hear what I had to say. No one cared that I wanted to focus on "me" and find my true self.

Bombarded with verbal attacks, no one understood. How could I expect anyone to understand when I did not fully understand why myself? I had an overwhelming need to go off on my own, and I did.

Although I had initiated the divorce, Danilo and I were best friends. What made our relationship last as long as it did was that neither one of us professed to be the boss of the household. We were true partners. We capitalized on each other's strengths. He took the lead in his areas of strength, and I in mine. We consulted each other on everything. Of course, we disagreed from time to time, so the one with the particular expertise had the last word. In some cases, we agreed to disagree and did nothing.

On December 31, 1999, my divorce was official. I had finally gotten what I wanted, but I did not feel good about it. I walked out of the lawyer's office feeling despondent, lost, empty, and alone. I had turned to my "best friend" for support and asked her to witness the execution of my divorce documents. The reaction I got from her was unexpected. It was judgmental and non-supportive.

I've never had a wide circle of friends. I could count my friends on one hand and have fingers left to count. We had been friends for about sixteen years. Kate was one of the few people in my life. I called a friend. She was more like a sister to me. Whenever I had news, good or bad, she was the first person I called. We shared many wonderful years of friendship. As such, I did not expect her judgmental reaction to my request. I was on my own with no friends or family support. Fortunately, a coworker I had been commuting with agreed to accompany me to the lawyer's office at the last moment.

Although I did not regret my decision, I still could not figure out what was missing in my life. As I walked out of the lawyer's office, I recognized that divorce was not the answer to whatever it was I was seeking.

Even though we were in the twenty-first century, I felt the stigma associated with divorce. Even as a well-educated, reasonable person, I felt the pressure of guilt from a faceless society that made me feel like a failure because I'd given up on a relationship. Why should people make you feel guilty about making a personal decision that you believe is in your best interest?

CHAPTER 28
SPIRITUAL AWAKENING

Since childhood, I've had trouble accepting the conventional religious dogma, questioning the nuns and my mother on religious topics. Of course, the answers I received discouraged me from asking questions. It was the way it was, and one had to accept them, no questions asked. Still, in my mind, I had a hard time processing the information. My gut feelings and intuition told me there had to be some other explanation.

I believed in many of the nonconventional philosophies that some religious groups condemned. I would seek bits of information from various sources, but it always fell short.

I questioned why I'd never overwhelming needed to go to church or seek the association of any religious institution. I had gone to church because my mother made us go. I stopped attending mass when I had found myself going through the motions. I had been there in body, but not in spirit, which led me to question the motives of those around me. Were they there because they were expected to or because they had a real calling?

Religion is one of the most polarizing and sensitive issues to discuss. Although religions encourage peace and tolerance, few can remain calm and tolerant when it comes to defending their religious beliefs.

When one analyzes religion through the historical lens, one notes that more people have been killed in the name of religion than any other type of war. History abounds in religious wars, with some continuing for years and claiming thousands of lives. There are also countless examples of those who have murdered their spouses because divorce is against their religion. But murder isn't?

Late 1999, my son told me about a woman he had seen on *The Larry King Show* named Sylvia Browne. I thought "how interesting" but took no action to follow-up. A week later, I saw one of her books, *The Other Side and Back,* while shopping. I thought, "Wow, what a coincidence," and purchased the book. I read the book and discovered that she had written about a lot of the philosophies that I had instinctively known and believed but hadn't been able to substantiate or articulate.

I later discovered *The Journey of the Soul Series.* In this series, Sylvia shares her forty years of investigation and research on religious and spiritual issues. I found the research profound, spiritually moving, and eminently logical. I attended events hosted by Sylvia Browne, where she shared her research and experience. Through those events, I found similar events hosted by Hay House and their Wisdom Community and authors.

The Hay House events and authors gave me the confidence to embrace my spirituality and come out of the "spiritual closet." Sylvia Browne put me on the path to spiritualism and changed my life most profoundly.

Sylvia Browne was the founder of the Society of Novus Spiritus, a community of Gnostic Christians. *Gnostic* is a Greek word, meaning "seekers of truth and knowledge." The Gnostic philosophy encourages you to think and question everything. It states that you should read it, question it, take what works for you, and leave the rest behind, even if "it" is a philosophy from another religion or region.

There is no condemnation, judgment, or demeaning of your soul. You are not a sinner; everyone is worthy in the eyes of God. It is about becoming a better person and perfecting your soul. The message is always positive and encouraging. Even though I could not identify or articulate what my instincts had been telling me, the Gnostic philosophy is what I had instinctively known and believed.

Since discovering this philosophy, I am elated about my spirituality. The Gnostic philosophy provided the wind that my sail needed to find its course. I had finally found spirituality without organized religion.

There comes a time for each of us when we have to decide the "truth" for ourselves. If what you consider to be the truth matches your religion, hooray! If not, then you have to find and align yourself with people and organizations that match your beliefs.

I had been divorced for three years, and although I was alone, I was not lonely. I took comfort and pure joy in discovering my spirituality. There was so much for me to learn and discover. I spent most of my time attending Hay House events in different cities, reading, researching, and writing. I needed this period of "alone time" to develop my spirituality without the distraction and burden of a relationship. I had enough distractions with my career, business travel schedule, and getting my children on the road to complete independence.

I loved my new life, spirituality, and the person who had emerged. The ironic thing about the metamorphosis was that I retreated from the people who were the closest to me, hence the divorce. Not that they were no longer good enough for me, but more about my trying to find myself and my place in life and trying to determine how those people fit into my life.

Following the Gnostic, philosophy had been rewarding and self-gratifying. I wish I had learned about it earlier in my life. It would have made a difference in how I had handled myself in critical situations. But then, my life was so busy with family, school, business travel, and career that I had not had the time to stop and think about anything else. In life, everything happens when it is supposed to. Not a minute earlier.

I had embarked on a journey of personal growth, transformation, and exploration. My experience was so profound that it allowed me to see my life and those of the people around me in a way I couldn't have done with the hectic schedule of the previous years. I could not have developed the foundation of my spirituality without the knowledge I gained from reading those Hay House books and attending the Wisdom Community events.

This shift in consciousness was part of my maturation as a spiritual being; it was part of my personal growth as Blanca De La Rosa. My professional, educational, and personal accomplishments paled compared to the spiritual awakening, enlightenment, shift in consciousness, and inner peace that finding myself gave me.

After three years, we had finally moved on to the final stage, where we were truly living independent lives but remaining best friends. We were no longer codependent having undone the tightly twined bonds of the last thirty years.

But here's the thing: that separate lives thing did not last long. After the holidays in 2003, four full years after the divorce and finding myself, Danilo and I started dating. What the hay was the purpose of the last four years? The separation, the divorce, and the drama.

Well, I recognized that the separation had been about reclaiming my identity and my individuality while finding myself and my spirituality. It had little to do with my relationship with Danilo. I had to step away from the hustle and bustle of my daily routine and look within to find enlightenment.

During the time of my divorce, I had changed my name, gone on a four-year sabbatical, and emerged as the person I am today. During those four years of metamorphosis, there had been a lot of turmoil in both my professional and personal lives, as I was transforming into the new "me." I had come to know and understand Blanca De La Rosa. Okay, so I'm a slow learner. But I learned a valuable lesson. Before being in a couple relationship, one must first be an individual. You have to know and understand your soul before you can commit to a soul mate.

It took a while to get back to being a couple, as we had spent the last four years leading separate lives. Danilo had been in two separate relationships during those years. After living the life of a bachelor for four years, it took some time for Danilo to slow down.

In April 2003, we made our relationship official and let family and friends know we would be remarrying. We remarried on June 28, 2003, but this time there were no controversies or second-guessing, and I walked down the aisle of my choice—we remarried in a chapel in

Las Vegas. There were no guests, no family. It was the most romantic time of our lives.

And we lived happily thereafter.

That could certainly be 'the end' of the story. But I had two lives. Two lives that, though intertwined and simultaneous, were kept separate on parallel tracks. I've had my share of major problems in both my personal and professional lives, but to the extent possible, I compartmentalized to keep each in their lane, not bringing my problems to the office or vice versa.

Compartmentalizing the major issues in my life was the only way I was able to manage a family, pursue an education, and a career. Whenever there was a convergence of major issues, my personal life was my priority, especially when my children were young.

In the next section: From the Projects Blossomed a White Rose, I detail my professional journey from New York City's projects to corporate America.

How does an immigrant born in an impoverished town in the Dominican Republic and raised in a New York City's public housing development wind up in a Fortune 5 corporation?

One day when we were in the South Bronx, my son was asked by someone who saw me walk into the building dressed in my business suit, "What does your mother do for a living?"

He responded, "She is a businesswoman at Mobil."

The person responded, "People like us do not get jobs like that."

Well, they do, and I did by not letting the naysayers get me down and by believing in myself and my abilities.

CHAPTER 29
THE END OF MY LIFE AS I KNEW IT

Throughout the years, my husband and I nurtured our love. We weathered storms, danced through seasons, and reveled in the simple joy of being together. Dancing and travel became the rhythm of our lives—a harmonious duet that echoed across continents and our kitchen alike.

As we planned the celebration of our 50th wedding anniversary, excitement bubbled within us. We were about to honor a magnificent tapestry—a labor of love woven with threads of commitment, shared memories, and cherished moments. Our children, grandchildren, and extended family would gather, and amidst laughter and tears, we'd celebrate the legacy we had created—a legacy that transcended time.

August 4, 2023, which marked the beginning of the end of my life as I knew it. The doctors diagnosed my Danilo with pancreatic cancer and gave him six to eight months to live.

We were both in shock, trying to come to terms with the fact that our lives would never be the same. The days seemed to blur together as we navigated through the whirlwind of doctors' appointments, treatment plans, and emotional turmoil.

As we digested the finality of the diagnosis, Danilo was afraid at the prospect of dying. I was delicately trying to appease him but to no avail.

I often shared with him my views on the afterlife, astral travel, celestial beings, and other mystical subjects. While he would listen, he seemed skeptical of these concepts. However, one morning in 2022, he awoke with a sense of wonder and excitedly said to me, "Blanca, I went to the other side last night. It was so peaceful. I saw my parents and friends and it felt so good to be there. I now understand what you have been telling me about the other side and soul travel. I was there." After sharing this profound experience, we moved on from the topic and never mentioned it again.

Early September 2023 as I was driving to the hospital in tears feeling helpless, not knowing what I could do to help him. I suddenly remembered that conversation from the prior year and knew that I had to remind him.

When I got to the hospital, I said to him, "Do you remember that dream that you told me about where your soul traveled to the other side? How it felt to be there, and that there was nothing to fear about going there. That was to prepare for this experience so that you wouldn't be scared." After we had that conversation, his attitude changed. He was no longer afraid and accepted his fate with courage.

As the months passed, we clung to each other for support, finding solace in the small moments of normalcy amidst the chaos. We tried to make the most of the time we had left together, cherishing every moment, never leaving one another's side.

Despite the overwhelming sadness that consumed us, we found moments of hope and strength in each other. We faced the challenges ahead with courage and resilience, determined to make the most of the time we had left.

As the days turned into weeks and the weeks turned into months, we found joy in the simple things, treasuring every smile, every laugh, every I love you, and every moment of peace we shared in the confinement of our home.

During the final two weeks of his life, Danilo talked about visions of his mother and other deceased loved ones, which provided profound comfort. He seemed to be very comforted by his mother's presence as he spoke with her telling her that he was depending on her to guide him in this journey. The communication with his mother helped Danilo approach the end of his life on earth with a level of acceptance that surprised many of his family members.

Danilo had always said that he wanted to die before me and when the time came, he wanted it to be just the two of us. The day before he passed Hospice had told us he would pass within the next 24 hours. His three sons and one of their wives were in the room. At about 11:00 p.m., I told everyone to go home get a good night's sleep and come back the next day. After they left, I said to him, "Everyone is gone now. It's just the two of us now, just like you wanted. Please let me know when it's time. Don't leave without saying goodbye."

As some cancer patients approach death, breathing patterns can change and secretions may collect in the throat. This creates a rattling sound known as the death rattle. It is a part of the dying process.

While the sound is unpleasant, the person emitting the death rattle usually feels no pain or discomfort. The death rattle signals that death is near. On average, a person usually lives for approximately 24 hours after the death rattle and the dying process begins.

I lay down by his side, holding his hand. Despite the loud sound of the death rattle, I dozed off. I don't know for sure what alerted me. I thought I detected a difference in the rattle and awakened at about 6:15 a.m. Somehow, he found a way to make sure I was awake and present when he took his last breath.

On January 29, 2024, at 6:35 a.m. my lifelong partner and best friend of 52 years departed from this world, creating an irreplaceable void in my heart. The profound sorrow I was feeling rendered my heart speechless, unable to express itself. The echoes of my husband's existence remain in my soul, reverberating in my chest every time I think of him.

Amid my grief, I found solace in the love we shared and the memories we created together. And though my life had taken an unexpected turn, I knew I would always carry his spirit with me, guiding me through the darkness and reminding me of the strength we had found in each other.

I am grateful for the years filled with heartfelt and unwavering love, along with the deep respect we held for each other. Together, we shed tears and reveled in the happiness and laughter that define a lifetime. Disagreements between us were infrequent, and when they occurred, they were petty quarrels over insignificant issues that quickly faded away, leaving behind no resentment or silent treatment. I will always cherish the memories of the little things and precious moments that made up our 52-year journey together.

When Danilo passed away, I felt disoriented. I had spent eight months nursing him and sitting by his bedside as he battled pancreatic cancer, disengaging from all other activities. After his death and dealing with final arrangements, I felt like a blank page with no direction, unsure of what I should be doing. I had no clue what the future had in store for me without my lifelong partner and best friend by my side.

His death marked a significant turning point, the final chapter of my life on earth with Danilo. Yet, I was confident that our bond would persist in a spiritual form. The bonds we share with our loved ones does not end with their death; they simply transform. Maintaining a positive connection beyond death is vital for the well-being of souls on both sides of the curtain of life on earth and the other side. I conveyed this belief, which brought great solace to Danilo in his final days. He would often tell me, "I will always be by your side and will be waiting for you on the other side, but you better not show up with another guy."

My partner's absence left me grappling with a mix of emotions - grief, confusion, and a sense of loss. I felt adrift and unsure of how to move forward without him by my side as his absence upended my life, causing the routine and familiarity of my life to disappear. I felt like a part of me was missing, and I struggled to envision a future without him. For example, we shared a deep connection through our travels to many different countries and the mere thought of boarding an airplane without him evoked powerful emotions.

There was no place I wanted to go and confined myself to our bedroom in an intentional search for solitude. I reduced my life to the simple things: reading, writing, watching Lifetime movies, and sleeping a lot. I'd spend days in my bedroom, as it was my sanctuary where I had spent quality time with him. Being in that room comforted me, as his presence was still palpable. I only ventured out of my bedroom to the kitchen to get something to eat.

Although I looked forward to talking to friends and family from time to time, I avoided meeting anyone, because I wanted to be alone in that kind of hermetic bubble I had created solely and exclusively for myself and my spiritual connection with Danilo. I did not want to know what was going on outside of my little bubble whether it was some else's personal drama or national drama on the news.

Intentionally isolating myself, creating a cocoon of solitude where the outside world would only intrude when I gave it permission to do so. I recognized that even as I secluded myself in my own isolated world, life continued to unfold. The world spins, seasons change, and stories unfold. As I was in hibernation, winter gave way to spring, and spring blossomed into summer, yet I stayed within my cocoon. Nevertheless, I recognized the need to reconnect gradually with the rest of the world. Peeking from the confines of my cocoon, I began to explore the world that had continued to evolve outside my secluded haven.

As I navigated the practicalities of life without him, I also had to come to terms with the emotional void his absence had left behind. Memories of our time together flooded my mind, both comforting and painful in their reminder of what I had lost.

Amid this uncertainty, I recognized that it was essential to reinvent myself and my existence in his absence. It became imperative for me to discover the new direction my journey should take now that I was on my own. It was a daunting task, but I knew I had to move forward, to honor his memory while also carrying on my own with my destiny for part two of my life. It was going to be a journey of self-discovery and healing, one that would ultimately lead me to a place of acceptance and peace.

PART V
FROM THE PROJECTS BLOSSOMED A WHITE ROSE

MY PROFESSIONAL JOURNEY

CHAPTER 30
TAKING THE GIRL OUT OF THE PROJECTS

For the most part, I spent the first eighteen years of my life in a predominantly Spanish-speaking environment within our slice of the Big Apple. We spoke Spanish at home, and most of the kids from my elementary and high school, the local businesses, and my circle of friends were of Hispanic descent. I had little to no exposure to other cultures.

I did not recognize the deficiencies in my lack of cultural diversity, communication, and social etiquette until I ventured into the professional working world of Midtown Manhattan. Granted, Midtown Manhattan is a world with a culture of its own. However, despite some similarities with my coworkers, I had missed a lot in translation. I quickly understood that I had a lot of catching up to do.

I attended an all-girls vocational public high school, which trained us in a trade that enabled us to enter the job market upon graduation. Our school had four trades to choose from: nursing, dental assistant, cosmetology, or business. I chose the business program.

After high school, I entered a nine-month co-op secretarial program, which was an excellent way to ease into the professional world of Midtown Manhattan. The program allowed me to attend school half the time and work the other half at the Marine Midland Bank's corporate office.

The secretarial co-op program focused on teaching students how to dress and behave professionally in an office setting—something I desperately needed. We were required to wear skirts, something I—Blanca, the tomboy—did not even own. My attire during my teen years was strictly jeans and sneakers.

I had excellent hands-on skills, typing 120 words per minute, taking dictation at approximately 140 words per minute, and understanding the protocols of crafting, developing, and producing business communication. I did exceptionally well in the classroom environment, but I failed miserably at my first corporate job. I was way out of my league.

In high school, they had taught us to master typing skills and the art of shorthand, but they had failed to educate us about the soft skills required to succeed: dress code, office politics, business phone etiquette, and other professional protocols.

When I think back to the group that graduated with me, few, if any, were ready to enter the workforce. We were rough around the edges.

After the completion of the co-op program, Marine Midland did not offer me a job. At the time, I did not fully understand why. I later recognized that the bank was looking for someone a bit more sophisticated. They recognized that I was not ready for the corporate environment. When I completed the secretarial school program, I was a tad bit more refined, but I still had a long, long way to go.

Fortunately, the secretarial school had a job placement program, and in June 1976, I got a job with a law firm in Midtown Manhattan that specialized in corporate litigation. The law firm was not looking for finesse; they were looking for someone with above-average intelligence who could type, take dictation, and file.

Amazingly, life has a way of directing our steps in such a way that we end up exactly where we need to be at each stage of our lives. The environment at the law firm was conducive to polishing some of the rough edges without being judgmental.

The law firm took the girl out of the projects, but it was extremely difficult to take the projects out of the girl. Unlearning the behaviors of eighteen years does not happen overnight. Behavior modification is a long, continuous, and arduous journey that may or may not fully eradicate those learned behaviors.

The behaviors, emotional reactions, and experiences I learned during the first eighteen years of my life became part of my personality. They are a subconscious part of who I am. It was the armor that protected me and helped me cope and survive in my environment.

These behaviors lay dormant in my subconscious as part of my personality, resurfacing when I feel threatened. There is a trace of that "old me" hidden deep in my subconscious. That "old me" resurfaces when some external event wakes it up and brings it forward. I've tended to fall back to familiar behavior when threatened, which, in many cases, has tended to be an overreaction.

When I started working in Midtown Manhattan, I was yet again thrust into a new world—an unfamiliar environment—that I did not know how to navigate. I did not understand the language or culture. I had to rely on my intuition to guide me.

When I lived in the projects, everyone was the same. I understood the environment and where I fit in. But, when I entered the professional working world, I saw the differences in speech, custom, and culture. At first, I was baffled, unsure of what to do. But as time passed, I started acclimating to the new environment.

Through the daily interactions with my coworkers, who had grown up in middle- to upper-middle-class environments, I gradually started shifting my perspective on social etiquette and professional behavior. I had to retrain my brain to think, speak, and react to situations. It was a long process, and I made many mistakes along the way.

The more educated I became, and the more time I spent in the professional world, the further I shifted from my culture. I was drifting from my roots and the people I'd grown up with, feeling as though I did not belong in either world. I did not have the same background as the people I was working with, while I also felt like I had less in common with the people with whom I identified. I became a part-time participant of two distinct worlds as I conducted day-to-day activities.

I had become a different person through the experiences of rejection and the clashing of cultures. I even struggled with my native language, as the ability to formulate a sentence in Spanish became harder.

Attempting to fit into an ethnic peer group, social networks, and familial relationships can be extremely difficult as one delicately straddles the traditions, values, and beliefs between the two worlds.

CHAPTER 31

FROM THE PROJECTS BLOSSOMED A WHITE ROSE

In 1982, I embarked on a journey, leaving the familiar environment of the law firm to venture into the immense world of Mobil Oil Corporation (Mobil). I had been married for seven years, had three young children, and was still working on my undergraduate degree at Pace University.

Leaving the law firm was another major decision that Danilo, friends, and family did not support. They were concerned that I was making a mistake by walking away from the security of a well-paying job for one that was not only paying less money but also required a six-month probationary period.

The concept of taking a short-term loss to get a long-term gain was foreign to my working-class friends and family. They could not understand that I had a vision of a corporate career. I could not blame them for not understanding since I had no tangible evidence that this vision would materialize. In their view, this vision was preposterous and unattainable, as we were working-class people. I should have been happy and satisfied with my job at the law firm.

I was grateful for the job security offered by the law firm, but the reason I had been working on my undergraduate degree was to pursue a corporate career. My intuition told me to disagree respectfully with my friends and family and follow that vision. There were no guarantees, but somehow, I was confident that this was the right time to move.

The six years I spent at the law firm were my formative years. During that time, I had polished some of the rough edges and learned some of the social skills required in the professional environment.

Leaving the law firm was difficult as the office had been my home away from home, and the people had become part of my extended family. I had started working there at the young age of nineteen—naïve, childless, and rough around the edges. I left at the age of twenty-five, much more poised and refined, and the mother of three children. I still had some maturing and polishing to achieve, but my smarts, skills, work ethic, and talents compensated for my lack of tact.

Leaving the law firm was a significant turning point in my life. Like the little bird that ultimately had to leave its nest and venture into the world on its own, I was going to explore how high I could soar.

The difference between the corporate environment and a small business is like night and day.

The law firm had fewer than thirty employees. It offered a nurturing, familial environment. It was a fast-paced environment, where I was involved in a variety of projects and gained well-rounded experience. I was much more than a legal secretary as I was required to provide a wide range of secretarial, administrative, and office management duties.

The corporate environment, on the other hand, was immense and impersonal, and its inner workings eluded me. Initially, I was not sure this bureaucratic environment was for me. Fortunately, the law firm had left its doors open for me. I always had the option to go back if the job with Mobil did not work out.

Besides the differences between the two environments and culture, the duties required were as stark. Accustomed to the intellectual stimulation of the work at the law firm, I found the secretarial job with

Mobil quite dull. It consisted of typing short telexes, delivering mail, and running some personal errands for the manager. Yuck!

Still, having a less demanding full-time job offered a few benefits. One advantage was being able to do my schoolwork during the day. In this position, I could complete my work and help the other secretaries with their work in a matter of hours.

One other significant advantage was the tuition reimbursement offered by the corporation, which eased the financial burden of tuition. This corporate benefit enabled me to take as many classes as I could handle instead of only enrolling for the classes I could afford.

Despite the benefits, my corporate experience with Mobil had a rocky start. Once again, the universe was testing my resolve. Besides struggling with balancing a budget, taking care of a family, and being a part-time college student, I was assigned to work for a less-than-supportive, emotionally abusive, mean-spirited, anal-retentive boss.

He was an exasperating and verbally abusive individual. He was a bully, and one did not know when he was going to blow up. On more than one occasion, I saw people walking out of his office in tears. From what I could surmise, senior management was aware of his abusive behavior and did nothing about it. They rewarded him with one promotion after another.

I hated that manager. It was an intense hatred, unlike anything that I had ever experienced in my life. The kind of hatred that eats away at you and the venom it releases most likely destroys your insides. I had to deal with this person daily, and his cruel behavior reinforced that hatred.

I even fantasized about getting one of the guys from the old neighborhood to teach him a lesson—street justice. Of course, I was able to control that girl from the projects, as logic prevailed, and he remained unharmed. But he was such a bully that it was fun to think of someone putting him in his place for once in his life. Instead, in a passive-aggressive way, I found different ways to get back at him.

One of the personal errands required of the secretaries was to do a coffee run. This manager liked to eat a bialy, which is a yeast roll similar to a bagel. Not only did I pick the one that looked the most pathetic, but I waited till the last minute possible to get his bialy. Petty, I know, but sometimes it's the little things that make for a pleasant day.

Not that I was a shrinking violet. If he pushed me, I pushed back harder. Respect goes both ways, and he did not deserve my respect. I'd go toe to toe with him. He was not accustomed to anyone standing up to him, especially a low-level underling who had recently walked through the door, such as myself. He hated that I dared to defend myself and that I would not let him break my spirit and resolve.

Most of the people who worked for him shrank away in fear ignoring his angry outbursts as he berated them. He knew that they would not retaliate for fear of losing their jobs, especially those shackled by the golden handcuffs of the corporation. Golden handcuffs are the financial benefits an employee would lose by leaving a corporation before a certain age or agreed period of time.

He once said to me, "You are wasting your time by working on your undergraduate degree and thinking that you are going to go up even one rung of this company's corporate ladder. I will make sure that no one in this company touches you with a ten-foot pole."

I confidently replied, "This company is not the only one hiring."

He looked at me with disdain and bewilderment in his eyes. He did not know what to make of that girl from the projects who came out swinging and was not afraid to lose her job.

He constantly threatened me with losing my job, stating that I would not make it past the first six months. The quality of my work was not the issue; it was that I dared to stand up to him and not tolerate his abusive behavior.

During those moments, the words of my friends and family reverberated in my mind, as I questioned my decision to leave the law firm. Based on my boss' feedback, I was going to be unemployed in a matter of months.

It was fortunate for me and my sanity that this horrendous situation lasted a little less than six months, as senior management promoted the abusive manager to his next assignment of terror. However, before he left our department, he recommended my termination at the end of the six-month probationary period.

I do not know what he told the manager who replaced him, but I had a distinct impression that the man was apprehensive as I introduced myself. Whatever he had said to the new manager did not work. The new manager of our department and I worked well together. He was extremely impressed with my skills and work ethic. He became my most ardent supporter, advocate, and informal mentor.

After the six-month probationary period, with the unwavering support of my manager, I became an official employee of Mobil. The dark cloud that had followed me suddenly dissipated.

Once I became a permanent employee, my goal was to move out of the secretarial job and into one of the contract administration positions. My understanding was that this type of move was not commonplace, especially for a secretary and someone new to the organization. I could honestly have retired ten years earlier if I had a dime for each time someone said that I was wasting my time by working toward my bachelor's degree.

Many of the other secretaries claimed that the company would not recognize a part-time university degree or allow me to move out of a secretarial position. They continued to drill into me that secretaries did not move into staff positions. The only move for secretaries was within the secretarial realm. Some claimed to be living proof as they had obtained their undergraduate degrees and were still within the secretarial hierarchy.

Fortunately, I was ignorant of the inner workings of the corporation and did not let their claims discourage me. I could not assess my possibilities for succeeding in the corporate environment based on the organization's mindset or those around me who had tried and failed. Maybe those who had failed were not as motivated as I was to succeed.

While they were busy naysaying, I was quietly working toward my goal. Why not? I had nothing to lose. I recognized that it was not going to be easy, but I was determined to put in the time required to get ahead in this corporate environment.

The group I supported was understaffed, and the analysts did not have sufficient time to run the required economics and spreadsheets.

I took full advantage of this deficiency by volunteering to help, which permitted me to start learning the business.

I started by simply entering data into the spreadsheets for the monthly economic report. Soon I had learned enough to support the group in running the actual economics and was no longer simply entering data. I took the time to understand and learn the logic and fundamentals behind the numbers. I became so proficient at developing the economics that I was soon running the economics and developing the written reports myself. The operations analyst was reviewing and signing off on the final report.

My efforts did not go unnoticed by my department manager. He was so impressed by my ability to perform duties assigned to analysts at a much higher level, that he lobbied to move me out of the secretarial job. He advocated that the corporation was not capitalizing on my skills and talents by keeping me in a secretarial position.

After two years, with a lot of hard work, determination, and a powerful mentor, I was promoted to the administration group as a contract documentation specialist, responsible for preparing contracts and other documentation associated with each cargo of crude oil.

I had accomplished what many had said was impossible: a promotion out of the secretarial realm and into an administrative staff position. My informal education and hard work were already working for me. A two-group promotion from a secretarial position and into the administration group was rare, and it was a significant milestone for me. As Alan Cohen once said, *"Blessed are those who are so naïve that they do not know what they cannot do."*

Ignorance is indeed bliss. Some say that information is power, but sometimes it is better not to have too much information. My colleagues had institutional knowledge that blinded them from entertaining a different trajectory for their career paths. I, on the other hand, trusted my inner guidance more than the external opinions of my colleagues.

The promotion was significant for other secretaries as well. My promotion out of the secretarial realm gave others the courage to apply for entry-level positions. I had set a precedent and became a trailblazer. As a result, management was inclined to allow others to showcase their talents. After my promotion, many others followed.

I am not implying that in the history of Mobil they hadn't ever promoted anyone out of the secretarial realm. But there were no recent examples to point to nor was it commonplace to be promoted outside of the secretarial hierarchy.

Nothing in my background had prepared me for a job in corporate America. Having grown up in a humble working-class environment, I entered the professional world with little to no knowledge of corporate etiquette and its unwritten rules. As I looked around our corporation, there were no role models, there was no one to emulate, and there was no one who looked like me or had a similar background.

Mobil had a defined career path and fancy paperwork for different groups of employees, such as women, African Americans, those recruited from Ivy League schools and other MBA programs. However, there was no career path or plan for someone who had started as a secretary with a part-time university degree.

With no one to offer advice on the dos and don'ts of navigating the corporate maze, I had to rely on my ability to sense the right path through trial and error, making a lot of mistakes along the way. Some of those mistakes cost me some career moves, and others I was able to overcome.

To carve a niche for myself, I had to have the guts to pursue what I wanted, following my instincts and intuition to forge my path and guide me through the corporate maze. I had to remain vigilant of opportunities that I could seize and capitalize. I had to exhibit the courage to put myself out there by networking and getting to know people so that they could get to know me and my abilities. And occasionally, I had to have the courage to request a meeting with a senior manager to let them know of my abilities and desire to progress my career within supply and trading.

I spent the first ten years of my corporate career paying my dues and learning as much as I could about the energy business. From 1982 to 1992, most of the positions I held within the administration group were clerical and, although not sufficiently challenging, served as excellent venues for learning the fundamentals of the energy industry.

It did not matter to me that some assignments were not glorious; some were quite mundane, but I believed that even the slightest action within each assignment was educating and propelling me forward toward the next position and plateau.

My modus operandi was to be consistent in my performance, work on increasing my responsibilities by mastering and capitalizing on each assignment and learning and thoroughly understand the fundamentals and priorities of our business.

Career opportunities within large corporations are boundless. A large corporation affords you the ability to learn, grow, and expand your horizons, all within the same company. Every time I moved up to the next level or into a different department, there was always a new culture and lingo to learn. Though it was the same company, the differences in the customs, mindsets, and focuses of the different groups never ceased to amaze me.

My new goal, moving into the supply and trading group, was not a common occurrence. Plenty of people said it was impossible, especially for someone from the administration group. Unfortunately, the group had a reputation of not being sufficiently professional.

The supply and trading jobs were considered the threshold of the professional level within our organization, a springboard for higher-level positions. They were reserved for MBA graduates from the top business schools in the US, highflyers on overseas assignments, and others who had been in the industry for many years.

In the early '90s, Mobil had a hiring freeze, and I was one of the beneficiaries of that policy. The networking I had been doing paid off, and in 1992, when a position opened up in supply operations, I was promoted out of the administration group and into supply and trading. The supply operations position was challenging, but I loved every minute of that stressful job, which brought with it a whole new set of challenges and opportunities.

When given the opportunity to work in the supply and trading group, I was elated. This group was extremely competitive with a 'sink-or-swim' and 'every-man-for-himself' attitude. This assignment was a significant test of my abilities. It was time to put up or shut up.

My elation did not last as I immediately started comparing myself to those around me. I felt less confident about my ability to do the job and compete with others. My cultural background, coupled with only three years of part-time graduate work from Pace University, I felt inadequate around the MBA graduates from the top business schools in the US: Wharton, Duke, Harvard, and Cornell.

I allowed the people around me, and the luster of their credentials, affect my self-esteem and confidence in my ability to engage. Nevertheless, I continued to plug along, staying focused on my goal.

My lack of confidence did not last long, as I noticed that some of the Ivy League MBA graduates could not cope in the stressful, competitive trading room environment. Some did not have the killer instinct required to survive in that dog-eat-dog environment.

They had Wharton, Duke, Harvard, and Cornell; and I had Pace University, ten years of experience in the industry, a killer instinct, and all the lessons I had learned from my humble beginnings, which had heightened my intuition and survival skills.

After the supply operations position, I went on to a crude oil trading job and then to a business development position.

Despite starting my career with so many obstacles, I made significant strides within the company from 1982 to 2000. I had been promoted ten salary groups in eighteen years. I had moved from one professional group to the next, excelling each step of the way.

I had that rocket in my pocket. But little did I know that sometime between 1999 and 2000, during one of my trips abroad, I had dropped the rocket somewhere over the Atlantic Ocean. My career with Mobil was fantastic; after the merger, it moved to not looking too good to bad to worse and, finally—as my grandson would say—to "the worstest."

In late 1999, Mobil merged with Exxon, and the merged company became ExxonMobil. The merger marked the end of the Mobil era. During the transition, many of Exxon's senior management and employees moved into Mobil's headquarters.

To me, it felt as if we had sold our home while continuing to live in the guest room. We no longer had any say on the how, when, and where of the management of the company. It was a strange feeling and a confusing and emotional time in our lives, as the cultures of the two companies were dramatically different. One could argue that they were polar opposites.

It became clear early on that this was no merger. It was quite clear who was calling the shots and which of the two cultures was going to dominate. Formally speaking, Mobil had been bought out by Exxon. Calling it a merger was much more palatable to those involved.

Besides the impact of the new culture, there were many unknowns about the organizational structure, the company's business strategies, operating practices, routines, roles, and responsibilities. The stress level was at an all-time high, and morale at an all-time low. Many employees lost their sense of purpose, self-esteem, credibility, and security. On top of those uncertainties, we were required to interview for our positions.

From 1997 to 1999, I had been the business development manager for Latin America in the Mobil aviation group. The learning curve was steep, but I honestly enjoyed the creativity and autonomy the job offered. The one challenge was the cultural mantra of Latin America.

During the '80s and '90s, the energy industry as a whole was predominantly male-dominated, and this was especially apparent in Latin America, where machismo dominates the culture. Most of the companies I was negotiating with were State-owned, and my counterparts were all male. When in negotiations, not once did I ever sit across the table from another woman. The only women I encountered were low-level staff—employees, secretaries, or cleaning ladies.

On the surface, gender roles and attitudes toward Latin women were clear and straightforward: A woman's place is in the home. It was apparent to me that many of the men I encountered did not feel comfortable with my role as a representative for a major US energy corporation.

Because I'm of Latin descent, many of the men assumed that I knew and understood the Latin culture, including a woman's rightful place in it. They used my heritage as a license to be disrespectful and make inappropriate comments and sexual innuendos. I have to admit that, at first, I was not sure how to handle this behavior. My male colleagues in the US never treated me with such disrespect.

I let the comments go the first couple of times. After the third time, inappropriate comments were made, I realized I had to put an end to this behavior. During one of our afternoon meetings, my first agenda item was sexual harassment. I opened our meeting with, "Let's get the sexual harassment out of the way so we can have a productive meeting without having to stop for foolish and inappropriate comments. I am sure that if I were not a Latina, you would not dare behave this way, for fear of reprisal." As I looked around the conference room table, waiting for someone to make the first comment, no one said a word. Everyone just kept looking down at their notes. Thankfully, that was the last time I had to deal with the harassment and innuendoes.

One other time, a senior person from a Latin American company speculated on how much money the company would pay for my release if I were kidnapped. During that era, kidnappings were prevalent in Latin America. My intuition told me he was not kidding. The entire encounter gave me chills and left me feeling extremely uncomfortable.

Despite some challenges, my experience as a business development manager for the aviation group was a rewarding one. As such, I advocated for and looked forward to another business development position with the merged company.

After several interviews, in January 2000, I was assigned a business development position responsible for the Latin American portfolio—the job I wanted. But you know what the adage says: be careful what you ask for because you might get it.

I failed to recognize the risk of venturing into new territory within a new company with new managers. For those of us brave enough to take the plunge, it meant starting our careers anew, as we had no history with the merged company.

About nine months after starting the business development for Latin America position, I was reassigned to manage the US portfolio. Transitioning the business from our Latin American affiliates to headquarters was intense. It meant understanding the salient aspects of each deal amid negotiations.

While managing the Latin American portfolio, I had traveled approximately 70 percent of the time, with a grueling workload. That year had been the hardest I had worked in my entire life. I'm not sure how long I could have kept up that routine without affecting my health.

After I completed the transition, management reassigned the Latin American portfolio to someone else, receiving zero credit for the grueling workload and schedule of the previous nine months. The reassignment blindsided me. Maybe I made too much of that reassignment, but to me, it was like being fired. Nothing like it had ever happened to me, and the worst part was that I was not told the *why* of the reassignment. I think I was entitled to a little hostility.

It wasn't so much the reassignment. It was the way our management handled it. It was as if they were moving pieces of furniture from one side of the room to the other without stopping to take into consideration the impact on those involved in the shift. The entire situation was shrouded in secrecy, with no explanations. The decision was final; case closed. I spent a lot of time trying to figure out and understand management's intentions and motives.

During this period, the corporation was evaluating and ranking the employees of the newly merged company, selecting those to be further developed and groomed for upward mobility.

In the corporate environment, this type of experience is exceedingly difficult to remedy, especially in a new company with new management evaluating my performance. There was nothing I could do or say to influence the outcome.

The business development job was the one I had advocated for, but the management structure of the group, coupled with the stress of getting a new organization up and running, was fertile ground for misinterpretations and frustrations for all. It was one of the most frustrating environments I've ever had to contend with in my career.

I consider myself a strong person who is not easily rattled or offended. But the management structure and the growing pains of the merged company broke my spirit and resolve. The domineering, paternalistic, and stifling management style of the new culture was extremely difficult and not conducive to a healthy work environment.

Within the Mobil environment, I was a well-known, highly respected professional with a career. Within the newly merged environment, I was an employee no one knew with a well-paying job. In effect, the ladder had been pulled out from under me. After eighteen years with the company and having made significant strides, I had to start over. It was a new beginning and another significant turning point in my career.

This oppressive environment suppressed my personal, professional, and career growth. I felt as if I were suffocating under the weight of the unnecessary pressure exerted by our management. I had to find a way to work my way out from under the oppression exerted by our management and reassert myself.

The one consolation was that this was a consensus; everyone in the group agreed that this management style stifled the creativity of the group with unnecessary stress and undue pressure.

Not wanting to go down without a fight, I challenged the misconceptions attributed to me by my manager. This manager had formulated an opinion without knowing me as a person or as an employee. No matter what I tried, there was no getting through to her. Once her mind was made up, or she had formulated an opinion, that was it. This decision—right, wrong, or indifferent—sealed my fate with the newly merged company. It is difficult to get ahead if you do not have a supportive management that believes in you and your abilities.

This new company was offering a job—a well-paying job—but I did not want to kid myself into believing I had a career. I had to reassess my aspirations of moving ahead because upward mobility at my level was reserved for a limited few. These were large and competitive rank groups, and any misstep, no matter how slight, could be detrimental or obliterate your chance of promotion. The higher up you go in an organization, the fewer the jobs and the fiercer the competition.

Corporations, like people, have distinct personalities. The culture of an organization is its personality, and its core values and beliefs can affect your career satisfaction and success. No amount of hard work and determination will help you get ahead if you are in the wrong corporate culture.

CHAPTER 32
A NEAR-MISS EXPERIENCE

By the summer of 2001, I had settled into the position of managing the US portfolio. Although my travel schedule was not at the 70 percent level like the previous year, I was still traveling two to three times per month.

As the business development manager for the US, I was required to fly to Los Angeles at least once per month. My preferred itinerary to Los Angeles was to take the first flight out, which was American Airlines Flight 77. This flight arrived into Los Angeles early enough on Pacific time to meet with my colleagues in the afternoon and prepare for any meetings scheduled for the following morning.

Although this had been my routine for months, each month, I found myself looking for an excuse not to go to California. This apprehension puzzled me, as I had done extensive travel for both personal and business reasons. I did not know what to make of my reluctance to fly. My unwillingness to fly only surfaced when it came time to travel to California.

At the time, I attributed the feeling to the five-hour flight to Los Angeles and ExxonMobil's travel policy, which required coach-class travel for domestic flights, regardless of distance. Before the merger, Mobil permitted business class for flights over three hours, whether domestic or international. As such, I associate my reluctance to fly to California with the change in policy.

During the week of September 3, 2001, the senior manager of our business development group walked into my office to discuss the possibility that I would be reassigned to another department by the end of the month. Given this information, I planned to complete any ongoing negotiations but defer any renegotiations of new contracts to the person who would replace me.

Taking full advantage of a legitimate excuse to cancel my travel plans to Los Angeles, I contacted my counterparts and confirmed that they had no problem with postponing the timing of our renegotiations. I waited until Friday, September 7, to cancel my scheduled trip to Los Angeles, California.

Many of us remember exactly where we were and what we were doing when we heard of the attacks on the twin towers of the World Trade Center in New York City on September 11, 2001. I was sitting in my office when I heard the news. I immediately walked over to our trading room, where the televisions were always on the news channel. I stood in the middle of the trading room, which was usually bustling with activity, among a crowd of colleagues frozen in place and silenced by the shock of the unfolding events.

As the American Airlines Boeing 767 crashed into the north tower around 8:45 a.m., I stood among my colleagues thinking, "This has to be a terrorist attack." As I continued to watch in horror and disbelief, a United Airlines Boeing 767 appeared on the screen and crashed into the south tower, approximately eighteen minutes after the north tower crash. At that time, I was certain this was a terrorist attack. We later witnessed in horror as the towers collapsed and thousands lost their lives before our eyes.

As millions of Americans watched the unfolding events on their televisions, an American Airlines Boeing 757 crashed into the west side of the Pentagon in Washington, DC.

If the senior manager of our group had not come into my office that afternoon to discuss the possibility of reassignment, I would have been on American Airlines Flight 77 on September 11, 2001, and part of the devastating inferno and rubble that killed 125 Pentagon employees plus the airline passengers.

When I first heard the newscast, I did not make an immediate connection, as it would not have taken a little over an hour for an airplane to get from Washington Dulles Airport to the Pentagon in Washington DC.

According to published reports, the airplane crashed into the western side of the Pentagon at 9:37 a.m. eastern time. Reports indicated that the aircraft left Washington Dulles Airport at 8:20 a.m., the hijacking occurred around 8:50 a.m., and the plane deviated from its normal flight path at approximately 8:54 a.m.

It wasn't until I heard the actual details that I finally made the connection. The airplane that crashed into the Pentagon was the same flight I took each month to travel to Los Angeles and the one I had canceled four days earlier. It took me a few weeks to get past the surreal feeling of disbelief and begin fully processing what had transpired. The magnitude of the unfolding events of the previous week did not immediately sink in.

Each time I had crossed the threshold and boarded American Airlines Flight 77, I had always had an ominous and foreboding feeling. It was like a warning of something to come, and I hadn't known what to make of it until the incident on September 11, 2001.

In addition to the foreboding feelings, the actions of the senior manager of our group, who was not my direct supervisor, were perplexing. I still can't explain it. At that time, there were two levels of management between us, and the responsibility for advising me of any potential career move rested with my direct supervisor, not the senior manager.

The senior manager of our group was a man that kept to himself and, for the most part, only interacted with his direct reports. It was entirely out of character for this senior manager to come into my office and sit at the conference table to discuss anything with me. Before that time, the most we had shared was mere pleasantries. So, when he came into my office that afternoon and sat down to talk to me about this potential move, I was surprised but did not give his actions any importance. He had the right to inform me of any possible reassignment.

My interaction with the senior manager was so strange and out of character that I didn't even share the conversation with my direct supervisor, whose policy involved not sharing information. She shared information on a need-to-know basis only, and, in her opinion, we usually did not need to know.

After I fully understood the events of September 11, I saw the discussion with the senior manager as divine intervention. Not only did I not move to the other department, but I also didn't hear another word about a potential move from anyone. Nor did I ask. At that point, it was irrelevant. It was the strangest thing.

In my view, the primary purpose of the conversation with the head of our unit had been to keep me off of the American Airlines flight on that fateful day. The universe had known that I would take any excuse presented to me to cancel my trip to California. Fortunately, I had listened to my intuition.

I had been receiving intuitive flashes of insight that had been warning me about something to come on this flight for months. Although I couldn't have predicted the events that transpired on September 11, the message had been clear that I needed to cancel my trip.

This insight had protected me, as it had encouraged me to stay away. Someone once said that "good instincts usually tell you what to do long before your head has figured it out." Sometimes, your intuition will deliver a message with words spoken through another person or situation, and you have to be able to decipher the clues.

Some might say it was not my time to go or explain it differently. But for me, this was divine intervention giving me the signals I needed to stay off of that fateful flight on September 11, 2001, through routine, daily workplace events that determined my fate.

A seemingly inconsequential decision to cancel a business trip made the difference between life and death for me.

CHAPTER 33
POSITIVE DISINTEGRATION

I had spent months wallowing in self-pity, doubting my abilities and worthiness, which had been a colossal waste of valuable time. But there's nothing like a near-miss experience to help you get some perspective on what's important in life.

I allowed self-pity to hold me hostage and blackmail me emotionally. This mindset did nothing for my personal or professional growth. The intriguing part was that this reaction was entirely out of character for me; I hadn't ever reacted in this manner before. It was the first time in my adult life I had let anyone break my spirit or let a situation define me as a person.

I genuinely believe that all our relationships and experiences play specific and pivotal roles in molding who we are and who we will be in the future. I learned a precious lesson from my relationship with this manager. I vowed not to allow anyone to break my spirit again.

That period was my dark night of the soul. My career, the one that had once given me comfort, support, and financial security, was being threatened by the unseen hand of fate. From my vantage point, I could not see where I would end up, so I fought the changes. As destiny forged a new path, I clung to the old. But here's the thing: the longer

I fought and tried to hold on to the old, the longer it took to embrace my new beginnings.

Humbled into acceptance, I stopped fighting my situation and faced the hard truths of my career. Destiny was keeping me in this job and this company. I sat back, stopped feeling sorry for myself, and waited to see what the future had in store for me.

I stopped to reflect on everything that I had to be thankful for, and the blessings outweighed this one devastating experience. I was grateful for everything I had accomplished.

The first eighteen years of my career were amazingly successful, with a long list of accomplishments. Also, I was thankful for my well-paying job with excellent benefits in such a highly respected corporation as ExxonMobil, which was so much more than many could claim.

At the time, I had been too angry to stop myself from judging the person and lashing out at the situation with knee-jerk hostility. Remember that girl from the projects? She came out swinging, and I'd had a hard time controlling her. Those defense mechanisms and behaviors I had learned while growing up in the projects had resurfaced and had not served me well.

I had not given the situation time to unfold, settle, and reveal its true insight and message. I had not taken the time to understand the bigger picture; didn't dig deeper to extract the lesson the situation had brought. I had let my emotions drive my responses, actions, and reactions. I had been reacting to the devastation and obliteration of my ego and self-esteem, not to the person who had been controlling my career.

If faced with this same situation today, I would put my ego and pride aside and not internalize or personalize the event. I would resist the temptation to go into victim mode and become a hostage to my hostility. Instead, I would try to get down to the *why* of the decision without wasting too much time rehashing the issue.

We shouldn't assume we always know why someone has done something, or why a particular decision has been made, especially in a large bureaucratic organization. People have their reasons for their behavior, and we can't jump to the conclusion that their actions are about us in particular.

At times, the politics and bureaucracy of a large organization dictate specific actions related to information we are not and never will be privy to, and we become collateral damage. There may be more significant issues that require resolutions, and specific actions may be required to ensure the desired conclusions. The reality is, in many cases, someone above you needed a scapegoat, and "tag, you're it."

Once I changed my mindset and attitude, my relationship with this manager began to improve for me. It wasn't an ideal situation, but we finally learned to respect and understand each other. There wasn't a formal apology, and I do not know for sure that one was warranted, but this manager acknowledging my strengths and abilities and adding that what had occurred early on was an "unfortunate situation" was good enough for me.

What we, at times, perceive as unfair, a roadblock or failure can at times be a blessing in disguise. Maybe this option was closed to me because I was meant to be doing something else, or to keep me from harm.

Nothing in life lasts forever, and in December 2001, we received the fantastic news that happy days were here again. The restructuring of our group's management was the best Christmas present I could have received. I was no longer angry or hostile, but somehow, I knew that restructuring was the best thing that could happen to my colleagues and me. Because of the restructuring, we reported directly to the senior manager of the group. The same one that had saved my life earlier that year.

Working directly for the decision-maker of our group was a turning point in lifting the dark cloud that had been hanging over me. The first thing I did was ask to have a few minutes of our manager's time. I asked that he view this as a new start for me. I requested the opportunity to prove what I could bring to the table. It was an open and genuine dialogue, and I was glad that he was receptive.

Unfortunately, the knee-jerk reaction of that girl from the projects and my manager's uninformed assessment had done a lot of damage to my career. It would take a long time and a lot of effort to restore and repair the damage from my self-inflicted wounds and the initial unfavorable assessment and evaluation submitted by this manager.

It took another two years to get past that "unfortunate situation." During the first year's evaluation, my manager said, "I see a vast improvement in your performance."

Although that girl from the projects was tempted to comment, this time, I was able to control her. I bit my tongue and said, "Thank you." The following year, during the second performance review, he was extremely complimentary and had nothing but glowing reports and feedback on my performance.

There are pivotal moments where the actions or words of a person have an immense impact on our lives. That feedback was one of those moments for me, as I had been vindicated, valued, and recognized. I had finally recovered physically and emotionally from the severe blow that had shattered my ego and my self-esteem and had left me feeling helpless and useless.

I now recognized and could identify with the person who had received the evaluation. I had regained my direction and my sense of self. I no longer had to mourn the loss of my career. I could now start making plans and hoping for a better and brighter future with the new company.

October 7, 2003, marked a new beginning for me. I had regained my confidence and emerged from that dark period a stronger and more confident person. I underwent a metamorphosis, during which I shed any insecurities and doubts about my abilities. I emerged feeling equal to everyone around me, even the Ivy League MBA graduates. I believed I was contributing as much and, in some cases, even more than some of the people around me.

My initial reaction was to judge and resist the change in my career path, as I perceived it as the deterioration of my career. But with the benefit of hindsight, I recognized that the disintegration of my career was necessary to make way for a new, positive path. It was destiny's way of pushing me in a different direction.

All of this turmoil was occurring at the same time that I was going through the divorce and getting to know myself as Blanca De La Rosa. My personal and professional lives were going through major transformations.

My career took on a whole new dimension and focus. My work became extremely rewarding and prepared me for the next phase of my life. I had to let go of the old model of what I "was" to prepare for who I would "become."

Though I still worked in the business development group, I spent much of my time mentoring. I ran for office within the company and served as vice president and then president of our employee resource group (ERG) for Latinos, which completely changed my focus and direction within the company.

As part of the leadership team of ExxonMobil's Latino ERG, I represented our company at universities and high school campuses promoting the company's commitment to diversity and higher education within the math and science fields.

My involvement with the ERG afforded me ample opportunity to give back and to pay it forward. I selflessly gave my time and wisdom to make a positive difference in the lives of people who could learn from my experience.

After thirty-four years in the industry, my most rewarding role was serving as a mentor to the young men and women in our company—guiding them through the corporate maze.

The dissolution of my career was life's way of pointing me in a different direction. I had mourned the loss of my long-held career. But in life, we are not always privy to why a situation falls apart or when it has played out its purpose in our life's journeys. Many times, the old has to be undone to clear the way for the new. I had to honor the dissolution of my career as I knew it to make way for new beginnings.

Once I learned to redefine what success meant to me, I could then move on to enjoy a fruitful career. I used to define success by the number of promotions I was getting, perceiving a lack of promotions as unsuccessful. I was basing my success on the conventional definition of being promoted every two years instead of defining it for myself.

The positive disintegration of my career taught me that my career was not defined by where I ended up. My career was a journey that would be assessed by my integrity, the people I met and inspired to reach their full potential, and the lessons and values I extracted from my experiences. Those lessons brought me full circle, making me the person I am today.

The journey of my career was defined by my choices, actions, reactions, and inactions, considering the opportunities and challenges I encountered.

The greatest lesson I extracted from the positive disintegration of my career was that, at its core, my career success was really about my self-evaluation, my sense of accomplishment, and my ability to define success for myself rather than clinging to some false definition dictated by those in the corporate environment.

Throughout my thirty-four-year career, I experienced my share of ups and downs, but the ups far outnumbered the downs. I had broken down the barriers that prevented a secretary from moving up to the administration group, jumped the hurdles that existed between administration and supply operations, and cleared the obstacles that existed between supply operations and crude oil trading, and trading and business development.

The many colleagues who shared my journey, and their support and friendship throughout the years, contributed to the success of my career. It was an honor to have worked with true professionals.

My career was a rewarding and amazing experience—an unimaginable corporate career—that started as a secretary with Mobil and culminated as a business development project manager at ExxonMobil, one of the most prestigious corporations in the US.

EPILOGUE

CHAPTER 34

IN PURSUIT OF A BETTER TOMORROW

What would you give up today for a better tomorrow? Would you give up your car, home, money, or career? Would you risk your life in pursuit of a better tomorrow?

Many individuals give up the only world they know to give their families a better tomorrow. They exchange family and friends for a lonely existence in a new world. Many put themselves and their families in harm's way by embarking on treacherous trips. They risk their lives to escape situations in their homelands that they perceive as much more dangerous than the trip itself.

Most immigrants pursue the basic needs many of us take for granted, such as safety, food, and shelter. They seek a better and safer life for themselves and their families and to accomplish what they would or could not attain in their homeland.

In 1492, Christopher Columbus started a process of migration that changed the face of the West. For over 200 years, over 750,000 Spaniards immigrated to the New World, and this influence reshaped the Western Hemisphere. The West became a land of immigrants, with the indigenous population as the only natives.

For centuries, people from other nations have been drawn to the US, the land of opportunity where anything is possible, in pursuit of a better tomorrow. All of those groups have contributed to the United States' success and diversity. For many years, the US has been slowly evolving into a multicultural and multireligious nation. The America of today is multi-racial, and the cultural influence of the various ethnic groups is experienced from shore to shore.

Our family emigrated from the Dominican Republic to New York City in 1963. We were fortunate to have gotten visas and green cards and traveled by airplane to enter the US.

Many others are not as fortunate. To escape the situations in their home countries, they employ people smugglers (known as coyotes) who promise safe passage into the US in exchange for a fee of approximately $3,000 to $4,000 per person. In reality, for some, the trip involves walking long distances in the hot, bleak, and desolate desert. Many of those attempting the trip die in their pursuit of a better tomorrow.

Other migrants gamble their lives at sea in rickety cobbled-together boats filled with too many migrants and too few supplies. Many do not make it to shore.

Because of the difficulty and expense of the journey, whether it is by crossing the desert, sea, or land in a smuggling truck, it is not an easy one, as it can be dangerous and deadly. In addition to contending with the elements, some migrants must deal with unscrupulous coyotes that physically and sexually abuse the migrants. The coyotes then extort family members, forcing them to pay a ransom for the migrant's release.

Once in the US, immigrants opt to live in communities with others from their native countries, or those who speak their same language, while adapting to the lifestyles of a new culture and language. The familiarity of custom offers a sense of security by providing the services, manners, and the native tongue of the old country while diminishing the likelihood of stumbling linguistically and culturally.

Despite a supportive community, the adaptation process can still be arduous, as immigrants must navigate educational challenges along with the psychosocial consequences that emerge as they struggle to learn a new language and fit into a new community.

In the search to discover a new identity without compromising the values of the old world, immigrants continually balance two worlds. As they struggle to learn the new language and culture, they delicately balance an English-speaking life for conducting day-to-day business and the native-language-speaking life of family and friends.

Unfortunately, some immigrants do not entirely assimilate into the mainstream, as they believe that this insidious process will rob them of their history and self-esteem. Many do not even learn to speak English, as their hearts, dreams, and desires are "back home." They live their lives planning and plotting the return to their native land. This lack of assimilation and diversity can make it difficult to excel outside of their immediate environment, as they do not have the social skills required to navigate a world outside their backyard.

My grandfather, José Fernández, left his village of Nocedo del Valle in Orense, Spain, at sixteen, hoping to build a better tomorrow for himself and his descendants. He gave up the only world he knew for a lonely existence in the New World. The process of acculturation at such a young age, without familial support, was extremely difficult for him. He eventually settled in the Dominican Republic at the age of twenty-eight and subsequently had a family of his own.

Although my family's journey was not a treacherous one, as immigrants, we faced the same challenges other migrants before and after have encountered.

My family's origin started with a humble, poor background, and I've often wondered what my life would have been like if we had not immigrated to the United States. When I visit this beautiful yet impoverished island of the Dominican Republic and see the need and want in the eyes of some of the people, I think, "That could have been me." So, I feel incredibly blessed and grateful for everything that I have been able to accomplish.

The lotus flower starts its life at the bottom of a pond, mired in mud and muck. As this flower slowly grows up toward the sunlight and the water's surface, it is patiently transforming and perfecting itself. Once it is out in the sunshine, it blossoms and turns into a beautiful flower, representing life, new beginnings, progress, and the possibility of people growing and developing into something beautiful.

Like the lotus flower, my family was able to rise above and overcome the challenges we faced as immigrants. We were able to rise above the negativity and hard times we encountered, emerging with a renewed sense of self.

I have come a long way from that poor, impoverished town in the Dominican Republic. If someone had told me that my life would unfold the way it has, full of untold blessings and opportunities, I wouldn't have believed them. A life that I, as an immigrant growing up in New York City's projects, could not have imagined, even in my wildest dreams.

We each have a choice about our future based on what we learn from our past, because: *"Life is lived forward …and understood backward." — Søren Kierkegaard*

BIBLIOGRAPHY REFERENCES

REFERENCES

1. "Lotus Flower Symbolism," Lotus Flower Meaning, accessed April 19, 2019, www.lotusflowermeaning.net/symbolism.php

2. "Good instincts usually tell you what to do long before your head has figured it out." ~ Michael Burke, https://www.quotes.net/quote/38642

3. "Frederick Douglass Houses," Wikimedia Foundation, last modified November 11, 2018, https://en.wikipedia.org/wiki/Frederick_Douglass_Houses.

4. "Cirrhosis" Wikimedia Foundation, last modified April 16, 2019, https://en.wikipedia.org/wiki/Cirrhosis.

5. "Dilation and curettage (D&C)," Mayo Clinic, October 26, 2016, https://www.mayoclinic.org/tests-procedures/dilation-and-curettage/about/pac-20384910.

6. "Numbers Game," Wikimedia Foundation, last modified April 13, 2019, https://en.wikipedia.org/wiki/Numbers_game

7. Suzanne Bates, "The 'Vision Thing'—Critical to Accelerating Women's Careers," *Work Bloom*, February 27, 2009, https://www.localjobnetwork.com/a/t-the-vision-thing--critical-to-accelerating-womens-careers-au-bates,-suzanne-articles-a2817.html

8. Victoria L. Rayner, "Getting Beyond Career Failure," *Skin Inc.* June 26, 2008, http://www.skininc.com/spabusiness/management/personnel/21804394.html

9. Miral Fahmy, "Career women are their own worst enemies: study," Reuters, August 19, 2008, http://www.reuters.com/article/2008/08/20/us-women-careers-idINSP29843720080820

10. Paul Grundy, "Paul Grundy: My Story," JW facts, last modified September 2018, https://www.jwfacts.com/watchtower/experiences/paul-grundy.php

11. Joyce E. Salisbury, "The History of Spain: Land on a Crossroad," The Great Courses, https://www.thegreatcourses.com/courses/the-history-of-spain-land-on-a-crossroad.html

12. Amy S., "Ways of Curing Meat & Smoking During The 1800s," Pepper Fortress, March 17, 2018, http://www.prepperfortress.com/ways-of-curing-meat-smoking-during-the-1800s/

13. "Province of Ourense," Wikimedia Foundation, last modified January 11, 2019, https://en.wikipedia.org/wiki/Province_of_Ourense

14. "Spain," Wikimedia Foundation, last modified April 17, 2019, https://en.wikipedia.org/wiki/Spain.

15. Steven Thomas, "Timeline for the Second Rif War 1909," Steven's Balagan, June 30, 2002, http://balagan.info/timeline-for-the-second-rif-war-1909

16. Kristen Allen, "Latin American Independence Movements of The Early 19th century," Prezi, February 9, 2002, https://prezi.com/tky5vuofxn0x/latin-american-independence-movements-of-the-earl.

17. Henry Louis Gates, Jr, "The African Americans: Many Rivers to Cross," PBS, last accessed April 19, 2019, http://www.pbs.org/wnet/african-americans-many-rivers-to-cross/history/on-africa.

18. "The Dominican Republic," Spain Exchange: Country Guide, last accessed April 19, 2019, https://www.studycountry.com/guide/DO-intro.htm

19. Bartolome de las Casas, *A Short Account of the Destruction of the Indies,* London, England: Penguin Books, 1992

20. "Caribbean Unit 6: Dominican Republic Flashcards," Quizlet, last accessed April 19, 2019, https://quizlet.com/110732844/caribbean-unit-6-dominican-republic-flash-cards/.

21. "Santo Domingo," Wikimedia Foundation, last modified March 10, 2019, https://en.wikipedia.org/wiki/Santo_Domingo

22. "Family and Kin," Country Studies, last accessed April 19, 2019, http://countrystudies.us/dominican-republic/32.htm.

23. Juan Pablo Duarte, "The Father of the Country" ("Padre de la Patria"); (181-1876) (Santo Domingo–. https://www.colonial-zone-dr.com/people_history-Duarte.html

24. "Introduction to Race in Cuba," History of Cuba, last accessed April 19, 2019, http://historyofcuba.com/history/race/RaceIntro.htm

25. Race and Inequality in Cuba, 1889–1981, *Journal of Contemporary History*, Alejandro de la Fuente, https://journals.sagepub.com/doi/10.1177/002200949503000106

26. "Hatuey," Wikimedia Foundation, last modified March 14, 2019, https://en.wikipedia.org/wiki/Hatuey

BLANCA DE LA ROSA - BIOGRAPHY

Blanca De La Rosa, born in the Dominican Republic and raised in the projects of the upper west side of Manhattan, is the daughter of Dominican immigrants. Despite cultural and linguistic challenges, she graduated from Pace University with a degree in international business management. She built a successful 34-year career at Mobil Oil and later ExxonMobil Oil Corporation, rising through various domestic and international roles that took her across the US, Europe, Central/South America, and Nigeria.

As a business development manager and president of the company's Employee Resource Group, De La Rosa represented ExxonMobil at the Hispanic Heritage Foundation's Regional and National Scholarship Awards. She also served as a host, keynote speaker, and panelist at numerous events supported by the company's charity foundation. Her most rewarding role was mentoring younger employees through the corporate maze.

De La Rosa is a self-published author:

Memoir/Autobiography: "Pursuing a Better Tomorrow" is an inspiring journey from Spain to the US, intertwining four stories that illustrate the challenges and opportunities of immigration, acculturation, coming of age, and self-discovery. De La Rosa shares her personal journey from New York City's projects to corporate America, highlighting her growth and achievements despite numerous challenges.

Fiction: "The Betrayal, A Lifetime of Regrets" Camila and Nic seemed to have it all—a loving marriage, two beautiful children, a cozy home, and a promising future. But beneath the surface, their perfect life was beginning to crack.

Career Self-help: "Empower Yourself for an Amazing Career" and "A Holistic Approach to Your Career" A holistic approach is essential for upward mobility. Develop a career plan with clear goals and a forward-looking perspective. Empower Yourself provides uplifting and inspiring insights with practical advice and inner wisdom for workplace success.

Spiritual Self-help: "Your Power Within – Inner Guidance" It explores themes of personal growth, the soul's journey, inner strength, and the quest for purpose. The book emphasizes patience and gradual progress, guiding readers toward understanding and evolving through their experiences.

BLANCA DE LA ROSA – BIBLIOGRAPHY

Fiction - Novel

Camila and Nic seemed to have it all—a loving marriage, two beautiful children, a cozy home, and a promising future. But beneath the surface, their perfect life was beginning to crack. Feeling neglected and unfulfilled, Camila embarks on a secret affair that threatens to unravel their world. As the truth comes to light, Nic is blindsided by the betrayal, left grappling with the disintegration of the life he once knew.

Self-Help / Spiritual

"Your Power Within—Inner Guidance" is a journey of self-discovery and healing. Through personal anecdotes and reflections, the book explores the quest for purpose and inner strength. It encourages readers to tap into their inner power, break free from limits, and create their dream life. This guide helps readers discover their passions, connect with their inner selves, and align with their greater purpose. Your inner power is limitless!

Memoir - Autobiography

¿A qué renunciarías hoy por un mañana mejor? Muchas personas renuncian al único mundo que conocen en busca de un mañana mejor.

A lo largo de más de cien años, En busca de un mañana mejor no es sólo una memoria que retrata la historia de tres generaciones, sino más bien un viaje intergeneracional desde España hasta Estados Unidos. La novela transporta al lector a una época largamente olvidada con una descripción histórica legible de los taínos, los conquistadores, los primeros colonos, el Imperio español y la República Dominicana, intercalados en la narrativa a través de la perspectiva del personaje de la época.

Self-Help / Career

A holistic approach is essential for upward mobility. Develop a career plan with clear goals and a forward-looking perspective.

Empower Yourself provides uplifting and inspiring insights. with practical advice and inner wisdom for workplace success.

Memoir / Autobiography

What would you give up today for a better tomorrow? This question fuels an inspiring cross-generational journey from Spain to the US, spanning over 100 years. Through the characters' stories, we see the challenges and opportunities of immigration, acculturation, coming of age, and self-discovery. De La Rosa's transition from New York City's projects to corporate America highlights her personal and professional growth.

www.ingramcontent.com/pod-product-compliance
Lightning Source LLC
Chambersburg PA
CBHW030256100526
44590CB00012B/416